This commentary on the Epistles of John is a splendid blend of sound exegesis of the original text and appropriate contextualization of its message for Asian cultures. A hallmark of biblical interpretation involves not only determining what the text meant in its own time, but translating the biblical message so contemporary readers can discern what the text is saying in terms of application. Serious students of the Bible, teachers, and pastors will benefit greatly from this important resource.

Clive Chin, PhD
Academic Dean of the School of Theology English Faculty
Singapore Bible College

The Epistles of John have aroused more and more scholarly attention recently. Dr. Gilbert Soo Hoo adds a voice to the many interpretations, especially from an Asian perspective. As a matter of fact, the culture and philosophy in Asian regions are very different from those in the West. Our Asian experiences will certainly enrich that of the West. In so doing, the author incorporates current scholarly opinions and joins their discussion in his commentary. Gilbert's work adds important salt to the pluralist interpretations of John's letters.

Eric Kun-Chun Wong, PhD
Associate Director, Divinity School of Chung Chi College
The Chinese University of Hong Kong

Asia Bible Commentary Series

1, 2, 3 JOHN

GLOBAL LIBRARY

Asia Bible Commentary Series

1, 2, 3 JOHN

Gilbert Soo Hoo
with
Pervaiz Sultan

General Editor
Federico G. Villanueva

Old Testament Consulting Editors
Yohanna Katanacho, Tim Meadowcroft, Joseph Shao

New Testament Consulting Editors
Steve Chang, Andrew Spurgeon, Brian Wintle

© 2016 by Gilbert Soo Hoo

Published 2016 by Langham Global Library
An imprint of Langham Publishing
www.langhampublishing.org

Langham Publishing and its imprints are a ministry of Langham Partnership

Langham Partnership
PO Box 296, Carlisle, Cumbria CA3 9WZ, UK
www.langham.org

Published in partnership with Asia Theological Association

ATA
QCC PO Box 1454 – 1154, Manila, Philippines
www.atasia.com

ISBNs:
978-1-78368-868-5 Print
978-1-78368-188-4 ePub
978-1-78368-190-7 PDF

Gilbert Soo Hoo has asserted his right under the Copyright, Designs and Patents Act, 1988 to be identified as the Author of this work.

All rights reserved. No part of this publication may be reproduced, stored in a retrieval system or transmitted, in any form or by any means, electronic, mechanical, photocopying, recording or otherwise, without the prior written permission of the publisher or the Copyright Licensing Agency.

All Scripture quotations, unless otherwise indicated, are taken from the Holy Bible, New International Version®, NIV®. Copyright ©2011 by Biblica, Inc.™ Used by permission of Zondervan. All rights reserved worldwide.

British Library Cataloguing in Publication Data
A catalogue record for this book is available from the British Library

ISBN: 978-1-78368-868-5

Cover & Book Design: projectluz.com

Langham Partnership actively supports theological dialogue and an author's right to publish but does not necessarily endorse the views and opinions set forth, and works referenced within this publication or guarantee its technical and grammatical correctness. Langham Partnership does not accept any responsibility or liability to persons or property as a consequence of the reading, use or interpretation of its published content.

To Weiki and Winyan, "my dear children,"
as I echo the author in addressing his readers.

To Ming with whom I, like the elder with his readers,
prefer to spend time "face-to-face" as partners in significant ministry.

CONTENTS

Series Preface xi
Acknowledgments xiii
List of Abbreviations xv
Introduction 1
1 John 27
   1 John 1 27
   1 John 2 40
   1 John 3 69
   1 John 4 91
   1 John 5 116
2 John 137
3 John 151
Bibliography 167

Topics

Tale of Two Realms – Standing on the Truth 114
Christian *Furz* – Our Religious Duty 135
Tale of Two Realms – Within the Church 166

SERIES PREFACE

In recent years, we have witnessed one of the greatest shifts in the history of world Christianity. It used to be that the majority of Christians lived in the West. But now the face of world Christianity has changed beyond recognition. Christians are now evenly distributed around the globe. This has implications for the interpretation of the Bible. In our case, we are faced with the task of interpreting the Bible from within our respective contexts. This is in line with the growing realization that every theology is contextual. Our understanding of the Bible is influenced by our historical and social locations. Thus, even the questions that we bring into our reading of the Bible will be shaped by our present realities. There is a need therefore to interpret the Bible for our own contexts.

The Asia Bible Commentary Series addresses this need. In line with the mission of the Asia Theological Association Publications, we have gathered Asian evangelical Bible scholars in Asia to write commentaries on each book of the Bible. The mission is to "produce resources for pastors, Christian leaders, cross-cultural workers, and students in Asia that are biblical, pastoral, contextual, missional, and prophetic." Although the Bible can be studied for different reasons, we believe that it is given primarily for the edification of the Body of Christ (2 Tim 3:16–17). The ABCS is designed to help pastors in their sermon preparation, cell group leaders or lay leaders in their Bible study groups, Christian students in their study of the Bible, and Christians in general in their efforts to apply the Bible in their respective contexts.

Each commentary begins with an introduction that provides general information about the book's author and original context, summarizes the main message or theme of the book, and outlines its potential relevance to a particular Asian context. The introduction is followed by an exposition that combines exegesis and application. Here, we seek to speak to and empower Christians in Asia by using our own stories, parables, poems, and other cultural resources as we expound the Bible.

The Bible is actually Asian in that it comes from ancient West Asia and there are many similarities between the world of the Bible and traditional Asian cultures. But there are also many differences that we need to explore in some depth. That is why the commentaries also include articles or topics in which we bring specific issues in Asian church, social, and religious contexts into dialogue with relevant issues in the Bible. We do not seek to resolve every tension but rather to allow the text to illumine the context and vice versa, acknowledging that in the end we do not have all the answers to every mystery.

May the Holy Spirit who inspired the writers of the Bible bring light to the hearts and minds of all who use these materials, to the glory of God and to the building up of the churches!

Federico G. Villanueva

General Editor

SERIES PREFACE

In recent years, we have witnessed one of the greatest shifts in the history of world Christianity. It used to be that the majority of Christians lived in the West. But now the face of world Christianity has changed beyond recognition. Christians are now evenly distributed around the globe. This has implications for the interpretation of the Bible. In our case, we are faced with the task of interpreting the Bible from within our respective contexts. This is in line with the growing realization that every theology is contextual. Our understanding of the Bible is influenced by our historical and social locations. Thus, even the questions that we bring into our reading of the Bible will be shaped by our present realities. There is a need therefore to interpret the Bible for our own contexts.

The Asia Bible Commentary Series addresses this need. In line with the mission of the Asia Theological Association Publications, we have gathered Asian evangelical Bible scholars in Asia to write commentaries on each book of the Bible. The mission is to "produce resources for pastors, Christian leaders, cross-cultural workers, and students in Asia that are biblical, pastoral, contextual, missional, and prophetic." Although the Bible can be studied for different reasons, we believe that it is given primarily for the edification of the Body of Christ (2 Tim 3:16–17). The ABCS is designed to help pastors in their sermon preparation, cell group leaders or lay leaders in their Bible study groups, Christian students in their study of the Bible, and Christians in general in their efforts to apply the Bible in their respective contexts.

Each commentary begins with an introduction that provides general information about the book's author and original context, summarizes the main message or theme of the book, and outlines its potential relevance to a particular Asian context. The introduction is followed by an exposition that combines exegesis and application. Here, we seek to speak to and empower Christians in Asia by using our own stories, parables, poems, and other cultural resources as we expound the Bible.

The Bible is actually Asian in that it comes from ancient West Asia and there are many similarities between the world of the Bible and traditional Asian cultures. But there are also many differences that we need to explore in some depth. That is why the commentaries also include articles or topics in which we bring specific issues in Asian church, social, and religious contexts into dialogue with relevant issues in the Bible. We do not seek to resolve every tension but rather to allow the text to illumine the context and vice versa, acknowledging that in the end we do not have all the answers to every mystery.

May the Holy Spirit who inspired the writers of the Bible bring light to the hearts and minds of all who use these materials, to the glory of God and to the building up of the churches!

Federico G. Villanueva

General Editor

ACKNOWLEDGMENTS

This commentary is the fruit of countless hours spent by a number of co-laborers who thought this endeavor is a worthwhile pursuit. Dr. Federico Villanueva, the general editor of the Asia Bible Commentary Series, encouraged me with his patient and wise counsel. The editors from Asia Theological Association and Langham Partnership gave very helpful feedback to make this work better. Dr. Pervaiz Sultan offered me a glimpse of his Asian world as contextual consultant. Dr. Clive Chin, my dean, and Dr. Michael Shen, my principal, both of Singapore Bible College, provided unconditional support as I balanced my teaching responsibilities with writing.

LIST OF ABBREVIATIONS

BOOKS OF THE BIBLE
Old Testament
Gen, Exod, Lev, Num, Deut, Josh, Judg, Ruth, 1–2 Sam, 1–2 Kgs, 1–2 Chr, Ezra, Neh, Esth, Job, Ps/Pss, Prov, Eccl, Song, Isa, Jer, Lam, Ezek, Dan, Hos, Joel, Amos, Obad, Jonah, Mic, Nah, Hab, Zeph, Hag, Zech, Mal

New Testament
Matt, Mark, Luke, John, Acts, Rom, 1–2 Cor, Gal, Eph, Phil, Col, 1–2 Thess, 1–2 Tim, Titus, Phlm, Heb, Jas, 1–2 Pet, 1–2–3 John, Jude, Rev

BIBLE TEXTS AND VERSIONS
Divisions of the canon
NT	New Testament
OT	Old Testament

Modern versions
ESV	English Standard Version
NIV	New International Version
NRSV	New Revised Standard Version

Journals, Reference Works, and Series
AB	Anchor Bible
ABCS	Asia Bible Commentary Series
Bib	*Biblica*
BSac	*Bibliotheca Sacra*
CBQ	*Catholic Biblical Quarterly*
EBC	Expositor's Bible Commentary
HTS	Harvard Theological Studies
JBL	*Journal of Biblical Literature*
JETS	*Journal of the Evangelical Theological Society*
JSNTSup	*Journal for the Study of New Testament Supplement Series*
JSOT	*Journal for the Study of the Old Testament*
LQ	*Lutheran Quarterly*

NCBC	New Century Bible Commentary
NIBC	New International Bible Commentary
NIDOTTE	New International Dictionary of Old Testament Theology and Exegesis
NIVAC	The NIV Application Commentary
NovT	*Novum Testamentum*
RelSRev	*Religious Studies Review*
ResQ	*Restoration Quarterly*
TNTC	*Tyndale New Testament Commentaries*
TynBul	*Tyndale Bulletin*
TMSJ	*The Master's Seminary Journal*
VT	*Vetus Testamentum*
WBC	Word Biblical Commentary

INTRODUCTION

The Asian church is faced with the critical challenge of clearly articulating the message that Jesus is the Christ, fully God and fully man. Our voice is that of a minority and is often drowned out by competing voices from majority cultures and religions. How are we to sustain our witness? Will the church be able to survive and even achieve a measure of victory? Will it present a united front, steadfast and unwavering, in a society where persecution is a given? How do we navigate the treacherous minefield of hostile neighbors, governments that are unsympathetic at best, and the majority religious profession, whether Islamic, Buddhist, Taoist, Hindu, or the like?

My prayer is that the Asian church will hear God's voice in the ancient letters of John and will strive to become yet another generation of disciples living in fellowship with the Father and the Son and with one another.

The church John was writing to in the first century AD was also facing serious challenge that threatened its survival. A number of leaders had become increasingly vocal about their interpretation of Scripture that differed from what the church held. They influenced a significant number of members to follow their teaching.

The dispute centered on Jesus' identity as related to his becoming human.[1] This is still an issue today for Christians with Hindu and Hindu-related backgrounds may naturally tend to think of Jesus as an avatar. However, the concept of an avatar, a mythological appearance of God in human form, does not align with the gospel's portrait of Christ. Unlike the Hindu Vishnu, who may have numerous manifestations (the principal ones being Krishna and Rama), Jesus did not simply assume a human form temporarily to visit humankind before returning to heaven. He became a real man permanently in order to die for the sins of the whole world and continue interceding for his followers as high priest. His personal standing with the Father serves as the only basis by which anyone may approach the Father.

There had been a breakdown in communication between the conservatives who maintained the original teaching about who Jesus was and those who wanted to honor the prevailing beliefs of the surrounding society and its culture. The latter left the church (1 John 2:19).

---

1. Although Judith M. Lieu remains cautious about the specific issue addressed, she discerns a dispute over Jesus in his relationship with the Father and his mission as the Christ (*I, II, and III John: A Commentary* [Louisville, KY: Westminster John Knox, 2008], 9–14).

This too is a problem we encounter. As leaders we want our church to grow. We strategize how best to invite newcomers. We seek ways to keep members from becoming disgruntled and leaving. We do not want our church to become a revolving door with a steady stream of people entering and another stream of members leaving. But in certain situations it may be best that some people leave, for the sake of the church, especially if their continued presence disturbs other members. The church must remain faithful to the unchanging truth of the gospel and yet be relevant to the local culture in which it worships. For it to attain that objective its members must be unified in their beliefs, objectives, and practices, otherwise it loses its testimony. Any disunity can spell disaster. The early church faced that challenge and struggled because of the two factions.

Today the Asian church ministers in a multi-religious and often multi-cultural environment and faces serious social problems, especially poverty. Thankfully we have a resource that offers guidance and encouragement as we do so – the ancient documents preserving the communication between a leader and the church known as 1, 2, and 3 John.

These three relatively short letters record something of the incorrect doctrine of those who left the church and the correct doctrine that the church must preserve in order to remain functional. The stakes were very high – incorrect doctrine can destroy members' faith in God and undermine their relationship with one another. The leader of the church addressed these concerns in writing to the church after the separatists departed. He reminded them that a correct understanding of who Jesus is should result in confession of one's sins and loving one another, rather than loving the world and its attractions. There is a clear correlation between truth and love that permits a person to fellowship with God and walk in his light.

Before we can look at 1, 2, and 3 John, however, we need to take care of some preliminary matters. Questions about the type of writing, original situation, the opponents of the church, and the identity of the author will influence our approach to and understanding of these writings. Because of the limited information about the original readers and their situation, some assumptions and conclusions must be made in order to proceed with a careful reading that can speak to us today.

Doing It with Style

Our style tells people something about us. In fashion, our style reflects our personality, tastes, status, and the way we like to present ourselves. When

Introduction

it comes to writing, authors' styles reveal their command of the language, knowledge of the topic under discussion, the type of relationship they have with their readers, and the literary purpose of the document.

1, 2, and 3 John are grouped among the general letters of the New Testament (NT). As such, they are commonly viewed as letters. However, they differ in form from modern letters, which we usually begin with an opening salutation like "Dear so-and-so" or, more casually, "Hi so-and-so." We usually greet the recipient by name, and then sign off at the end with a signature. When writing formal or business letters, we carefully select stationery with a letterhead that indicates the institution that we represent. The language of the letter will reflect the degree of formality appropriate to the nature of the correspondence. The more formal the situation, the more formal, dignified, and proper the language used. Conversely, the more personal and informal the occasion, the more conversational and even colloquial our language will be. We may even use terms of endearment that facilitate intimacy. Finally, the closing signature reflects the relative formality of the letter, being more or less personal according to the letter's tenor.

As soon as we turn to 2 or 3 John, we see a difference between these letters and modern letters. Instead of beginning with the name of the recipient, these two letters refer to the author first. He is identified only as "the elder," which gives us the title of the writer but does not help identify who he was.[2]

In 1 John, however, there is no greeting of any kind. The writer immediately launches into the body of the letter. The conclusion is equally abrupt, with no closing signature. Surprisingly, this format aligns well with emails and text messages, which often do not begin with a greeting and end with a signature. A key aspect of such modern modes of correspondence is brevity and the assumption that both parties know each other without explicit acknowledgment. But in the case of 1 John, although it is relatively short compared to other NT letters, it cannot be characterized as brief in the present-day sense of a short, quickly composed note that features a host of sometimes bewildering shorthand notations.[3]

---

2. See a full discussion on "elder" in Raymond E. Brown, *The Epistles of John* (AB 30 [Garden City, NY: Doubleday, 1982], 647–651). The term appears to be a title devoid of any personal reference (Martin M. Culy, *I, II, III John: A Handbook on the Greek Text* [Waco, TX: Baylor University, 2004], 141).

3. NetLingo lists the more commonly used shorthand notations. See http://www.netlingo.com/acronyms.php (accessed April 13, 2015). For example, LOL (laugh out loud or lots of love), NRN (no reply necessary), SGTM (sounds good to me), and u8 (you ate). But like any

Certainly there was some pre-existing relationship exists between author and reader which, in the case of 1, 2, and 3 John, evidence recognition of the author's spiritual authority. Addressing his readers as "children" (1 John 2:1, 12, 28; 3:7, 18; 4:4; 5:21) and as "beloved" (the plural form in 1 John 2:7; 3:2, 21; 4:1, 7, 11 and the singular in 3 John 5, 11), the writer conveys authority and affection. As a "father" he may be chronologically older, spiritually more mature and hold some position of inherent authority, potentially as an apostle, although that possibility can only be inferred. His reference to himself as "elder" (2 John 1; 3 John 1) confirms that assessment. The frequent occurrence of directives and admonitions throughout the letters presume the recognized authority of the writer and the expectation of compliance from the readers.

These ancient letters preserve the writer's response to some real-life matters that are important both to him and to his readers.[4] The importance of the issues explains why 1 John is much more formal than our emails and text messages, despite the clear signs of familiarity between the writer and the readers. In fact, all three of letters stand somewhere between formal and personal communication. Since they deal with weighty matters, they cannot be mistaken for light-hearted banter between friends and yet they are not impersonal memos from a CEO to his/her employees. There is a familial feel.

Looking for the Wordsmith

Calling someone a wordsmith recognizes that they have a skill with words, similar to the skill a goldsmith has in working with precious metals. We can label Shakespeare, for example, a wordsmith. People today hold to one of two basic theories about the wordsmith(s) of the Gospel of John and 1, 2, and 3 John. Either the same person wrote both the Gospel and the three epistles, or one person wrote the Gospel and a second person wrote the epistles.[5]

---

language that continuously evolves, shorthand notations constantly change so that what list of shorthand writers use may mark their age. For example, the 1960s generation signaled "A-OK" to indicate things were going well as compared to a later generation that employed "cool."

4. Although David Rensberger does not view 1 John to be a letter, he still sees it "written by a particular author to a particular group in regard to a particular situation" (*1 John, 2 John, 3 John* [Abingdon New Testament Commentaries; Nashville, TN: Abingdon, 1997], 30). Also, Judith Lieu, *The Theology of the Johannine Epistles* (Cambridge: Cambridge University, 2001), 4.

5. John 21:20–24 clearly identifies the author of the Gospel as the beloved disciple, whom early church tradition correlates with the Apostle John, as confirmed by the patristic writers from Irenaeus onward. Only recently have scholars proposed other authors. Different theories have emerged – the same author for all four writings; one author for the Gospel and another

Introduction

Generally, people see the Gospel and epistles sharing a common bond that makes them a group of four writings to be treated together.

Uncertainty surrounds the issue of authorship and so there is no consensus among scholars about who produced these writings. But fortunately this mystery does not hinder our reading and application of the text.

Sequels

In the movie industry, sequels often fail to live up to the hype of marketing or to the standard established by the original. But before we even evaluate whether a sequel proves to be worthy of its predecessor or a disappointment, we need to establish the relationship between the two films that justifies making the comparison. Typically, if two films bear similar or clearly related titles, feature the same actor(s), and evidence plot continuation, we have confidence that the two represent a sequence. Absolute confirmation comes when the director and producers themselves make the declaration that such is the case.

But when we ask whether our three epistles are in some sense a sequel to the Gospel of John, we find no such authoritative testimony. We have no recourse but to rely on circumstantial evidence. So we look for similarities of writing style, concepts, and language, especially if such similarities serve to distinguish the four writings (the Gospel and the three epistles) from the rest of the NT. While these clues do not result in absolute certainty, they do suggest a high probability that there is a relationship between the Gospels and the epistles.

The Power of One

Recognition that there is a sequence between the Gospels and the epistles requires the modern church to read the four together as one. The Gospel of John initiates the story of Jesus coming into the world as the Father's emissary to declare that he is the promised Christ and Son of God.[6] Every encounter in that Gospel invokes a personal response that reveals faith or unbelief with regard to Jesus' claim. No character in the unfolding drama of the Gospel can remain neutral for long. Eventually, their inner convictions surface.

---

for the epistles; some combination of writers for all four, but all produced by the same faith community. Robert W. Yarbrough affirms that John the son of Zebedee authored the Gospel and the three epistles (*1–3 John* [Grand Rapids, MI: Baker Academic, 2008], 5–7).

6. David Rensberger regards the Gospel's depiction of Jesus as having "come into the world" and "being sent by God" as pointing toward his divinity ("The Messiah Who Has Come into the World," in *Jesus in Johannine Tradition*, ed. Robert T. Fortna and Tom Thatcher [Louisville, KY: Westminster John Knox, 2001], 15–23).

Jesus' mission in the world is to initiate a community and a movement. In gathering the first disciples, he forms the nucleus of what will become the church with the coming of the Holy Spirit after his return to the Father. As he prepares the first disciples for their mission in the world, he charges them to love one another and to abide in him (that is, to depend on him) in his farewell speech, recorded toward the end of the Gospel of John. Although no longer physically present, he will continue his presence in the world through his disciples collectively as the church.

The three epistles address the church of a later generation, probably after the first generation of disciples has passed on (including possibly the author of the Gospel), and repeat the same charge to love one another.[7] In addition, Jesus' warning that the world will hate the disciples as it has hated him resurfaces in the epistles. Hence, an adversarial relationship exists between the church and the world, first seen in its hostility toward Jesus himself, stemming from reaction to the truth about his identity – the church subscribes to that identity but the world rejects it.

Perceiving the epistles as a sequel to the Gospel deepens our understanding of the continuity between the two.[8] The Gospel finds its logical extension and continuation in the epistles, and the epistles depend on the Gospel for foundational truths that provide doctrinal orientation. Each is incomplete without the other. Significantly, the Gospel provides the rationale for the epistles. Why love one another and stand for the truth about Christ? Why bother with church? What is its mission and role in the world? The epistles presuppose these fundamental questions being answered by the Gospel.

In particular, the church finds its marching orders from these four writings. Its very presence and ministry in Asia show that disciples have heeded Jesus' command to go into all the world to testify "that the Father has sent his Son to be the Savior of the world" (1 John 4:14bc). As Asian Christians, we confirm the still ongoing movement that Jesus initiated with the first disciples in Jerusalem.

---

7. Scott M. Lewis views the letters as the author's attempt to correct misinterpretation of the discourses in the Gospel, especially of the farewell discourse (John 14–17) (*The Gospel According to John and the Johannine Letters*, New Collegeville Bible Commentary 4 [Collegeville, MN: Liturgical, 2005], 108–109).

8. Tricia Gates Brown is representative of a number of contemporary scholars who perceive the continuity (*Spirit in the Writings of John: Johannine Pneumatology in Social-Scientific Perspective*, JSNTSup 253 [New York: T & T Clark, 2003]). She studies the teaching on the Holy Spirit in the Gospel and 1 John.

Introduction

Three points in the timeline show the continuity in terms of community and movement. First, the Gospel documents the starting point as Jesus looks forward to the immediate future of the disciples once he leaves the world. Secondly, the three epistles portray a later point in history with a new generation of disciples carrying on the mission Jesus charged the first disciples to implement. And thirdly, today we are the latest generation to go into the world as his emissaries facing our present context and striving to be the missional church he desires. So the Gospel and epistles represent something of our heritage and history, the basis on which we as Christ's church proclaim him to our world.

By virtue of our identity as Asian Christians, we substantiate the vitality of the movement Jesus began and that has persevered throughout church history. Jesus' charge to the early disciples to practice love and truth becomes our charge to obey through these writings. And we must take to heart his warning about the world. The situation reflected in these ancient documents does not significantly differ from ours today. If anything, our society is even more complex, being so multifaceted. Thus, reading the Gospel and epistles becomes not only a spiritual exercise for personal growth but also a recommitment to the love our Lord harbors for Asia. We love whom he loves.

In the next few sections, we will examine the factors that bind the four writings as one. Reviewing them strengthens our resolve to read the documents collectively for the full story and teaching contained in them. This is the only way to prepare ourselves adequately for the challenge before us.

A Common Tradition

One factor that promotes confidence in a relationship between two or more documents is evidence that they come from a common tradition. Commentators have proposed that the writer (or writers) of the Gospel of John came from a church (or possibly a community of churches) who were early disciples devoted to the teaching of the Apostle John.[9] Such a situation would help to explain the similarities and differences between the Gospel and the epistles, and would make the question of authorship less critical.[10] The

---

9. The concept of the community is most fully explained in Raymond E. Brown, *The Community of the Beloved Disciple: The Life, Loves and Hates of an Individual Church in New Testament Times* (Mahwah, NJ: Paulist, 1979). See also Robert Kysar, *John, The Maverick Gospel*, 3d ed. (Louisville, KY: Westminster John Knox, 2007), 171.
10. C. Haas, M. de Jonge, and J. L. Swellengrebel, *A Handbook on the Letters of John* (New York, NY: UBS, 1972), 5.

common tradition or background of teachings based on the Gospel of John emerge as the pre-eminent influence.

Some independent Bible churches today, for example, may maintain a tradition of insisting on a minimal statement of faith that omits detailed requirements on church practices and beliefs about the end times. Only the essentials of the faith – teachings about God, Christ, Holy Spirit, the Bible, salvation, church membership, and Christ's return – find their way into the statement. Some matters crucial for other traditions are excluded, for example, the mode of baptism, permissible roles for women, charismatic practices, and church governance. One church I know deliberately made its statement about faith in relation to regeneration so vague that those from a Reformed and a Wesleyan background could both subscribe to it, each interpreting it according to their own convictions, and be fellow members. The underlying intent is to foster fellowship between believers from a broader diversity of church backgrounds than would otherwise be permissible.

I believe a tradition of some kind to be a reasonable explanation for the relationship between the Gospel of John and 1, 2, and 3 John. Instead of a direct literary relationship, the Gospel and 1 John independently drew from common sources, whether oral or written.[11] Then 2 and 3 John depended on the first two.

A Common Situation and Opponents

Another factor that argues for a literary relationship between the Gospel of John and the three epistles is the common situation addressed and the common opponents faced. A number of polemical statements in 1 and 2 John reveal a struggle with unnamed opponents, with both groups claiming a common heritage based on the Gospel of John.[12] The conflict revolves around two points – one centered on Christ and the other moral. In 1 John 5:1–2, for example, we find both points present: "Everyone who believes that Jesus is the Christ is born of God, and everyone who loves the father loves his child as well. This is how we know that we love the children of God; by loving God and carrying out his commands." Any confession that Jesus is the Christ must be backed by love and obedience.

A clear statement about the opponents appears in 1 John 2:18–19, 22–23:

---

11. Lieu, *I, II, & III John*, 17–18.
12. Charles E. Hill discusses the reception of the Johannine corpus (the Gospel, three epistles, and Revelation) in the second century (*The Johannine Corpus in the Early Church* [Oxford: Oxford University Press, 2004]).

INTRODUCTION

> Dear children, this is the last hour; and as you have heard that the antichrist is coming, even now many antichrists have come. This is how we know it is the last hour. They went out from us, but they did not really belong to us. For if they had belonged to us, they would have remained with us; but their going showed that none of them belonged to us. . . . Who is the liar? It is whoever denies that Jesus is the Christ. Such a person is the antichrist – denying the Father and the Son. No one who denies the Son has the Father; whoever acknowledges the Son has the Father also.[13]

Apparently some former members had left the church and formed a new group, or possibly a new church. In separating themselves out, they proved beyond doubt that they were never really a part of the first church nor shared its theological convictions. Clearly the point of theological contention was about Christ, in particular the splinter group rejection of the messianic identity of Jesus. For that reason, the author refers to them as antichrists (although not in the end-time sense of the antichrist of prophecy). Rather, their stance against Jesus being the Christ made them antichrists theologically. Given that this group had left the church, those who remained in the church were those who professed Jesus as the Christ. As a result, according to the author, the first church alone possessed the Father. Because of the intimate relationship between the Father and the Son, when they professed allegiance to the Son, they also professed allegiance to the Father. As a direct consequence of denying Jesus to be the Christ, the splinter group inadvertently denied the Father. Their denial made them liars, a label found elsewhere and a clue that, whenever "liar" is used, the author may well be thinking of the splinter group (2:4; 4:20).[14]

The fact that these two groups once formed one church implies that they shared a common heritage. Even after the split some common ground, though drastically reduced, may still exist. One possible scenario for the historical development of the situation that birthed 1, 2, and 3 John has both

---

13. A fuller exposition of these verses is deferred to a later chapter.
14. On two other occasions the label "liar" is used with reference to God (1:10; 5:10), and is rejected as blasphemous. This is the case when by denying personal sin a person disputes God's judgment of sin in his life (1:10) and when in rejecting the Son a person rejects God's testimony about his Son (5:10). Thus, the person, not God, is a liar by rejecting the truth about personal sin or the Son.

groups accept the Gospel of John but differ in their interpretation of it.[15] Each group thought the other had broken fellowship with it.

The point of contention appears to center on the implications of the Gospel's teaching about Christ. Apparently, no reconciliation between the two groups ever happened. Those who separated out from the church appear to deny that Jesus' life and death served as the basis for humanity's salvation and de-emphasized the importance of moral behavior. They even claimed moral perfection that results in sinlessness.[16]

We really do not know who the separatists may have been.[17] Yet, clues in the form of labels offer provocative suggestions. The author calls them antichrists (1 John 2:18, 22; 4:3), false prophets (1 John 4:1), and deceivers (2 John 7). They have gone out into the world (1 John 4:1, 3; 2 John 7) – the author's way of saying that the separatists left the church and perhaps allied themselves with the world and its beliefs.[18]

What happened a long time ago might happen again today, perhaps even in your church. We hope and pray that never occurs because such events threaten to tear the church apart. No one wants that. And yet, are we prepared? Are we clear on who Jesus is and the importance of why he went to the cross? Do we understand our stewardship as leaders to teach our people vital truths about Jesus and to safeguard the flock of God from false teachings about Christ? Are we prepared to confront those who teach things contrary to Scripture, even if they are fellow leaders in the church?

Church discipline seems extreme but proves absolutely necessary if those teaching untruths do not repent when confronted. It takes courage and a lot of energy and time to rebuke false teaching. But we cannot do other necessary ministry until the problem is addressed. We cannot afford to delay in hopes the problem solves itself. If unchecked, the problem will get worse.

---

15. See John Eifion Morgan-Wynne, *The Cross in the Johannine Writings* (Eugene, OR: Pickwick, 2011), 218–240.
16. Ibid., 79–86.
17. Bruce G. Schuchard finds the letters' portrait of them fluid and vague (*1–3 John* [St. Louis, MO: Concordia, 2012], 16–17). That concern, however, has not stopped Stephen S. Smalley from proposing several distinct groups that may have lived then (*1, 2, 3 John*, WBC 51 [Waco, TX: Word, 1984], xxiv–xxv).
18. The author describes them as "they went out from us" (1 John 2:19), "they had come out into the world" (1 John 4:1), and "now it [spirit of the antichrist] is in the world already" (1 John 4:3). Two realms, mutually exclusive, connote the location of a person. The location metaphorically identifies that person as being an adherent to the gospel truth or a deviant from the gospel truth. Either he is part of the church or part of the world that rejects the gospel truth.

Introduction

Key Concepts

In the first sequel to the blockbuster movie *The Matrix*, entitled *The Matrix Reloaded*, a computer program known as the Keymaker generates shortcuts, portrayed as keys, which provide quick access to different regions in the simulated reality of the Matrix. With the right key, the protagonists of the movie hope to reach their objective and complete their mission.

In a parallel way, our objective and mission center on identifying the keys, the collection of fundamental concepts and teachings that first emerge from the Gospel of John and reappear in the epistles. These keys open for us a vista to understand the import of the epistles. They put us in a position to use these writings as the lens to examine our present-day context and make informed decisions about matters of faith and practice.

Concept 1: Portrait of Jesus

In the Gospel, Jesus consistently distinguishes himself from everyone else with such statements as "The one who comes from above is above all; the one who is from the earth belongs to the earth, and speaks as one from the earth. The one who comes from heaven is above all" (John 3:31). "But he continued, 'You are from below; I am from above. You are of this world; I am not of this world'" (John 8:23). "And the Father who sent me has himself testified concerning me. You have never heard his voice nor seen his form" (John 5:37).

Jesus' self-identification highlights his origin and his relationship with the Father. Jesus comes from heaven above, making him unique. His intimate relationship with the Father, expressed in terms of being sent by the Father, likewise establishes his uniqueness. This claim to uniqueness, equivalent to an affirmation of deity, confronts all whom Jesus encounters in the Gospel. Each person must either exercise faith and accept the claim or manifest unbelief in rejecting the claim.

This belief is essential for salvation. Until we believe in the divine origin of Christ, we cannot appreciate the significance of the cross. No mere prophet, Christ mediated between God and humanity.

Two implications come to the fore. First, the divine intervention highlights the impoverished condition of humanity, unable to save itself from sin and its consequences. Secondly, realizing that God's love was manifested historically, Christians should commit themselves to the service of others, seeking to deliver them from sin and suffering through Christ. Only when we embody the message of salvation through our sacrificial lifestyle will there be reconciliation among the broken of humanity in Asia and other parts of our globe.

The Gospel also portrays Jesus as the Christ/Messiah. Jesus declares to Martha, "I am the resurrection and the life. . . . Do you believe this?" And she replies, "Yes, Lord, I believe that you are the Messiah, the Son of God, who is to come into the world" (John 11:25–27). Martha affirms a connection between the resurrection and eternal life with Christ coming into the world. She further identifies Jesus as the Christ. The author of the Gospel states the purpose for writing: "But these [signs] are written [in this Gospel] that you may believe that Jesus is the Messiah, the Son of God, and that by believing you may have life in his name" (John 20:31).

Christ, then, is the one whom the Father sends into the world in order that those who believe in him may have eternal life. Then those who refuse to believe do not have eternal life. Christ's origin is above where the Father resides, and he comes into the world as the object of faith and as the one who makes known the unknowable God.

In the epistles, the author constantly speaks of "Jesus Christ."[19] The author of 1 John proclaims the potential for fellowship with the Father and his Son Jesus Christ ("our fellowship is with the Father and with his Son, Jesus Christ," 1:3). An invitation to enter into the relationship between the Father and the Son now extends to the believer.

Salvation means more than simply possessing eternal life, which is what we often emphasize in evangelism. It signifies the potential for fellowship with God the Father and God the Son. Indeed, eternal life connotes a union of God and believer. It ought to be a present reality; but is it this in your church? As in any relationship, the interaction should show signs of growing intimacy through ever greater familiarity and closeness. Commitment, love, trust, and dependence should mark believers as they commune with the Lord, individually and corporately, through church fellowship. Entering into his presence with other believers ought not to be routine, but an experience eagerly anticipated and uplifting. We can experience a little of eternity now through fellowship. What will you need to change about the way your church fellowships in order to experience a slice of heaven this week?

---

19. The Gospel features "Jesus Christ" twice in 1:17; 17:3. This compares to the eight times the double name occurs in the epistles (1 John 1:3; 2:1; 3:23; 4:2; 5:6, 20; 2 John 3, 7). Given how much longer the Gospel is compared to the epistles, the difference in frequency gains importance.

Introduction

Moreover, a moral aspect emerges in association with Jesus as the Christ as can be noted in the following passages. "If anybody does should sin, we have an advocate with the Father – Jesus Christ, the Righteous One" (1 John 2:1). "This is his command, to believe in the name of his Son, Jesus Christ, and to love one another, as he commanded us" (1 John 3:23). "Everyone who believes that Jesus is the Christ is born of God; and everyone who loves the father loves his children as well" (1 John 5:1). "Grace, mercy, and peace from God the Father and from Jesus Christ the Father's Son will be with us in truth and love" (2 John 1:3). This invocation expresses the desire for believers to abide in truth and love through the blessings of grace, mercy, and peace from the Father and the Son. And "anyone who runs ahead and does not continue the teaching of Christ does not have God; whoever continues in the teaching, has both the Father and the Son" (2 John 1:9).

This moral aspect pervades the epistles (at least 1 and 2 John), and contrasts with its absence in the Gospel.[20] The contrast brings out a fundamental difference between the Gospel and the epistles – the Gospel is oriented to readers who have not yet been saved, while the epistles are for those who have already been saved. The Gospel seeks to evoke faith in Jesus as the Christ sent from the Father above; the epistles presuppose that faith and challenge the believer to live out its moral implications.

Because of the separatists, the epistles articulate a faith statement confessing Jesus as the Christ, reminiscent of the Gospel. A number of statements make this profession. "Who is the liar? It is whoever denies that Jesus is the Christ. Such a person is the antichrist – denying the Father and the Son" (1 John 2:22). "This is how you can recognize the Spirit of God: Every spirit that acknowledges that Jesus Christ has come in the flesh is from God" (1 John 4:2). "This is the one who came by water and blood – Jesus Christ. He did not come by water only, but by water and blood. And it is the Spirit

---

20. For example, after healing the man born blind, Jesus declares, "For judgment I have come into this world so that blind will see and those who see will become blind" (John 9:39). Through both literal and metaphorical use, Jesus refers to spiritual perception for the physically blind and a lack of perception for those physically able to see. In the context of 9:35-38 where the healed blind man professes faith in Jesus, Jesus' judgment focuses on faith in him or the lack of such faith. Overhearing Jesus' pronouncement, the Pharisees ask him, "Are we blind too?" (9:40). They phrase their question to expect a negative affirmation – that they are not blind. But Jesus responds, "If you were blind, you would not be guilty of sin; but now that you can claim you can see, your sin remains" (9:41). Jesus rebukes them for not admitting their spiritual blindness which would result in forgiveness. And because they refuse to confess, their guilt remains. The particular sin in question is the refusal to confess Jesus as coming from God (see 9:33). So the central issue is not a moral/ethical one but one of saving faith.

who testifies, because the Spirit is the truth" (1 John 5:6).²¹ "We know also that the Son of God has come and has given us understanding, so that we may know him who is true. And we are in him who is true by being in his Son Jesus Christ. He is the true God and eternal life" (1 John 5:20). "Because many deceivers have gone out into the world, those who do not confess Jesus Christ coming in the flesh; this is the deceiver and the antichrist" (2 John 1:7).

In essence, the confession acknowledges that Jesus is the Christ who became a man. Rejecting this truth denies the Father and the Son, and counters the witness of the Spirit. As a consequence, those who deny this will lack eternal life. Not only are they deceived, they go forth to deceive, actively swaying others to adopt their position. They may acknowledge Jesus and Christ separately, but they fail to regard the two individuals as one and the same person. This is their error.

In contrast with the Gospel's proclamations about Jesus as the Christ, the epistles do not depict Jesus' cosmic journey from above, where the Father resides, to the world below and eventually his return to the Father above. In the epistles, Jesus' identity is less bound up with his origins and his being sent and more with his incarnation in becoming the Christ. This is the point of dispute with the separatists.

Concept 2: Portrait of the opponents

Those opposed to Jesus in the Gospel differ dramatically from those in the epistles. The Gospel depicts "the Jews"²² confronting Jesus seemingly at every turn, particularly with regard to Sabbath "violations" (e.g. 5:16; 6:41; 7:11; 8:48; 9:18; 10:19). The confrontation comes to a climax when Jesus accuses them of having the devil as their father because they seek to kill him without justifiable cause and reject the truth about him (8:44). Likewise, the Pharisees posed a continuing threat (e.g. 7:47–48; 8:13; 9:15–16; 11:46–47; 12:19; 18:3). Both "the Jews" and Pharisees never expressed faith in Jesus and emphatically opposed him, culminating in his condemnation and crucifixion.

Those opposed to Jesus in the epistles, however, once enjoyed fellowship in the church. Unlike "the Jews" and Pharisees of the Gospel, these opponents had been in the inner circle of devotees. They had all shared a common profession of faith and derived their understanding of Christ from a common

---

21. I defer a fuller discussion on the significance of "water" and "blood" until a later chapter.
22. I use quotation marks for "the Jews" to mark them as the group that consistently opposes Jesus in order to distinguish them from the Jews as a people. For example, John 2:13 speaks of "the Passover of the Jews."

Introduction

source, the Gospel of John or, at least, the tradition from which the Gospel arose. However, a split became inevitable because of their differences when it came to interpreting the Gospel.

This difference may not always have been visible, but it was certainly real. As the author of 1 John notes, "They went forth from us, indeed they were not part of us. For if they were part of us, they would have remained with us, but because they departed it became clear that they were not part of us" (2:19). The traditionalists never embraced the truth fully, as did the conservatives who remained behind. In spite of the overlap in their understanding of Christ, the differences resulted in the church splitting as some departed. The author hints that the split was actually healthy for maintaining the purity of the confession of Jesus as the Christ. Had the two groups tried to remain in fellowship, internal strife would have erupted, resulting, no doubt, in further casualties.

The end result for Jesus' opponents in the Gospel and for the traditionalists in the epistles is the same. Both rejected the truth of Jesus being the Christ and so both are labelled "liars." For both, their sins remained.

The epistles take the consequences a step further. They depict the traditionalists as deficient morally and ethically. They do not love other believers, and hence cannot love God. They disobey the commandments and they fail to show hospitality to travelling ministers (3 John 5–8).

The programs, attendance, or even the vitality of the worship services are no measure of whether a church is fulfilling its purpose and role. An accurate measure involves the relationships the members foster with one another, how they care for others, the wholesomeness of their life-witness marked by truth and love, their obedience to the teaching of Scripture, their conduct in the marketplace with integrity and competence – all these together provide the measures by which the church's leaders should evaluate and correct as necessary. When people enter your church, will they be noticed, get connected, and feel a sense of belonging? And when they leave to resume life in the world, will they influence or be influenced?

Concept 3: Call for discernment

The author of 1 John calls on his readers to exercise discernment in testing the spirits for truth and falsehood (4:1–6). Such an invitation represents a Christian responsibility that the Gospel hints at. A Gospel parallel can be extracted from Jesus' statements: "My teaching is not my own. It comes from the one who sent me. Anyone who chooses to do the will of God will find out whether my teaching comes from God or whether I speak on my own. Whoever speaks on their own does so to gain personal glory, but he who seeks the glory of the one who sent him is a man of truth; there is nothing false about him" (John 7:16–18).

Jesus calls upon his audience to discern whether his teaching comes from God or not. If, as Jesus claims, his teaching comes from God, then he is true and righteous, that is, he is sent by God to glorify God through his teaching.

The readers of the epistles, on the other hand, have an objective benchmark to assess whether a teaching comes from God or not. "This is how you can recognize the Spirit of God: Every spirit that acknowledges that Jesus Christ has come in the flesh is from God, but every spirit that does not acknowledge Jesus is not from God" (1 John 4:2–3a).

The Gospel and 1 John are not presenting two radically different criteria. Both focus on recognizing Jesus' authenticity as the one sent by God in human flesh.

Another mark of a healthy church is the vigilance necessary to recognize, propagate, and defend the truth. Truth defines the church and fuels its continued growth. Falsehood destroys the church. The teaching of church leaders must conform to truth or be found wanting. The first line of defense against false doctrine is the leadership. But the church membership also has an important role to play in opposing untruth and upholding the truth. The leadership must teach, disciple, and discipline their members in order to ensure that everyone is prepared and ready to discern whether a teaching is from God or not.

Concept 4: Love

On the eve of his departure to return to the Father, Jesus issues a new commandment to his disciples: "A new command I give you: Love one another. As I have loved you, so you must love one another. By this everyone will know that you are my disciples, if you love one another" (John 13:34–35). But the disciples were not yet ready to comply. Two considerations suggest that the commandment would be obeyed only after Jesus' departure. First, Peter vainly boasts of his willingness to lay down his life for Jesus (John 13:37). Jesus responds with an accusatory question, "Will you really lay down your life for me?" (John 13:38a), before predicting Peter's denial (John 13:38b). Secondly, later in his farewell, Jesus states: "My command is this: Love each other as I have loved you. Greater love has no one than this: to lay down

Introduction

one's life for one's friends. You are my friends if you do what I command" (John 15:12–14).

Putting the two considerations together yields the following thought. Jesus regards his disciples as friends (John 15:15) and will demonstrate his love for them by laying down his life for them (John 13:1, 12–17, 31–33).[23] He, in turn, commands that they do likewise, being ready to lay down their lives for him and for each other. This sacrificial act satisfies the love commandment and demonstrates true friendship with Jesus and with one another. It shows the world what discipleship means. But the capacity to love as Jesus loves will not materialize until later, for he predicts: "A time is coming and in fact has come when you will be scattered, each to your own home. You will leave me [to be] all alone" (John 16:32a). Only after his crucifixion and resurrection, and indeed only after his departure to the Father, will they obey the commandment to love one another.[24]

The readers of the epistles, however, lived after the ascension and Pentecost. They, unlike the disciples of the Gospel narrative, are ready now to love one another. "Anyone who loves their brother and sister lives in the light, and there is nothing in them to make them stumble" (1 John 2:10). If the readers honor this commandment, the following truth applies: "But if we walk in the light, as he is in the light, we have fellowship with one another, and the blood of Jesus, his Son, purifies us from all sin" (1 John 1:7). Loving one another enables one to live in the light where fellowship with one another and with the Father and the Son (1 John 1:3) takes place and, at the same time, where one's sin is cleansed by Jesus' blood.

In fact, expressing love for one another by laying down one's life for others (John 15:12–14) resurfaces in 1 John 3:16 ("This is how we know what love is: Jesus Christ laid down his life for us. And we ought to lay down our lives for our brothers and sisters").

---

23. Francis J. Moloney explains that 13:1–30 concerns the passion of Jesus (*The Johannine Son of Man*, Biblioteca di Scienze Religiose 14 [Rome: Libreria Ateneo Salesiano, 1978], 190–194). The end of 13:1 reads, "He loved them to the end." The word "end" can mean "to the end of his life" or "to the fullest extent." Probably both meanings are implied. Leon Morris views Jesus' words in 13:31–33 as alluding to his death and ascension (*The Gospel According to John* [Grand Rapids, MI: Eerdmans, 1995], 560–562). Fernando F. Segovia, however, regards the verses as alluding to departure back to the Father (*The Farewell of the Word: The Johannine Call to Abide* [Minneapolis, MN: Fortress, 1991], 69–74).

24. Only with the coming of the promised Spirit of truth (John 16:7–15) will the disciples understand the full import of Jesus' teaching and commandment.

Hence, the love commandment is universally applicable to disciples for all time, although the ability to comply would be in the future in the Gospel and is in the present in the epistles.

A time differential signals the different reference points of the narratives of the Gospel and epistles.[25] Jesus labels his commandment "new" (John 13:34), but the author of 1 John regards it as "old" (2:7). The author recalls Jesus' initial giving of the commandment as something that happened in "the beginning." The prologue (1 John 1:1–5) implies that the readers belonged to a later generation of disciples who did not have direct contact with Jesus.[26]

Today we do not normally think about laying down our lives for others we love. We provide for their needs, spend time with them, treat them to a meal, and support them in their time of crisis. Recently an entire congregation was mobilized to intercede for a young mother facing a rare life-threatening condition triggered by her pregnancy. Her lungs developed cysts that caused her to be short of breath and cough up blood. At one point the doctors informed her husband that he might have to decide between saving his wife or the unborn baby, for both could not be saved. What a terrible decision to face! The husband would rather have suffered this disease himself than watch his wife endure it.

Love does not mean that we inevitably will die for someone, but that we are willing to do so. Such a sacrificial attitude characterizes what Jesus meant in his commandment. A church that loves members this way shines a powerful beacon of light. Who wouldn't want to join such a gathering?

A survey of the use of the word "love" in the Gospel and the epistles yields an insightful correlation.[27] The Gospel portrays God loving the world in order to redeem the world (3:16). He loves the Son[28] by giving and showing him all things (3:35; 5:20), and because the Son lays down his life (10:17) and obeys the Father (15:10). God also loves the disciples (17:23) who obey Jesus' commands (14:23). Jesus loves the Father (14:31) and also his

---

25. By narrative I mean the stories or narratives embedded in the Gospel and the epistles. As an example, Richard B. Hays analyzes the embedded narrative in Galatians (*The Faith of Jesus Christ: The Narrative Substructure of Galatians 3:1–4:11*, Biblical Resource Series [Grand Rapids, MI: Eerdmans, 2002]). He distinguishes between Paul's personal story as secondary to the primary gospel story (30). In a similar way, we are looking for the thread of Christ's story running through the Gospel of John and the epistles.
26. Schuchard points out the differentiation between the eyewitnesses of Jesus ("we") and the readers ("you") (*1–3 John*, 89–92).
27. The word "love" may be a verb or noun. I am interested only in the concept being conveyed and the particular literary form used.
28. 15:9 [first occurrence of "love"]; 17:23 [second occurrence], 24, 26 ["love" appears twice].

Introduction

disciples,[29] provided they keep his commands (15:10). The disciples ought to love one another[30] and Jesus[31] by keeping his commands[32] (14:28).

Negatively, the world loves darkness (3:19) and is incapable of loving God (5:42) and Jesus (8:42). The world can only love selfishly (12:25, 43) or only its own (15:19).

Love as a defining attribute characterizes God, Jesus, the disciples, and the world. The love of God, Jesus, and the disciples is always depicted as directed toward others – God loves the world, Jesus, and the disciples; Jesus loves the Father and the disciples; and the disciples are to love one another and Jesus. Often the love portrayed expresses itself through appropriate action. God sends his Son. Jesus lays down his life for the disciples. They obey Jesus' commandments. The world, however, directs its love toward self, seeking personal glory or gain. It proves incapable of loving "others" – God, Jesus, or the disciples. Because the world loves only its own, it fosters a gap between itself and the realm above. Anyone belonging to the other realm is hated. A "we versus them" mentality reinforces two things: a self-condemning preference for darkness (symbolic of being devoid of the life only the Word can give, 1:4–5), and an inherent inability to span the divide between the two realms in order to know God. The world cannot love God or Jesus because it refuses to believe in Jesus.

The epistles generally agree with the Gospel in stating God's love for his children[33] that achieves its intended purpose when they obey his commandments[34] and provide for one another's needs (negatively 1 John 3:17–18). But 1 John goes further in declaring his essential quality, "God is love."[35] He

---

29. 11:3, 5, 36; 13:1 [twice], 23, 34 [the second of three occurrences]; 14:21 [fourth occurrence]; 15:9 [second and third occurrences], 12 [second occurrence]; 19:26; 20:2; 21:7, 20.
30. 13:34 [first occurrence], 35; 15:12 [first occurrence].
31. 21:15 [second occurrence], 16 [twice], 17 [thrice].
32. 14:15, 21 [first two occurrences], 23 [first occurrence], the negative expression in 14:24.
33. 1 John 3:1; 4:7 [second occurrences], 16 [first occurrence], 19 [second occurrence]; 2 John 3.
34. 1 John 2:5; 4:12 [second occurrence], 4:17–18 [second and third occurrences].
35. 1 John 4:8 [second occurrence], 16 [second occurrence]. Also see Schnackenburg, *Epistles*, 210–216.

demonstrates his love by sending his Son.[36] His children too are to love one another.[37] They are also to love God.[38]

Love for the world disables one from loving God (1 John 2:15 [first two occurrences]). A related love would be love for prominence (3 John 9).

Continuing the Gospel theme of God's love, the epistles narrow the object of that love from the world (John 3:16) to his children (1 John 4:10). Indeed, the majority of Gospel references allude to his love for the disciples. But the Gospel's depiction of the Father's love for the world expressed by sending his Son aligns with the invitation to believe (John 20:31). The epistles, on the other hand, have moved beyond the invitation to address those who have already accepted the invitation. Moreover, 1 John makes a statement: "God is love." That is something the Gospel may hint at but stops short of stating openly. 1 John advances the Gospel concept of God loving his children by articulating the purpose of his love – that they fulfill his purpose by loving one another. Again, the Gospel implies this thought that 1 John explains plainly.

The Gospel theme of loving one another continues unabated in the epistles. Indeed, for the Gospel and epistles, the major characteristic of God's children and disciples highlight compliance with this commandment. Obedience implies love for God himself. The negative corollary becomes "if one fails to love the brethren, even at the cost of his life, he fails to love God." Love for God takes an indirect path – love for fellow children of God in tangible ways as the means of loving God.

The love theme features two complementary aspects for which one must maintain a balanced compliance. Children of God must love God by loving one another and, at the same time, avoid loving the world and the things in it. The general tenor of the epistles suggests that the unnamed "things" refer to worldly attractions and the erroneous teachings about Christ by the separatists.

At a missions conference, a missionary couple shared their experience of returning home after years on the field working with a primitive tribe.

---

36. 1 John 4:9–10 [first and third occurrences], 11 [first occurrence].
37. 1 John 2:10; negatively 3:10, positively 3:11, 14 [first occurrence], and negatively 3:14 [second occurrence]; positively 3:23; 4:7 [first and third occurrences], negatively 4:8 [first occurrence], positively 4:11 [second occurrence], 12 [first occurrence], 16 [third occurrence], 18 [first occurrence], 19 [first occurrence], negatively 20 [second occurrence], 21 [second occurrence]; 5:1 [second occurrence], 2 [first occurrence]; 2 John 1, 5–6; 3 John 1, 6.
38. Negatively 1 John 2:15 [third occurrence] and 4:20 [first and third occurrences], positively 21 [first occurrence]; 5:1 [first occurrence], 2 [second occurrence], 3.

INTRODUCTION

During the afternoon before the evening service, they visited a local mall teeming with shoppers. They took in the glitter, sounds, and impressive merchandise on display. That evening they shared about their visit. Taking stock of what they had missed while away, they noted an absence of any desire for anything the mall offered. They were content and happy. The joys of family, supportive churches, and an unwavering conviction that they were exactly where God wanted them to be gave a peaceful sense of fulfillment – something the world cannot give.

Concept 5: The world

The Gospel uses the term "world" in a multifaceted fashion, as do the epistles.[39] One Gospel use refers to humanity (more precisely Israel according to the narrative), the object of God's love and saving gesture through his Son.[40] A second use alludes to the public in a general way, where, for example, Jesus' brothers urged him to show up in public at the Feast of Booths.[41] Yet, a third use regards the world, as represented by "the Jews" and Pharisees, that rejects and hates Jesus.[42] Another use connotes the physical realm[43] or the life in the physical realm.[44] A fifth use appears in a contrast of two realms, the realm above where the Father resides and the realm below populated by humanity, between which only Jesus traverses.[45]

The above survey yields the following summary for the nuances of "world" in the Gospel: humanity (Israel) as the object of God's love [29], public or out in the open [2], opposition to Jesus and his disciples [24], the physical realm [6], and the realm below [14].[46] The two prominent uses of "world" focus on humanity/Israel as the object of God's love and the opposition against Jesus and his disciples. These two uses give a rough overview of the Gospel – in love God makes contact with the world through his Son Jesus but, except for the disciples, the world rejects the Son.

---

39. See Schnackenburg's discussion on "world" in 1 John 2:15–17 (*Epistles*, 125–128).
40. 1:9–10 [first two occurrences], 29; 3:16–17, 19; 4:42; 6:14, 33, 51; 8:12, 26; 9:5 [twice], 39; 10:36; 11:27; 12:19, 46–47 [twice]; 14:17, 19, 22; 17:6, 9, 21, 23.
41. 7:4; 18:20.
42. 1:10 [third occurrence]; 7:7; 12:31 [twice]; 14:30–31; 15:18–19 [five times]; 16:8, 11, 20, 33 [twice]; 17:14 [thrice], 15–16, 25.
43. 11:9; 17:5, 24; 21:25.
44. 12:25; 16:21.
45. 8:23; 13:1 [twice]; 14:27; 16:28 [twice]; 17:11 [twice], 13, 18 [twice]; 18:36 [twice], 37.
46. The number in brackets represents frequency of occurrence of "world" for that particular nuance.

The epistles evidence a similar nuance of humanity, the object of God's salvific activity.[47] A second use speaks of the world system, its ideology and attractions.[48] Another nuance reflects opposition to God as seen in opposition to his disciples.[49] A fourth use relates to the physical realm without any moral or ethical aspect (1 John 3:17).

The nuances of "world" in the epistles divide into four categories: humanity as the object of God's redemptive activities [3], the world system [5], opposition to God and his disciples [14], and the physical realm [1]. The most frequent use highlights opposition to God, followed by the world system that stands contrary to God's truth.

The Gospel and the epistles share the common and quite prominent nuance of the world opposing God. In the Gospel, the world opposes Jesus now and the disciples later and, in the epistles, the world opposes the disciples now. The epistles introduce a new category, the world as an ideological system that denies the Gospel truth, particularly as it relates to Jesus as the Christ. Humanity as the object of God's love boasts the lion's share of occurrences in the Gospel. In contrast, the epistles feature only a few such occurrences. Another significant difference between the Gospel and epistles resides in the Gospel's Jewish orientation of humanity, whereas the epistles appear to broaden the scope to include Gentiles.

Concept 6: Light and darkness

This dualism marks the Gospel and the epistles. The Gospel prologue (1:1–18) introduces the ever-existing Word as the light that comes into the world (1:5, 7–9) to give life (1:4). It comes to enlighten every person; but men preferred the darkness in order to hide their evil deeds (3:19–20). However, those who practice the truth come to the light in order to reveal their deeds accomplished in God (3:21). Later, Jesus proclaims that he is the light of the world (8:12; 9:5). Hence, the Gospel presents Jesus as the light coming into the world in order to give the gift of life. Those dwelling in the world live in darkness without the light that signifies life from above. Two possible responses greet the light's arrival – a shrinking back into the darkness to hide one's evil deeds and a coming forth into the light to reveal one's deeds performed with God's enablement. The light exposes each person and reveals the nature of their deeds. This exposure serves as judgment (3:19).

---

47. 1 John 2:2; 4:9, 14.
48. 1 John 2:15 [thrice], 16 [twice], 17.
49. 1 John 3:1, 13; 4:1, 3–4, 5 [thrice], 17; 5:4 [twice], 5, 19; 2 John 7.

Introduction

Even the literal sense of light (11:9–10) takes on a metaphorical sense. Contrasting day and night, Jesus declares that people easily stumble at night, not because it is dark but because they lack guiding light within.

More explicitly, Jesus claims to be the light for a little while longer in the world and urges his audience to believe in the light, that is, to believe in him (12:35–36, 44–46). What shortens his stay in the world is his imminent being lifted up from the earth (12:32–33). By rejecting him as the light, a person stands condemned to darkness, separated from Jesus and losing eternal life (12:50).

The imagery of light and darkness continues in 1 John. In addition to the statement "God is love" (4:8), the author proclaims that "God is light, and there is no darkness in him" (1:5), another essential attribute of God. What the author connotes by these metaphors can be inferred from the following verses. In order to enjoy fellowship with God, believers must not live in darkness but in light (1:6). Only if they practice the truth and do not lie, can they enter into that fellowship. This conduct suggests that a correlation exists between light and truth. The moral/ethical dimension surfaces with another affirmation that the blood of Jesus the Son cleanses from all sin (1:7). The thrust of 1:8–10 points to confessing one's sin and being forgiven, rather than to denying that sin. Then to walk in the light requires an honest and open relationship with God where personal sin is dealt with in the prescribed manner.

1 John 2:8–11 brings forth another moral/ethical aspect of walking in the light, loving fellow believers. Facilitating horizontal relationships with fellow children of God, characterized by love, ensures that the true light continues to shine and that any impediment that causes stumbling be removed.

In 1 John, then, the metaphor of light and darkness signifies a proper life lived in truth and love, having sins forgiven and loving the brethren. These ideas differ from the Gospel idea of believing in Jesus having come into the world offering eternal life. A common bond, however, forges a bridge between the two writings with regard to the truth. The Gospel indicates that those whose deeds are truth (3:21) come to the light, whereas 1 John equates walking in the light with practicing the truth (1:6). Truth specifically centers on acknowledging one's sins and loving the brethren. These echo Jesus' implied invitation to confess sin in order to be forgiven (9:39–41) and his new commandment to his disciples to love one another (13:34; 15:12–13, 17).

Simply being a long-time churchgoer and speaking Christian jargon give no assurance that a person has the light of Christ. Many church statements of faith require members be a Christian, born-again, regenerate, or believer – various ways of specifying the same thing. Besides asking questions about a person's relationship with Christ and understanding of Scripture, what do church leaders look for? Evidence of high moral and ethical practices, loving relationships with fellow believers, and a record of serving the church rank high on the list. We ask about a person's spiritual disciplines and manner of life in the world. In summary, we want members who love the Lord and his children, and who keep themselves unstained by the world.

Conclusion

This chapter has shown that the Gospel of John provides the indispensable foundation for a proper understanding of the epistles. The key concepts that characterize the Gospel reemerge in the epistles, tying them together. In fact, the Gospel is the grand key to unlocking the message of the epistles. The good news is the Father sending his Son Jesus Christ into the world so that those who believe in him may experience a change of association – no longer belonging to the world that harbors hostility toward the Lord and his disciples but now belonging to a community marked by forgiveness of sins, love for one another, truth, and a mission of being sent into the world like Jesus was sent.

The pluralistic world that is Asia presents a challenge for disciples whom Jesus sends to bear the message that he is the Christ to be worshiped and acknowledged as sovereign Lord. However, a diversity of culture, language, and religion deeply entrenched in the minds and hearts of the people competes to define an alternative truth and caricatures the Christian faith as foreign, invasive and, hence, a purveyor of untruth.

Addressing this scenario, 1 John 4:1 lifts a prophetic voice cautioning: "Beloved, do not believe every spirit but test the spirits [to discern] whether they are from God, because many false prophets have gone out into the world." The church in Asia must heed this admonition if it hopes to not merely survive but to succeed in its mission. Confidence comes from faith in the certain victory that has overcome the world (1 John 5:4). In the present context, that means overcoming our Asian world system of thought, beliefs, and practices that deny Jesus as the Christ, Savior of mankind, and Son of God.

And how does the church gain such faith? Scripture supplies the answer: "Then faith comes from hearing the message, and the message is heard through the word about Christ" (Rom 10:17) – in the present case, the word

Introduction

of Christ in 1, 2, and 3 John. So it is with a sense of urgency that we read these ancient letters for a still relevant truth that addresses a comparable situation we face today.

1 JOHN

1 JOHN 1

"Lone wolf" describes a wolf which lives alone, separated from the pack. When applied to people, lone wolves prefer to do things independently, often disregarding the group's plans and activities. This behavior goes against the concept and aims of fellowship and can undermine the ministry of the local church. 1 John 1 focuses on a particular aspect of fellowship that values vibrant relationships with God the Father and Son and with other believers. Such fellowship can only be achieved through lives characterized by truth and personal righteousness.

Representing the older generation of disciples, the author passes on his experience and wisdom to his readers, the younger generation. In particular, he introduces them to the Father and the Son based on a personal relationship.[1] Using the language of physical intimacy – hearing, seeing, and touching – the writer depicts a closeness that trumpets: "God is near and immediately accessible." With each succeeding generation inviting the next to meet God, the church can transcend any one lifespan of believers as younger disciples eventually replace their predecessors, thereby maintaining fellowship with the Lord and with one another long term.

A quick survey of the term "church" in the book of Acts confirms the idea of a community of believers who experience various situations together and act in a synchronized manner.[2] Conceptually, 1 John 1 portrays the believing community as walking in the light or truth, a metaphor for a right moral relationship with God who is light. Light is a common symbol in other religions. Buddhist art, for example, depict a rainbow light radiating out from within Buddha that confirms the attainment of enlightenment. But the light in our letter refers to an attribute of God himself. At most, the

---

1. Christopher Cowan examines the issue of the relationship between the Father and the Son in response to recent assertions that the Son is not subordinate to the Father in their respective roles and reaffirms Jesus' subordination by assessing the language of Jesus being sent, his dependence and obedience, and the "Father" and "Son" terminology ("The Father and Son in the Fourth Gospel: Johannine Subordination Revisited," *JETS* 49 [2006]: 115–135).
2. Richard P. Thompson, *Keeping the Church in Its Place: The Church as Narrative Character in Acts* (New York: T & T Clark, 2006).

devotee can aspire to live in harmony with that divine light as a testament of reconciliation between a holy God and a forgiven believer.

A stark distinctive emerges as we read this letter. Whereas the religions of Asia represent an integral part of society, its culture, beliefs and practices, Christianity signals a clear separation as when 1 John 2:15 warns: "Do not love the world or anything in the world." These ancient writings, the Gospel of John and the three epistles, demand a choice – believe in Jesus as the Christ and separate from the world's beliefs or reject Jesus and remain affiliated with the world – because association with the world disrupts fellowship, vertically with the Father and the Son and horizontally within the community of disciples.

1:1–5 Hit the Ground Running

The initial section, 1 John 1:1–5, omits any greeting by immediately delving into the main topic.[3] This omission makes this epistle and Hebrews unique among NT letters. The "we" in the opening verses may refer to the author and other historical witnesses to the Christ event or signifies a faith statement and hence is not a reference to eyewitnesses.[4] Although interpreters are divided on the matter,[5] both possibilities fit the context and so both are adopted in the following discussion. The author, in a collective sense, encompasses generations of disciples who have experienced Jesus in a spiritual encounter, including the first disciples, and who have successively passed on their legacy to the next generation.

---

3. Modern interpreters tend to regard 1 John 1:1–4 as the prologue. See, for example, Thomas F. Johnson, *1, 2, and 3 John*, New International Biblical Commentary (Peabody, MA: Hendrickson, 1993), 25–27; and Martin M. Culy, *1, 2, 3 John: A Handbook on the Greek Text* (Waco, TX: Baylor University, 2004), 1–10. However, Charles H. Talbert includes v. 5 (*A Literary and Theological Commentary on the Fourth Gospel and Johannine Epistles*, rev. ed. [Macon, GA: Smyth & Helwys, 2005], 6–7). I favor Talbert's view because of the recurrence of "we have heard" in 1:1, 3, 5, and of the close affinity between "we declare to you" (1:2) and (1:5), although different verbs are used.
4. A related issue is whether to interpret the "we" as an editorial plural or as a reference to a collection of witnesses. However, given the author's regular use of the singular when referring to himself (for example, 2:1, 7–8, 12–14, 21, 26; 5:13) and the occasional reflexive "let us love one another" (4:7), I lean toward the company of witnesses.
5. Rudolf Bultmann, for example, argues that the late date for 1 John precludes eyewitnesses of the historical event being still alive, offering instead that the "we" were eschatological eyewitnesses (*The Johannine Epistles: A Commentary on the Johannine Epistles*, trans. R. P. O'Hara, L. C. McGaughy, and R. W. Funk, Hermeneia [Philadelphia: Fortress, 1973], 9–11). Taking the more traditional view, Scott M. Lewis locates the author and his readers in the end of the first century and early portion of the second (*The Gospel According to John and the Johannine Letters*, New Collegeville Bible Commentary 4 [Collegeville, MN: Liturgical, 2005], 108–109).

1 John

This biblical pattern ought to be replicated in the church if the church is to continue long term. Many churches conscientiously strive to preach the word faithfully and reach out into the surrounding community by being incarnational. Yet a third trait, that of intentional fellowship, ensures continuity of the faith. The tragic commentary on the generation that succeeded Joshua and his contemporaries haunts the pages of Scripture (Judg 2:10–12). Joshua's generation failed to pass on the legacy of revering and serving the Lord. Sadly, their children did not have a relationship with the Lord. The church can avoid this tragedy through fellowship.

This initial section (1:1–5) may be divided into five components: verses 1–3b, 3c, 3de, 4, and 5.[6] I will discuss each component in turn. First, I jump to 1:3c, then 1:3de, before turning to 1:1–3b. This order of discussion treats the main clause (1:3c) first, followed by 1:3de. Then verses 1–3b would become easier to understand.

The main clause in 1:3c reads: "We proclaim to you." The one generation of disciples passes on what they have experienced to a younger generation. The content of the communiqué is in verses 1–3. The form of the verb "proclaim" suggests an unfolding process.[7] The identity of the writer and the reader assume center stage.[8] The writer represents disciples who have something important to share. Sharing signifies fellowship.

The writer states the purpose for sharing: "so that you also may have fellowship with us" (1:3d). The basis for fellowship is shared experience, whether actual or vicarious. A testimony invites a reader to enter into the

---

6. To point out syntactical nuances of 1:3, I refer to my own translation. But for the rest of 1:1–5, I refer to the 2011 edition of the NIV. Commentators regard vv. 1–4 as a single sentence. See, for example, Raymond E. Brown, *The Epistles of John: Translated with Introduction, Notes, and Commentary*, AB 30 (Garden City, NY: Doubleday, 1982), 153; and Bruce G. Schuchard, *1–3 John*, Concordia Commentary (Saint Louis, MO: Concordia Publishing House, 2012), 65.

7. "Proclaim" is in the present tense to convey, from the speaker's point of view, an ongoing process of declaring. The idea emphasizes more than the mere fact of communication. The focus ferrets out the different aspects of the content communicated in some sequence.

8. We simply identify them as two successive generations of disciples. Raymond E. Brown refined his hypothesis of a Johannine community behind the Gospel and three epistles in *The Community of the Beloved Disciple: The Life, Loves, and Hates of an Individual Church in New Testament Times* (Mahwah, NJ: Paulist, 1979), *Epistles of John*, and *An Introduction to the Gospel of John*, ed. Francis J. Moloney (Garden City, NY: Doubleday, 2003). Scholars, like Paul N. Anderson, accept the hypothetical community ("The Community That Raymond Brown Left Behind: Reflections on the Johannine Dialectical Situation." Online: http://www.bibleinterp.com/PDFs/Anderson.pdf [accessed May 2, 2015]). But see Richard Bauckham, ed., *The Gospels for All Christians: Rethinking the Gospel Audiences* (Grand Rapids, MI: Eerdmans, 1998). I find Bauckham's position cogent.

story. Stories have an almost magical effect as the reader can readily identify with the writer, feeling the writer's emotions and seeing the event with the imagination. The writer's point of view and values are shared and accepted.[9]

The benefit of entering into fellowship with the writer rests on 1:3e: "And our fellowship is with the Father and with his Son, Jesus Christ." The designation "his Son Jesus Christ" occurs four times in the NT with three of those appearing in this epistle (1:3; 3:23; 5:20). The only other incidence is in 1 Corinthians 1:9, expressing a very similar idea. But what makes 1 John 1:3 unique is the double construction "with the Father and with his Son, Jesus Christ." In using the preposition "with" twice, one for each person of the Godhead, the writer carefully distinguishes between the Father and the Son as two separate persons.[10]

Fellowship with the Father and with the Son comes through an intimate relationship with the writer and other disciples. But the disciple must separate from the world in order to bond. Indeed, the means to have fellowship with the Father and the Son is through church fellowship.[11]

A profound change occurs through an encounter with Jesus as the Word of life. A person changes membership from that of the world to that of the community of disciples across generations and of the Father and the Son. A change in allegiance also signals moral responsibility and conduct. Status depends on being part of the community. Departure from the community sacrifices the status (1 John 2:19).[12]

The structure of this subsection (1:1–3b) is complex. I lay out the subsection in the following manner to highlight the flow:
- that which was from the beginning (1:1a)
- that which we heard (1:1b)

---

9. Judith M. Lieu observes that the exchange is non-reciprocal, one-directional where the recipients' implicit acceptance of the author's authority gives him that authority and not from any inherent authority resident in the author himself ("Us or You? Persuasion and Identity in 1 John," JBL 127 [2008]: 805–819, especially 808–810)

10. Brown notes that the double preposition avoids "a confusion of identities" (*Epistles*, 171). Rudolf Schnackenburg speaks of "a mutual interpenetration" in which God and man maintain their distinctive personalities while abiding in one another (*The Johannine Epistles: Introduction and Commentary*, trans. Reginald and Ilse Fuller [New York, NY: Crossroad, 1992], 63–69). He confirms that fellowship with the Father can only be achieved through the Son.

11. Zane C. Hodges points out that fellowship with God requires fellowship with other believers as a precondition ("Fellowship and Confession in 1 John 1:5–10," *BSac* 129 [1972]: 48–60).

12. Taking the perspective of the author, Dirk van der Merwe labels those who left as opponents with harsh descriptives that imply that they are not of God but of the world, deceivers, lacking life ("The Identification and Examination of the Elements that Caused a Schism in the Johannine Community at the End of the First Century CE," *HTS* 63 [2007]: 1153–1154).

- that which we saw with our eyes (1:1c)
- that which we beheld and our hands touched (1:1d)
- concerning the word of life (1:1e)
- and the life was revealed (1:2a)
- and we saw (1:2b)
- and we bear witness (1:2c)
- and we proclaim to you (1:2d)
- eternal life which was with the Father (1:2e)
- and [it] was revealed to us (1:2f)
- that which we saw (1:3a)
- and we heard (1:3b)

The grammatical relationship 1:1–3b has with the main clause (1:3c) determines the role of this opening subsection. Clearly it encompasses the content of what the author desires to declare to his readers. Sharing this content enables the readers to enter into fellowship with the author and with the Father and the Son. The repetition of "that which" emphasizes the focus of the content shared.[13] The reference to physical sense perception – seeing, touching, hearing – suggests that the focus is not some abstract concept but a concrete, physical object.

The phrase "concerning the word of life" (1:1e) identifies the focus of the content declared. Yet, "the word of life" itself is a metaphorical pointer to an ultimate reality. Given the relationship between the Gospel of John and 1 John (see the Introduction), we look for clues particularly as we compare the prologues of both writings. Toward the end of the Gospel prologue the writer identifies the Word as Jesus Christ (1:14–18). Thus, we correlate Jesus as the Word, the source of life, who is intimately related to God the Father. But one significant difference lies in the temporal reference "in the beginning" (John 1:1a; 1 John 1:1a). John 1:2–3 clarify that John 1:1a depicts the Word's pre-existence. However, 1 John 1:1b–3b signify that 1 John 1:1a describes the personal encounter with the Word.

For the first disciples, who were apostles, "the beginning" alludes to their encounter during Jesus' earthly ministry.[14] In fact, a defining qualification to

---

13. "That which" is a relative pronoun that points to a referent. The referent is the real focus of the content shared.
14. D. Edmond Hiebert, "An Expositional Study of 1 John, Part 1 (of 10 parts): An Exposition of 1 John 1:1–4," *BSac* 145 (1988): 201. Also, Richard Bauckham, *Jesus and the Eyewitnesses: The Gospels as Eyewitness Testimony* (Grand Rapids, MI: Eerdmans, 2006).

be an apostle numbered among the first disciples required the person to have accompanied Jesus from his baptism to his ascension (Acts 1:21–22). The disciple's primary function is to be a witness of Jesus' resurrection.

For later disciples, "the beginning" refers to an encounter with Jesus through the witness of earlier disciples. Faith is required whether the encounter was physical, as for the earliest disciples, or spiritual, as for all future disciples. One must believe that Jesus is the Word of life.

Significantly, the manner by which the author expresses "which was with the Father" (1 John 1:2e), recalling "and the Word was God" (John 1:1b), depicts a dynamic relationship.[15] This depiction serves as the pattern to be repeated in the relationship the disciple has with Jesus. The disciple is ever moving toward Jesus in a similar expression of love and devotion.

An implicit invitation to a similar encounter with Jesus as the Word of eternal life extends to the readers. They too can meet Jesus as did the writer. They too can "see," "hear," and "touch" Jesus. They do so through the witness of the writer. Implicit too is the potential that the readers can witness to yet others who will be able to encounter Jesus. The chain reaction is potentially endless and further suggests that succeeding generations of disciples may witness to the next generation and so pass on their legacy concerning the Word of life. Theoretically, the succession can be endless except for Christ's return.

The author of this epistle represents an authority figure who links the old generation with the new in passing on a spiritual legacy. He calls to mind a *pir* (literally "elder," a spiritual mentor for many in the Islamic context of India and Pakistan) with the role of guiding and blessing in socio-spiritual and political matters. Given deep-seated corruption in parts of Asia, the leadership challenge focuses on integrity. The author models how church leaders should lead.

The author adds another element to the fellowship between disciples and with the Father and Son, that of joy to complement life eternal (1:1e, 2e): "We write this to make our joy complete" (1:4). As life has an eternal quality, so too does joy. The "this" refers to 1:1–3, all that the author experienced in the encounter with Jesus the Word of life. Strikingly, the author contrasts "write" with "testify" and "proclaim" (1:2cd and 1:3c). The latter two modes

---

15. The preposition "with" in both places normally pictures movement toward something. Then the "Word" or "eternal life," both metaphorical descriptions of Jesus, facilitates a dynamic and vibrant relationship by moving toward the Father. Jesus is ever moving toward the Father, a pictorial representation of his love for the Father.

of communication usually allude to speaking in an oral society.[16] However, maintaining the coherence of 1:2–4 connotes that the author testifies and proclaims what he encountered through the written medium. A written communiqué suggests permanence.

The concept, Word of life, has great significance for the people of Asia, particularly for those struggling with poverty, prevalent in Asia. In the case of Pakistan, for example, in spite of some economic development over the decades, the unequal distribution of resources creates a situation for many such that "the Sun rises but light does not shine." Sickness, suffering and deep impoverishment raise a question in the minds of many: "What difference to me does Jesus as the Word of life make?" Does his proclamation, "I have come that they may have life, and have it to the full" (John 10:10), mean full stomachs? The mission and ministry of the church are to meet felt needs. It must share Jesus in tangible ways where scarcity of food and especially water create another layer of impoverishment.

In the midst of increasing insecurity in the present world, particularly in areas of intense persecution like in some regions of West Asia, India, and East Asia, the church of Christ has a calling to proclaim and manifest the Word of life.[17] First, it is the message of salvation from sin and, secondly, it is the message of sustainability of material resources, development, and peace. This calls disciples to stand for development and peace, love, and respect for all the down-trodden in society. The message of life breeds hope for many believers who constitute the poorest of the poor. They often lack the basic necessities of life, face social discrimination, and are stigmatized by their menial jobs that no one else wants. The message of life, both for the immediate present and for the more distant future, challenges disciples to engage in mission and to contextualize their religious practices.

---

16. David Carr discusses how important teachings were transmitted from generation to generation in the Ancient Near East, particularly the Jewish Law ("Torah on the Heart: Literary Jewish Textuality Within Its Ancient Near Eastern Context," *Oral Tradition* 25 [2010]: 17–40). Carr focuses on the education and enculturation process in a familial context. His study holds particular relevance in that the author(s) addressed readers as "children" (1 John 2:1, 12, 13e, 18) and "beloved" (1 John 2:7; 4:7; 3 John 5), thereby invoking the picture of family communication.

17. A partial listing of countries in West Asia includes Afghanistan, Pakistan, Iraq, Iran, Syria, Sudan, and Jordan (Online: http://www.un.org/Depts/Cartographic/map/profile/westasia.pdf). Another partial listing for East Asia includes China, Brunei, Vietnam, Indonesia, Myanmar, North Korea, and Malaysia (Online: http://www.state.gov/p/eap/ci/).

In 1:4 the author seeks the readers' joy in the fullest possible sense.[18] The source of their joy would be the fellowship they may have. Negatively, a disciple cannot achieve full joy apart from fellowship. Living in isolation and cut off from regular contact with other disciples would also disrupt one's connection with the Lord. Then one cannot access the only source of joy, God.

The church represents an effective means to achieve promised joy. Living in the world but not affiliated with the world in any compromising way garners tension and conflict. The challenge that the church must accept, then, is to strive for a living encounter with Jesus as the Word of life through vibrant worship and fellowship. Only then will disciples experience the fullness of joy even when struggling with the trials of life.

The author particularizes the content of his message to his readers when he states: "This is the message we have heard from him and declare to you: God is light; in him there is no darkness at all" (1:5). This verse serves as a "bridge" that transition from the prologue into the body of the epistle that discusses the significance of God as light.

The declaration "God is light" portrays God's character in metaphorical language.[19] Regarding "light" as life finds support in the nearby occurrence of "the Word of life" (1:1e) and "eternal life which was with the Father" (1:2e). And yet we suspect more may be meant given "in him there is no darkness at all" (1:5e). We will keep reading this epistle to uncover additional aspects of this concept of light. But at this point we may conclude that those desiring fellowship with God must possess eternal life and share in his character morally.

1:6–7 Light, Metaphor for Fellowship

Lighthouses represent hope and guidance for ships navigating treacherous waters in the dark. The light beaming out from them helps seafarers to steer the right course and avoid the dangers threatening to sink their ships.

Similarly, the contrasting metaphors of "walking in darkness" and "walking in the light" in 1:6–7 signify the dangers of a darkened path and the

---

18. The reference to joy being fulfilled recalls four similar expressions in the Gospel (3:29; 15:11; 16:19–24; 17:13). For a fuller discussion, see Raymond E. Brown, *The Gospel according to John (i–xii), Introduction, Translation, and Notes*, AB 29 (Garden City, NY: Doubleday, 1966), 156; and Francis J. Moloney, *The Gospel of John*, SP 4 (Collegeville, MN: Liturgical, 1998), 448–451
19. D. Edmond Hiebert, "An Expositional Study of 1 John Part 2 (of 10 parts): An Exposition of 1 John 1:5–2:6," BSac 145 (1988): 331. Syntactically, the definite article accompanies "God" but not "light," thereby making it clear that "God" is the subject and "light" describes his attribute metaphorically.

blessedness of traversing a lighted path. The author writes: "If we claim to have fellowship with him and yet[20] walk[21] in the darkness, we lie and do not live out the truth" (1:6). Darkness connotes falsehood and denial of the truth. In contrast, 1:7 highlights three characteristics of a true disciple – "walk in the light,"[22] "have fellowship with one another," and purified "from all sin." Walking in the light implies conformity to a life of uprightness, enabling fellowship with God who is light, the perfection of uprightness.

"Truth" in the present context is not a set of doctrines to know, believe, and confess as a catechism. Here, truth delineates a life lived in obedience to God's instruction and commands. It is tangible and can be observed by others.

Fellowship according to this epistle involves a community of disciples characterized by the common trait of uprightness, living in conformity with God's word. The cleansed community seeks fellowship with God through the central reality of Jesus' efficacious blood.

With 1:7 connoting a contingency,[23] a choice rests with the reader – walk in the light or walk in the darkness. The decision has moral overtones. One choice results in sins forgiven and being cleansed.[24] The other choice leaves one's sins to fester.

These verses highlight a dualism that continues from John's Gospel, namely the contrasting metaphors of light and darkness, truth and falsehood.

---

20. The conjunction "and yet" normally links items to form a collection or group of some kind. Here, however, there seems to be a concessive thrust that conveys a contrast between what is verbally claimed and action that does not align with that claim.
21. In the subjunctive mood, "walk" conveys a possibility. In the present tense, the verb further depicts the event as a pattern of normative behavior. The previous verb "say" is also subjunctive but aorist in tense. The tense simply views a person's verbal action in its totality, that is, the person makes a statement without regard to how it was said. The two subjunctive verbs frame a compound protasis ("if" statement).
22. Commonly "to walk" depicts metaphorically a person's manner of life and conduct in the OT. See, for example, Pss 1:1; 15:2; 26:1, 3, 11; 39:6; 78:10; 81:12–13; 82:5; 86:11; Prov 2:7, 13, 20; 6:12; 8:20; 10:9; 11:20. Darkness, then, symbolizes a wicked lifestyle devoid of any desire to honor God by obeying his laws and perverting justice. Truth, on the other hand, aligns with God's word and instruction, thereby characterizing such a person as righteous.
23. This is the same kind of conditional statement as found in 1:6 but with a simple protasis. There is no verbal claim. Apparently, the author portrays the disciple who "walks the talk" as not feeling any compulsion to make a claim since his conduct confirms his character and his association with God.
24. In the present tense, "cleanses" signifies ongoing, continuous activity. And given the present tense of the other two verbs "walk" and "have," the author conveys an ongoing coordinated set of activities, interrelated and interdependent. As disciples "walk" in the light, that is, as they live uprightly, they enjoy fellowship with one another and, at the same time, each are cleansed from every sin. And as they continue in fellowship and cleansing, they continue living upright lives.

Disciples continually face a choice, and have no possible recourse to an intermediate third option. Scripture does not envision a half-way disciple. We either follow the Lord wholeheartedly or we turn away.

Church fellowship is integral to the Christian life. It cannot be confined to regularly scheduled gatherings of the faithful. It showcases a life lived in submission to God and his word. It further confirms a reconciled life, continually cleansed by Jesus' blood, where the believer enjoys continuous fellowship with the Lord. The believer understands the necessity of fellowship with other believers as life-sustaining and being responsible to each other. Disciples need the church and the church needs them.

1:8–9 Truth or Dare

An old game called Truth or Dare demands that a player choose between answering a question, often an embarrassing one, truthfully and taking a dare, usually doing something difficult or even dangerous. The contrastive concepts of truth and falsehood that move center stage in the following discussion deal with a very serious matter.

Again, a pair[25] of contrastive conditional statements portrays a situation, first negatively (1:8) and then positively (1:9).[26] Verse 1:8 states that failure to confess[27] one's need for God's grace embodied in Jesus results in condemnation. To deny sin in one's life shuts the door on forgiveness from God.

Recognizing the parallelism between verses 6–7 and verses 8–9, we correlate "walk in the darkness" (1:6) to "claim to be without sin" (1:8), and "we lie and do not live out the truth" (1:6) to "we deceive ourselves and the truth is not in us" (1:8). To use modern parlance, such a person lacks self-awareness. Darkness perverts the truth in labelling injustice as justice, wickedness as righteousness, and falsehood as truth.

1 John 1:8 implies that no disciple ever achieves sinless perfection in this life. No matter how spiritually mature or how long they have been as disciples they still sin, although, hopefully, they attain a consistency of moral

---

25. A contrastive conjunction "but" beginning 1:7 joins 1:6 and 1:7 as a pair. However, no conjunctions appear at the beginning of 1:8, 1:9, and 1:10, each of which contains a probable conditional statement. This asyndetic feature quickens the pace of reading through these verses. Without conjunctions to indicate possible pairing of verses, we have to examine the content of each verse and to discern the logical relationship between verses.
26. These probable conditional statements are of the same form as those in vv. 6–7 and so present definite possibilities of occurring in the life of a disciple.
27. The two verbs denoting speech, "claim" (1:8) and "confess" (1:9), help frame the antithetical relationship between 1:8 and 1:9. We detect pride or lack of self-awareness behind the verb "claim" and humility behind "confess."

uprightness being ever dependent on divine grace. One must remain humbly realistic, because one occasionally succumbs to temptation. Sinless perfection describes God who alone is light without any darkness whatsoever.

Acknowledging that we are not God but human and subject to human frailty, we are to actively confess our sins (1:9). A promise is given, conditioned on our confession. God is faithful and just. And because he is so, he forgives our sins and cleanses us from all unrighteousness (1:9).[28] So knowing and understanding the implications of God's character and actions consistent with that character emboldens us to avail ourselves of his grace through confession. Indeed, confession as a spiritual discipline enables us to draw close to our Lord.[29]

Although the primary thrust of these verses urges confession to God in private prayer, the broader context of fellowship suggests accountability within the community of disciples. One's manner of life affects others and sin can have a rippling effect that will hurt them. Confession begins with the realization of sin in one's life and the acknowledgment of personal responsibility. It calls for verbalizing the sin to God and those affected. Proper remorse and contrition must accompany the confession. Then one can be forgiven and take steps toward reconciliation.

Will the church accept the challenge of openness and transparency, humbly confessing their sins in the context of fellowship with one another and with the Lord? These verses call for authenticity both individually and corporately.

1:10 Making God a Liar

This verse nearly repeats 1:8. The writer concludes the chapter with "if we claim[30] we have not sinned,[31] we make him out to be a liar and his word is

---

28. The conjunction normally translated "in order that" to convey purpose probably expresses result here. That is, as a result of God's faithfulness and justice, a reference to his covenant responsibilities to forgive and cleanse upon the worshiper's confession, the believer can trust the covenant stipulations and expect God to atone for his sins. The NIV renders it "and will."
29. In examining Dietrich Bonhoeffer's writings, Nicola J. Wilkes notes the critical place personal confession had in his spirituality, ministry, and theology ("Life and Health: Bonhoeffer's Normative and Divergent Accounts of Private Confession of Sin," *Theology Today* 71 [2014]: 58–68). Martin Luther was another advocate for private confession. See Ronald K. Rittgers, "Luther on Private Confession," *LQ* 19 (2005): 312–331.
30. This is the third time the author uses the same verb "claim" in the subjunctive (1:6, 8, 10). Each time we can render it interpretatively as "claim" or even "boast." What is claimed is false in view of the inconsistency between the boast and the lifestyle actually lived out.
31. The verb "have sinned," in the perfect tense, denotes a state of being or condition. Individual acts of sin or even the entire collection of sinful acts is not the emphasis. Rather,

not in us." This is no mere repetition of the earlier verse but a progression of thought. If disciples declare that they have no sin (1:8b), they are really implying that they are sinless, a characteristic that only God possesses. Such an implication levels a blasphemous charge[32] against God by calling him a liar. The previous verse (1:9) implies a covenant of grace through which God forgives, a covenant ratified by the blood of Jesus (1:7). Boasting a state of sinlessness spurns the need for the covenant and the blood of Jesus. It implies a life totally independent of God's grace. Hence, the statements "the truth is not in us" (1:8d) and "his word is not in us" (1:10d)[33] represent the danger of losing one's status of being a disciple, a most serious consequence. Then 1:10 sounds a loud and clear warning.

The readers, however, have not lost their status as disciples. Presumably, the invitation to enter into fellowship with other disciples and with God remains available (1:3). Otherwise they would not be warned. But they face an important decision. They must take two positive actions – walk in the light (1:7) and confess their sins (1:9). Then they can claim the promises of fellowship, cleansing from all sin, and forgiveness. If they fail to take appropriate action, they forfeit the promises and incur condemnation.

The hand of fellowship extended by the author invites his readers to join a spiritual and confessional togetherness leading to church unity. Only then can the church impact society effectively. As a small minority in many regions of Asia, disciples must rally around one another for mutual support and accountability if they hope to fulfill their mission as agents of grace and mercy.

Fellowship happens when all participants take an active role where stories play out for review, meditation, and inspiration. Disciples live out the story of their lives, facing the many issues and challenges of life, and yet experiencing divine grace through a functional relationship with the Lord. How each

---

character or condition emerges through actions. Thus, it is not so much that a person sinned as that person is a sinner.

32. The present tense verb "do/make" portrays continuous activity, which implies that the person making the erroneous claim of being sinless continually blasphemes God by disputing his word that condemns all as having sinned (e.g. Rom 3:23). So long as someone maintains a false innocence, that person continues to blaspheme God by implying that God did not speak the truth.

33. The preposition in the phrase "in us" conveys a locative idea – the realm within. Rudolf Schnackenburg takes "his word" to mean "the word of God" that implies the witness of the Holy Spirit within (*The Johannine Epistles: Introduction and Commentary* [New York, NY: Crossroad, 1992], 84). If Schnackenburg is correct, then the person not having the word of God within does not have the Spirit within or has silenced the Spirit's inner witness. Either way that person stands in danger of not being a disciple.

disciple fares affect other disciples. Fellowship serves as the vehicle by which that influence may be felt by all. All share what they have heard, seen, and touched concerning the word of life. Authenticity preserves the stories shared without falsification or embellishment so that human inadequacy and divine sufficiency emerge to underscore a common theme – grace. Encountering Jesus makes available in abundance grace to live fully, fearlessly, and purposefully. In that sense, the Asian church is counter-cultural.

1 JOHN 2

Recently the prime minister of Singapore identified the external threats the country faced and the need to be united.[34] He listed terrorism, the weakening economy in certain regions of Southeast Asia, and the haze drifting in from a neighboring country. Being a small nation, Singapore has limited resources and so must maintain a united front.

In 1 John 2, the author analogously addresses the external threat facing Christians as he continues his focus on personal morals from the previous chapter. His discussion shifts to the world and the danger it poses for the disciple. The threat features both a moral element in the allurement away from purity of the faith and a doctrinal element in its denial of Jesus as Christ.

But first the writer concludes his treatment of sin in 2:1–2 begun back in 1:6.

2:1–2 Our Advocate with the Father

The author reassures believers that they "have an advocate with the Father – Jesus Christ, the Righteous One" (2:1). The "these things" refers back at least to 1:10 or 1:6–10.[35] The danger of "walk in the darkness" (1:6), "the truth is not in us" (1:8), and "his word is not in us" (1:10) casts a shadow over our reading. Could these things apply to Christians? What are the implications?

Yet, with words of assurance the author instills hope but affirms that we must respond appropriately.[36] He softens the harshness of 1:6, 8, 10.[37] What can be construed as accusations in 1 John 1 becomes a warning and caution in 2:1. He expresses the fervent hope that his readers will not sin by giving heed to this letter. At the same time, however, he anticipates the possibility of sin. Disciples still sin and they ought to confess (1:9). Linking that promise with the present verse, we infer that Jesus Christ as our advocate will

---

34. Siau Ming En, "External Threats Aplenty, but a United Nation Will Overcome Them: PM Lee," *Today*. Online: http://www.todayonline.com/ge2015/external-threats-aplenty-united-nation-will-overcome-them-pm-lee (accessed January 3, 2016).
35. C. Haas, M. de Jonge, and J. L. Swellengrebel regard 1:10 as the primary reference of "this" but more generally to 1:5–10 (*A Handbook on the Letters of John* [New York: United Bible Societies, 1972], 34).
36. Thomas R. Schreiner and Ardel B. Caneday assert that "the apostle writes 1 John to assure believers that they truly belong to God . . . that assurance is the primary goal of the letter" (*The Race Set before Us: A Biblical Theology of Perseverance and Assurance* [Downers Grove, IL: InterVarsity, 2001], 278).
37. But Karen H. Jobes finds the "harshness" instructive (*Letters to the Church: A Survey of Hebrews and the General Epistles* [Grand Rapids, MI: Zondervan, 2011], 424–426).

intervene when we confess. The identification "the Righteous One" ties Jesus with "he is faithful and just" (1:9).

The writer continues with the declaration that "he is the atoning sacrifice . . . for the sins of the whole world" (2:2).[38] This fuller explanation of Jesus' redemptive significance clarifies how he functions as our advocate. If a disciple should sin again, Jesus can restore the broken relationship upon confession.

The author's expansion of the scope of Jesus' redemptive activity to include the world strongly hints at a missional aspect. This possibility stands in sharp contrast to the world's hostility depicted later in the chapter as we will see. This adversarial relationship has already surfaced earlier in 1:10 for those who deny sin and claim sinlessness.

Stating that Jesus is the appeasement of God's wrath "for the whole world" echoes John 3:14–16. As the lifted serpent had salvific value so does the lifted Son. Faith recognizes Jesus' ministry as advocate.

2:3–11 Keeping the Commandment

The triad of obedience, love, and knowing Jesus highlights 2:3–11.[39] Following the dualistic pattern of the Gospel, this section contrasts three pairs of extremes with no intermediary alternative. Those claiming to be disciples keep Jesus' command or they do not. They either love or hate. They know Jesus or they do not. All three ideas are interrelated so that being characterized by one aspect determines how one is associated with the corresponding aspect in the other two pairs. Hence, those obeying Jesus' command also love others and know Jesus. The opposite holds – disobedience links with hate and not knowing Jesus.

What they claim may or may not align with what they do. Alignment signifies integrity; the opposite marks the hypocrite. The author affirms that we can know the Lord if we keep his commands (2:3). The form of the two verbs (the first "know" and "keep") depicts a continuing confidence and practice.[40] Given the previous chapter, this knowledge is grounded in and fortified by a relationship with Jesus. Like any relationship, the time element

---

38. Leon Morris advocates "propitiation" more accurately places the appeasement of God's wrath center stage (*The Apostolic Preaching of the Cross*, 3d ed. [Grand Rapids, MI: Eerdmans, 1965], 144–213, especially 205–213).
39. David Rensberger, *The Epistles of John* (Louisville, KY: Westminster John Knox, 2001), 24–29.
40. The two verbs are present tense. "We know" connotes not just ongoing activity but a settled confidence in a present reality. "Keep" describes a practice or habit, a repeated obedience that characterizes the person. See John L. Anderson, *An Exegetical Summary of 1, 2, and 3 John*, 2d ed. [Dallas, TX: SIL International, 2008], 42–43.

determines the depth of our familiarity with him – the longer the relationship, the deeper our knowledge experientially.

As we obey his commands consistently, we can be certain that we are in a functional relationship with him.[41] No thought of perfect obedience, however, can be inferred particularly in view of 1:10. Human frailty predisposes us to sin, and only constant vigilance and accessing grace will keep us on the moral high road.

Then 2:4 states: "Whoever says,[42] 'I know him,' but[43] does not do what he commands is a liar, and the truth is not in that person[44]" (2:4). The tenor of 2:4 parallels that of 1:8. If what people claim proves they are liars and the truth is not in them. The form of "know" portrays a state or condition.[45] Claiming intimacy with the Lord presupposes compliance with his commands.

The final declaration, "the truth is not in that person," points to an operative principle within a person.[46] Possessing the truth concerns more than simply the issue of honesty. Indwelling truth appears to be an operative principle within that directs and even empowers one to a life of integrity and transparency. No deception clouds that person's demeanor. Character is perceptible, most evident in one's choices, values, speech patterns, and habits.

Christian educator Howard Hendricks once famously said: "The greatest crisis today is the crisis in leadership. And the greatest crisis in leadership is

---

41. Charles H. Talbert expresses this idea in covenantal terms (*Reading John: A Literary and Theological Commentary on the Fourth Gospel and the Johannine Epistles* [New York: Crossroad, 1994], 23–25).
42. The substantive participle, "whoever says," is in the present tense, depicting a regular practice of saying such things. The participle can also be descriptively translated "whoever claims" to suggest a fraudulent statement.
43. The conjunction usually translated "and" functions to group items together that may share some common trait but here I have rendered it "but" to highlight a contrast between the two clauses joined by the conjunction.
44. The near demonstrative pronoun "that person" makes fraudulent claims and so proves to be a liar. A. E. Brooke observes a pattern in the Gospel and epistles that when the pronoun refers backward "it always denotes the subject or object, *as previously described*" (*A Critical and Exegetical Commentary on the Johannine Epistles* [repr., London, New York: T & T Clark, 2004], 31). The italics appear in the original.
45. In the perfect tense, the verb describes a person familiar with the object which here refers to the Lord.
46. The preposition of "in that person" bears a locative sense denoting sphere of influence or operation. Truth may describe sincerity (Stephen S. Smalley, *1, 2, 3 John*, WBC 51 [Waco, TX: Word, 1984], 48). It may also be an operative principle that orients and guides. Given that "the Spirit is the truth" (5:6f) and the mutual indwelling of God and the disciple through the Spirit (3:24d; 4:13c), 2:4 may allude to the Spirit's ministry in the disciple.

the crisis of character."⁴⁷ The issue of character may be a modern challenge, but it has ancient roots as documented in this letter.

In some Asian societies, people's identity and sense of self ties intimately with affiliation to a group, be it family, ethnic clan, professional guild, religious beliefs or something socio-economic.⁴⁸ But their association with others who lead exemplary lives does not exonerate them from being personally accountable for their character. They must still live in like manner. Being a member of the believing community is important, but personal morals in conformance to God's commands are equally important (2:3–6).

Living in a shrinking global community with mobility a fact of life, a person may move to another region of the world. Hence, tracking people's lifelong spiritual journey, even with the connectivity afforded by the ubiquitous Internet, becomes daunting.⁴⁹ More importantly, they must strive toward maturity where they assume personal responsibility for their own lives and growth. They pursue fellowship with the Lord and with others because they realize the necessity of doing so for continued character building and make appropriate choices.

The verb "obey" in 2:5 is the same term as "keep" in 2:3 and "does [not] do" in 2:4.⁵⁰ The verse (2:5) affirms that obedience demonstrates the maturity of one's love for God and that one abides in him. The parallel expressions in 2:3 and 2:5 imply that "his commands" and "his word" have the same referent. Compliance with the Lord's commands or word provides the outward confirmation of an inward reality – truth directing the disciple's life. Because

---

47. Message at Xenos Discipleship Conference, Columbus, Ohio, July 17, 2003. For a book-length treatment of character building through mentoring, see Howard G. Hendricks and William D. Hendricks, *As Iron Sharpens Iron: Building Character in a Mentoring Relationship* (Chicago, IL: Moody, 1995).
48. References to this group identity can be found in discussions about human rights in Asia, for example. See Bilahari Kim Hee P. S. Kausikan, "An East Asian Approach to Human Rights," *Buffalo Journal of International Law* 2 (1995–1996): 265. Online: http://tembusu.nus.edu.sg/docs/East_Asian_Approach.pdf (accessed May 5, 2015). In psychological studies this concept also emerges. See Catherine Tien-Lun Sun, *Themes in Chinese Psychology* (Singapore: Cengage Learning, 2008), 50–56.
49. For articles on the social and cultural impact of the Internet, see Philip Brey, "Evaluating the Social and Cultural Implications of the Internet." Online: http://ethicsandtechnology.eu/wp-content/uploads/2012/10/a1-brey.pdf (accessed May 6, 2015). Brey astutely observes that one's assessment of the Internet's potential benefit or harm depends on one's value system or worldview. The church, then, needs to take an informed stand on this technology to teach its members (particularly the youth) appropriate use and to determine how best to utilize it for ministry. This consideration becomes a moot point in areas of Asia where electricity is unreliable or unavailable.
50. The NIV presents three different translations of the same verb normally rendered "keep."

this truth comes from God and expresses his will, it assumes a metaphorical role. The truth is God's authoritative presence. The love of God being made complete[51] is the result for the disciple who obeys his word.

The clause "love for God is truly made complete" (2:5) signifies completion or the satisfaction of some intention or effort. God loves the disciple intentionally. The desired result is the disciple's submission to God's word or commands. Given that obedience is a fundamental trait of disciples, God loving them serves as an impetus that prompts them to love God by aligning with his will and so confirms their identity as disciples. And as they so move then God's love functions as an operative principle or power in them in a similar fashion as indwelling truth. But the parallelism breaks down in that truth is not said to be perfected as love is. Rather, love encompasses purpose or motivation and truth provides direction.

Understanding these two concepts and their interdependence informs the church as it defines its mission/vision and maps its ministerial strategy. Both concepts balance each other and so both must be present. Having love without truth fosters passion and zeal but no sense of direction. In the same way, having truth without love yields only direction but lacking the necessary fervor or proper motivation to move.

The final portion of 2:5 states: "This is how we know we are in him."[52] The word "this" alludes back to "love for God is truly made complete."[53] Fulfillment of God's loving purpose in the life of his disciples gives assurance that they are in him. No greater proof that a person has entered into a relationship with God can be found than by being both the object and result of

---

51. "Is made complete" in the perfect passive form communicates a resultant state or condition due to a process which, in this verse, is divinely orchestrated ("theological passive"). God's love sanctifies the disciple that produces a state of being perfected. The idea of a divine purpose is evident. D. A. Carson distinguishes between two aspects of God's love, the relational and constitutional components (*Difficult Doctrine of the Love of God* [Wheaton, IL: Crossway, 2000], 25–43, especially 40–41). We will discuss this divine love more when we look at 1 John 4.
52. W. E. Vine explains the phrase "in him" as "spiritual relationship and unity of life" (*The Epistles of John: Light, Love, Life* [Grand Rapids, MI: Zondervan, 1970], 25). According to Rensberger, the disciple pursues a personal and intimate relationship with God, resulting in knowing the one who is infinite in a finite manner (*Epistles*, 26).
53. Although Hiebert acknowledges that "by this" which the NIV compresses into "this" may refer to what preceded or what follows in the text, he favors the latter citing a similar occurrence in 2:3 ("Exposition of 1 John 1:5–2:6," 342). However, 2:3 features "and" just ahead of the phrase that effectively separates the phrase from what preceded. No such conjunction appears in 2:5 and so syntactically the phrase likely refers backwards.

his love. God's love transforms. Transformation, then, indicates that his love is perfected.

If believers are not growing toward spiritual maturity, one questions whether God's love has penetrated into their heart. The fact that obedience to God's word is the means of accomplishing his purpose undergirds an important principle – the Lord's love gives opportunity to fulfill his purpose but that opportunity must be seized and acted upon by the disciple. We are not robots programmed to act in the prescribed manner nor do we live primarily by instinct as do the animals. Having a say in the process, we collaborate or refuse to cooperate. A choice or decision awaits us. Opportunity implies stewardship.

Integrity speaks of consistency between what one professes and practices. The author demands that disciples "must live as Jesus did" (2:6) if they claim to abide in him. As noted in the previous chapter, "to walk" metaphorically describes a person's conduct and manner of life. Abiding in the Lord is another metaphor depicting fellowship with the Lord.[54] Fellowship depends on the proper conduct and manner of life. Regardless of what one may say, actions confirm or deny the truthfulness of the words.

Conduct consistent with high morals is an essential discipline that contributes toward intimacy with God. Our Lord loves us for a purpose – that we seek intimacy with him through a manner of life that conforms to his word and commands.[55] To walk as he walked implies synchronization of purpose, goals, values, convictions, and conduct.

The direct address, "beloved," begins 2:7 and marks the parallel address "my children" earlier in 2:1. Then the writer states that he is not writing[56] a new command but an old one, the message[57] which his readers heard when they first encountered the Lord. In addressing them thus, the author maintains affection typical of close relationships.

---

54. Ruth B. Edwards believes "abiding" connotes perseverance (*The Johannine Epistles* [Sheffield: Sheffield Academic, 1996], 73). This idea, however, probably relates more to consistency in walking in the ways of the Lord because of the immediate context.
55. As Thomas L. Constable notes, obedience and Christ-like manner of life confirm an abiding relationship with the Lord ("Notes on 1 John," 25). Online: http://www.soniclight.com/constable/notes/pdf/1john.pdf (accessed May 6, 2015).
56. In the present tense, the verb "write" may allude to the current letter that the author is now composing. Gary M. Burge labels the writing as "a fresh, impassioned tone" (*The Letters of John*, NIV AC [Grand Rapids, MI: Zondervan, 1996], 100).
57. The NIV renders "word" as "message." In 1:10 and 2:14 the NIV translates the term as "word."

Being a written communiqué, 1 John reveals that the author made an effort to minister to his younger charges. Unlike email today, taking ink to papyrus or possibly animal skin and writing his thoughts out in longhand (possibly employing a scribe), and then sending his note by courier, took significant time, not to mention his not knowing their response for perhaps weeks or longer. It was a laborious process.[58]

The phrase "from the beginning" recalls Jesus' words in John 13:34.[59] When Jesus uttered this command for the first time, it was new. But for each new generation of disciples hearing the command for the first time, it is also new, as the expression "which you have had from the beginning" implies.[60] But by the time of the composition of 1 John some time later, the command is "old" (or familiar). Implicitly, a relaying of the command must have taken place in order for later generations of disciples to receive it. With the ascension, Jesus cannot command later disciples directly. In his place, each generation of disciples faithfully lives out and passes on the command to the next. In a sense, disciples represent Jesus in discipling younger disciples.

In the latter portion of 2:7, the writer identifies the "old" command explicitly as "the message you have heard." The term "message (or "word")" appears five times in this letter (1:1, 10; 2:5, 7, 14). Only here (2:7) does "message" refer to the love command (John 13:34).

Obedience nurtures a loving disposition that propagates through the fellowship of believers who love one another. Love is bidirectional – submission to God through obeying his command and submission to one another in love. The kind of love demanded is modeled by Jesus who laid down his life for the disciples. Accordingly, disciples are to lay down their lives for one another. Jesus' sacrifice bore a redemptive thrust. That of the disciples bears the imprint of Jesus' love and thereby conveys the fruit of Jesus' redemptive love.

As God's love is intentional so is our love. We love others into fellowship with the Lord and with his disciples. Love invites and includes.

---

58. E. Randolph Richards, "Reading, Writing, and Manuscripts," in *The World of the New Testament: Cultural, Social, and Historical Contexts*, eds. Joel B. Green and Lee Martin McDonald (Grand Rapids, MI: Baker Academic, 2013), 349–363.
59. As D. Edmond Hiebert notes, the phrase cannot refer to the beginning of the human race or to the OT Law in Lev 19:18 but to the early church, in particular to the time when the readers "first heard and accepted the gospel preached to them" ("An Exposition of 1 John 2:7–17," *BSac* 145 [1988]: 422).
60. As an imperfect, "have had" conveys a progressive or continuous sense of ownership in the past that continues into the present. The syntax of "from the beginning" also reinforces action from the past that continues onward.

1 John

Startlingly, the author then declares that he writes a new command (2:8). Its truth can be seen in Jesus and them, because the darkness is receding and the true light shines. The switch to a "new" command suggests something new and different from the original or "old" command.[61] In order to make sense of the contrast between the "old" (2:7) and the "new" (2:8), we need to contrast the content of the old command (2:7) with a new reality (2:8). The old reality portrayed Jesus sacrificially loving on the night of his arrest and the hope that the disciples will love in like manner. But in 1 John that hope has been realized – the disciples now love sacrificially. That this new reality is an established fact finds confirmation in the recession of darkness and the radiance of the true light.[62] The dualism reflects the opposing lifestyles or conducts that can describe the disciples. Darkness marks those who disobey the command or truth, deny their sins and so are not forgiven and cleansed by the blood of Jesus. Light labels those who obey, confess, and are forgiven and cleansed. The former lives outside of fellowship; the latter reside in fellowship.

The special designation "the true light" echoes John 1:9 and the verb "gives light" calls to mind light shining in darkness (John 1:5). How the Gospel prologue describes Jesus metaphorically now describes both Jesus and the disciples in 1 John. Jesus' coming results in disciples shining his life as the spark has passed through to each succeeding generation.

What 1 John presents as hope realized challenges the church today. Does Jesus' light shine in and through the church? Do members love one another sacrificially? Or does darkness cling to some aspect of our fellowship with one another and of our relationship with the Lord?

The author now condemns those claiming to be in the light and yet[63] hate brother or sister to reside in darkness (2:9). The forms of all the verbal

---

61. Raymond F. Collins explains that newness of the old command refers to the new age, the end times ("'A New Commandment I Give to You, That You Love One Another . . .' (Jn 13:34)," *Laval théologique et philosophique* 35 [1979]: 244). Schnackenburg, however, offers another explanation based on the text at 2:8 – the new command "is true in him and in you" (*Epistles*, 105). The newness stems from the command being fulfilled in Christ and in the readers.

62. The present tense of "is passing" connotes the process of being fulfilled – darkness is diminishing but not completely gone. Even though "is shining" depicts the same kind of action, the adverb "already" confirms that true light is presently shining in a full. Smalley suggests that the "new law" is operative because the darkness is fading (*1, 2, 3 John*, 57). I concur that the "true light" refers to Christ (*1, 2, 3 John*, 58). He is fully operative in the disciple in whom darkness is fading away.

63. The conjunction normally translated as "and" usually joins items sharing some trait to form some kind of collection or group. Here, however, the author makes a contrast or

terms depict a pattern of behavior that characterizes the person making the claim.[64] "Still" expresses an ongoing situation from the past that continues into the present without any hint of ending. The coupling of light and loving fellow believers contrasts with the coupling of darkness and hating fellow believers.[65]

An affirmation follows: love for fellow believers means living in the light, and[66] no stumbling block hinders (2:10). This declaration functions like a conditional statement, an "if-then" type of expression.[67] Loving fellow believers expresses the condition to be satisfied. If met, then two consequences result: (1) such people abide in the light and (2) nothing would cause them to stumble. Surveying the key term "to make stumble" in the NT gives us a solid indication as to its meaning. "To make to stumble" here in 2:10 refers to sin, that is, the disciple who loves fellow believers, and thereby abides in the light, will not commit sin.

The dualism of light and darkness powerfully proclaims only two manners of life – either a person characteristically loves or hates. Manner of life reveals a person's character and relational trait. People's ability to relate/fellowship with others depends exclusively on their ability to love. Without love there can be no fellowship.

---

perhaps implies a concession ("the one who claims that he is in the light even though he hates his brother").

64. The participles, "anyone who claims" and "[anyone who] hates," are present tense connoting habitual activity. Such people persistently make false claims and consistently hate believers. Their regularity showcases a settled attitude marking character.

65. The imagery of light and darkness is prevalent in Second Temple literature, close to the writing of these epistles. But the epistles may postdate the period (see Craig L. Blomberg, *From Pentecost to Patmos: An Introduction to Acts through Revelation* [Nashville, TN: Broadman & Holman, 2006], 486–487). Yet their proximity to the period permits a look at literature from then for insight on the concepts of light and darkness in 1 John. Peter H. Davids, Douglas J. Moo, and Robert W. Yarbrough review some of the literature and find ethical overtones (*1 & 2 Peter, 1, 2, & 3 John, Jude* [Grand Rapids, MI: Zondervan, 2002], 70–71). Also Talbert, *Reading John*, 24.

66. "And" bears a consecutive nuance, given the causal relationship between the two clauses joined. The first clause provides the necessary conditions to invoke the action or condition depicted in the second clause. So long as a person abides in the light s/he will not stumble. We can translate the conjunction "so/and so/hence."

67. William E. Elliott treats in full conditional statements ("Conditional Sentences in the Greek New Testament" [ThD diss., Grace Theological Seminary, 1981]). He standardizes classification of conditions in the NT based on what he calls "determination," the mood of the verb in the "if" clause. Mood conveys the author's view on the relationship of action to reality or potentiality. The category most pertinent to 2:10 is the simple condition with the indicative verb that regards the condition as real (73–105). However, perception may not align with reality.

In contrast, the author then laments that those who hate fellow believers live in the darkness and blindly grope about in life (2:11). Since this statement stands in contrast with 2:10, it may be helpful to compare corresponding clauses of the two verses:

- those who love their brother and sister live in the light (2:10a)
- those who hate their brother or sister reside in the darkness (2:11a)
- nothing in them makes them stumble (2:10b)
- live in the darkness not knowing where they are going (2:11bc)
- because the darkness blinded them (2:11d)

The first pair (2:10a, 11a) forms a clear contrast.[68] Based on "to live in him" (2:6), "live in the light" in 2:10 conveys the concept of a relationship.[69] What this means becomes clear when we recall 1:6–7 that affirms fellowship with God and with fellow disciples is possible only if we walk in the light as he is in the light. Light signifies the realm where God dwells and operates. Then the loving brother/sister nurtures an enduring relationship with God.

The contrast between the second pair of clauses (2:10b, 11bc) yields a picture of those who stumble about in the dark. Helpless, they will not reach their desired destination. The remaining clause (2:11d) has no comparable clause in 2:10 and simply provides the reason why they stumble – they cannot see ahead.

A number of metaphors serve to complete the picture. Darkness seems to imply opposition to the light which probably symbolizes God and his work (1:5, 7, 9).[70] The blinded eyes may describe incapacitated ability to discern and to follow God's way and path, ethical uprightness. Blinded, they live in denial, failing to acknowledge their sins and need for Christ as advocate.

2:12–17 Overcoming the World

The author addresses the hostile interaction between the disciples and the world. He will transition to a christological discussion in 2:18–29 with the point of conflict being Jesus' true identity. But here the author examines the disciples' struggle with the world and its temptations.

---

68. Anderson finds that "live" emphasizes duration and "maintaining a constant, habitual, permanent relationship with the light" (*Exegetical Summary*, 55).
69. Rensberger, *Epistles*, 26.
70. Lieu interprets "darkness" as "active force for evil, wilfully opposing God's work of bringing light" (*I, II, & III John: A Commentary* [Louisville, KY: Westminster John Knox, 2008], 81–82)

Before we can understand the author's thoughts in this section, we need to address two issues. First, the verb "I am writing" or "I write" that begins each verse in 2:12–14 appears in two different forms.[71] That may suggest two different compositions. However, nothing in the text would support such a possibility. So it seems best not press for some kind of differentiation but to regard the difference as stylistic variation. Secondly, the author references several groups – children, fathers, and young men. What do these groups represent? They may refer to church office or roles in the church, but the author does not clarify that potential interpretation with any specific mention of church functions. Rather, the groups recall passages such as 1 Timothy 5:1–2 that differentiate by age.[72] A related issue concerns the actual number of groups referenced – two or three. If three, the age breakdown leads to children, young men, and fathers or older men. Two groups imply that the address "children" alludes to all the addressees with a twofold segmentation of young men and fathers.[73] That the author had two groups in view may be confirmed by his general labelling of all his readers as "children" elsewhere.[74]

By calling his readers "children," the author keeps visible the affectionate and fatherly relationship he has with them. He represents the earlier generation of disciples who have nurtured and taught the younger generation of disciples. Given the distinction established in the prologue between the generations (1:1–5), we might surmise that the author makes a distinction between "fathers" and "young men" among his readers. Yet, certain considerations tend to eliminate that option.

The author makes a categorical statement that all disciples ("children") have been forgiven (2:12). The form of the verb "have been forgiven"

---

71. It assumes the present tense twice in 2:12–13 and the aorist in 2:14. Commentators debate the significance of the difference. If a temporal idea should be involved, although that is not a primary consideration of the Greek tense, then the present tense may allude to a current writing and the aorist looks back at a previous writing – possibly two compositions. Brown concludes that different tenses represent stylistic variation with no interpretative significance (*Epistles*, 294–297). Also, Johnson, *1, 2, and 3 John*, 48–49. Smalley, however, thinks the tense shift advances the argument (*1, 2, 3 John*, 78). But advancement comes by elaborating the young men's overcoming the evil one.
72. Lieu lists some additional passages with regard to household/family codes of conduct (*I, II, & III John*, 86–87).
73. Brown discusses the possibilities of one, two, or three groups (*Epistles*, 297–300). But nowhere else does the author use all three names to address the same readers. So the possibilities remain at two or three groups addressed.
74. The author uses two terms, both translated "children" – *teknion* (2:1, 28; 3:1–2; 5:21) and *paidion* (2:18). There is no real difference, although the author favors the former in frequency of use. This variation appears to be stylistic.

connotes a condition or resultant state.[75] The concluding phrase "on account of his name" alludes back to Jesus as our helper who accomplished propitiation (appeasing God's wrath against sin) (2:1–2). God is favorably disposed toward us because of Jesus' redemptive activities that appease his wrath. Jesus' name refers metaphorically to his propitiatory actions.

Then the writer addresses the "fathers" who know "him who is from the beginning" (2:13abc). Recalling "that which is from the beginning" (1:1a), we identify the referent as Jesus whom the first disciples encountered in a life-transforming way. The beginning points back to Jesus' earthly ministry.[76]

A number of issues face us as we try to interpret. The two groups, fathers and young men, that constitute the children whom the writer addresses, can connote two categories of age as in 1 Timothy 5:1–2 or two categories of spiritual maturity.[77] Both groups share the common trait of being forgiven, suggesting they practice confession (1:9). Most likely age is not the distinguishing factor in view of the two verbs describing each group. The fathers "know" Jesus and the young men "have overcome the evil one." The verbs characterize the two groups.[78] Both traits bear a spiritual imprint. Interestingly, one addresses the vertical relationship with Jesus and the other speaks of the horizontal relationship with the world. The young men are not in the process of overcoming the world, as if to imply that some uncertainty remains until the process is complete, but they are described as victors.[79] Victory is secured.

---

75. Being in the perfect tense, "have been forgiven" connotes those forgiven, no longer under condemnation, whose sins no longer count against them. The passive voice suggests the gracious divine activity behind the scenes.
76. Contra Lieu who takes the reference back to John 1:1 (*I, II, & III John*, 88). However, she acknowledges 1 John shows no interest in Jesus' pre-existence. But Schnackenburg notes knowing Jesus depends on "personal contact" with him (*Epistles*, 117). Hence, "from the beginning" points specifically to a transforming encounter with Jesus.
77. The latter option is Marshall's position (*Epistles*, 139–140). Contra Kenneth Grayston who regards the referents as two different church groups in conflict with the author (*The Johannine Epistles*, NCBC [Grand Rapids, MI: Eerdmans, 1984], 70). However, 2:12–14 represents the author's evaluation of the groups not their own claims.
78. In the perfect tense, both verbs connote a condition or state that marks the distinctiveness of each group. "From the beginning" may be associated with "know" or the standalone definite article following the verb. If the phrase relates more to the verb, the author states that the fathers have known the Lord from the beginning. But if the phrase relates more to the standalone article, then the author is characterizing the Lord. Since the article stands between the verb and phrase, it is more viable to connect the article and phrase together. This letter's prologue supports that.
79. The real opposition is "the evil one" which may refer to "the ruler of this world" (John 16:11, NRSV). The various terms (devil, antichrist, evil one) coalesce into one entity. See Kysar, *I, II, III John*, 54–55. In the Gospel and 1 John, "world" can symbolize the system, empowered by "the evil one," that opposes Jesus and his disciples.

Then the fathers refer to those who cultivated a deep relationship with Jesus, marking them to be on a par with the writer himself and his generation of disciples. Hence, "know" is equivalent to and encompasses all the interactive verbs in 1:1–3, 5 that describe the writer's encounter with Jesus. Such an encounter results in fellowship with the Father and his Son.

The young men, on the other hand, have overcome the evil one or world. They have resisted successfully the allurement of the world (2:15–17). We ponder the significance of this characterization. Why focus on young people's interaction with the world?

In a recent global survey (2012), people in other countries were questioned about their receptivity to American soft power (US music, movies, and television), democratic ideals, business practices, and advances in science and technology.[80] Especially pertinent, the survey contrasted the responses by age according to three broad ranges: 18–29, 30–49, and 50+. The following table depicts the percentage of those who liked American music, movies, and TV.

	18–29	30–49	50+
Germany	94	83	47
Britain	88	80	53
Poland	79	76	52
China	56	43	30
Japan	83	81	58

A second table depicts the percentage of those who were open to American ideas and customs.

	18–29	30–49	50+
Germany	41	24	16
Britain	42	37	24
Poland	49	40	27
China	50	44	34
Japan	67	61	53

---

80. "Pew Research: Global Attitudes Project." Online: http://www.pewglobal.org/2012/06/13/chapter-2-attitudes-toward-american-culture-and-ideas/ (accessed July 20, 2014).

1 JOHN

Although the survey limits its coverage of nations covered and only examines the American cultural influence, the emerging pattern supports the contention that younger people are more open to and potentially more influenced by ideas, customs, and way of doing things in the world. Now I am not equating America with the world at all. This survey simply illustrates the openness of young people regardless of whether they are Western or Asian. Age seems to be of greater significance than one's place of origin. However, I hasten to add that the survey did not address moral or spiritual issues.

But the challenge the church faces in cultivating the next generation of disciples, typically targeting the young (youth and young adults), requires understanding and appreciating the forces of influence at work in their lives.[81] Competing with the church's desire to influence its young people is the so-called "third place" that complements the first two primary places of a person's life, the home and office (or school for students).[82] This "third place" may be geographical or digital. The digital space people enter in order to interact with others is called social media. Dominating the landscape of the twenty-first century, rapid change and global connectivity define the reality of our world. If influence is power, and it is, then social media would be a leading contender for the title "most powerful influence" among young people today.

The church needs to know and understand the influences and how its young people are being influenced. Can it counter the influence effectively and arm them for spiritual warfare?

The writer recognizes the entire readership because they know the Father (2:13c).[83] Apparently he makes a distinction between knowing the Father and the one who is from the beginning (2:13). Hence, he makes a distinction of persons, the Father and Jesus whom the disciples encountered earlier. The parallel between the earlier "your sins have been forgiven on account of his name" (2:12) and the present "you know the Father," both describing the

---

81. A. Rae Simpson identifies three age categories for young people: adolescence (puberty through age 18), young adulthood (18 to 22/25), and later adulthood (mid-20s and older) ("Young Adult Development Project." Online: http://hrweb.mit.edu/worklife/youngadult/changes.html [accessed July 20, 2014]).

82. Ray Oldenburg claims that people need the "third place" for a healthy, balanced life (*The Great Good Place* [New York: Paragon, 1989]). This third place includes cafes, coffee shops, community centers, malls, bars, or other places people hangout for social interaction. He has authored a more recent book telling stories of third places (*Celebrating the Third Place* [New York: Marlowe & Co., 2001]).

83. Lieu, *I, II, & III John*, 90. Schnackenburg simply makes a general allusion to Christians who are saved and forgiven (*Epistles*, 118).

readers, suggests that the two corresponding conditions or characterizations – being forgiven and access to the Father – are mutual.[84] Being forgiven gives access to the Father and that access affirms that one is forgiven.

Then the writer repeats 2:13a in 2:14b about knowing the one from the beginning. Why he does so is unclear since he does not add new content. Repetition may be for rhetorical purposes, that is, emphasis. However, the writer introduces significant additions when he next addresses the young men as being strong, having the word of God in them and, as a result,[85] overcoming the evil one (2:14cd). He explains how they overcome the evil one – through being strong and having God's word abide within. More likely, the second clause explains the first: "you are strong in that the word of God lives in you."[86] The operative indwelling presence of God's word parallels the contrastive expressions "the truth is not in us" (1:8) and "his word is not in us" (1:10).[87] The crucial key to young people overcoming the evil influence of the world rests in the truth of God's word residing within. This speaks of personal maturity and responsibility in making the right choices and decisions and taking the appropriate action consistently.[88] An internal sense of right and wrong governs one's life, demonstrated by obedience and submission to God's authority as the norm.

The church strives to nurture young people by facilitating their personal growth and development to prepare them for living without compromise in the world with its allurement and belief system. The challenge is daunting in view of the ubiquity of the world's influence, especially in digital form and through entertainment. Marketers specifically target the youth segment of society. It would be unrealistic to employ a monastic mindset and to demand that young people cut off all contact with the world. Paul clearly did not advocate that option (1 Cor 5:10). The only viable alternative, then, is for

---

84. Rensberger goes further to state that being forgiven signifies defeat of the evil one (*Epistles*, 30–31).
85. The second occurrence of "and" in this verse appears to facilitate a consecutive relationship between the two clauses. We may render it as "so/and so/as a result" to highlight the logical sequence where the indwelling word enables the disciple to overcome the world.
86. The first conjunction "and" linking the two clauses functions epexegetically in explaining more explicitly the more general first clause by the more specific second clause.
87. In view of earlier comments on "his word is not in us" (1:10) in our previous chapter, the word of God within may refer to the indwelling Holy Spirit. His presence authenticates the indwelt person as a true disciple.
88. Smalley observes the predominate use of the perfect tense in 2:12–14 that characterizes disciples (*1, 2, 3 John*, 80). Verbs in the perfect tense include "forgiven" (2:12), "know" and "overcome" (2:13), and again "know" twice and "overcome (2:14). Additionally, the present tense of "is" and "abide" in 2:14 also describes disciples.

the church to prepare its members to live in the world as a compelling and winsome influence rather than to be influenced.

In 2:15–17, the writer cautions his readers against the threat the world poses. He begins with the admonition to not love the world or anything associated with it (2:15a).[89] The danger lies not in the world but in the disciple. Love represents a powerful inner force that compels a person to make a choice that results in a sequence of actions that impacts that person's life and character. The thrust of the verse highlights strong attraction and submission. To love the world signals accepting the world's power in one's life and consequently being enslaved.

A mutual exclusion prevents anyone from loving the world and the Father at the same time (2:15b). The question is not whether a person loves but the object of the love.[90] The Father and the world stand diametrically opposed to one another. This dualism demands a decision – submit to the Father or to the world – reminiscent of Jesus' admonition (Matt 6:19–24). The phrase "in them" indicates an inner reality that controls a person's life choices and values.[91] The love of the Father resides within and functions as an operative power or principle. "Love of the Father" may connote one's love for the Father or the Father's love for that person. Practically speaking, both nuances are probably intended. Love for the world precludes the ability to love the Father and to acknowledge his lordship and prevents any sanctifying effect the Father's love may have. The world cannot influence the disciple who loves the Father and submits to his transforming love. Only the love for the world gives the world access to the heart and mind.

The next verse specifies the particular aspects of the world that can exert an influence: the lust of the flesh, the lust of the eyes, and the pride of life

---

89. The traditional understanding that the present imperative refers to continual action or forbids current activity if negated or that the aorist imperative prohibits action from starting if negated cannot be sustained given counter examples in the NT. See Stanley E. Porter, *Idioms of the Greek New Testament*, 2d ed. and repr. (London: Continuum, 2007), 225. The negated present imperative in 2:15 prohibits the practice of loving the world. Buist M. Fanning concludes that the present imperative focuses on the internal details of the action which for 2:15 is spelled out in 2:16 (*Verbal Aspect in New Testament Greek* [Oxford: Clarendon, 1990], 325–388).
90. The two verbs "love," the first a present imperative negated and the second a present subjunctive, indicate that a person loves no matter what. The only difference is the object of the love. The present tense of both verbs portrays a norm or pattern of behavior where the subject consistently loves, perhaps in various ways, the object.
91. Culy labels the phrase as a metaphorical locative, the realm within which something happens (*I, II, III John*, 43). More specifically, Kysar identifies the connotation as a person's basic orientation (*I, II, III John*, 56).

(2:16). The writer clarifies the origin of these three. They come from the world and not from the Father. Here "flesh" assumes a Pauline nuance of a person living apart from the Spirit's leading and influence (Gal 5:16–26).[92] Once a person chooses the world, the love of the Father becomes inert – the Spirit recedes and the flesh takes control. "Lust" signifies a motivating force that directs a person toward a certain orientation in order to acquire the object of the desire. It represents movement away from the Father toward the world. "Lust of the eyes" depicts one's personal orientation. In actuality, the two lusts are one. The third aspect of the world, the pride of life, portrays an arrogance of life apart from the life only Jesus can offer.[93] All three descriptions of the things in the world may not allude to substantially different concepts but to the same idea – anything that is not from the Father and comes from the world, that indicates love for the world.[94]

Then 2:17 declares that the world and its lusts are passing away,[95] but the doer of God's will, will live forever. Concluding his short discussion on the mutual exclusivity of the love of the Father and the love for the world, the writer contrasts the temporary nature of the latter and the permanence of the one who submits to the will of God.[96] The true value of anything depends on permanence or the lack of. Temporary satisfaction in the end fails to satisfy. What does not insure one's permanence holds little value and, in fact, proves deceptive because it misleads a person away from what is of true value.

From the perspective of eternity, we understand the author's argument and realize no counterargument can be effective. However, we live in the world of the temporary and feel bounded by time. We cannot imagine eternity for it is too abstract. Too often we focus on the here and now. Even long-range planning or projection beyond this year or the next few years proves too much to handle because of the tyranny of the urgent.[97]

---

92. Contra Schnackenburg, *Epistles*, 121.
93. The word for "life" in 2:16 differs from the term in 1:1–2 that stems from Jesus and also appears in the Gospel consistently to refer to the life that he offers to all who would believe in him. The term in 2:16 refers to the life the world offers as a counterfeit to the reality that only Jesus can provide.
94. Talbert, *Reading John*, 25.
95. The verb "are passing away" is present passive, depicting an ongoing process that is occurring right now and does not point to an exclusively eschatological event. Even though the world represents a threat to the disciple, it is already judged and, as a result, suffering the consequences historically. In essence, the world is transient (Smalley, *1, 2, 3 John*, 86). The passive voice suggests possibly the divine superintending of the process.
96. Lieu, *I, II, & III John*, 96.
97. Charles E. Hummel, *Tyranny of the Urgent*, rev. ed. (Downers Grove, IL: InterVarsity, 1994).

Making life choices with eternity in mind is a creed confessed but not practiced. The challenge churches face is to translate love for the Father and overcoming the world into practical life habits and mindset that demonstrate knowing the Father and the Son. That can only become reality when the church excels in fellowshipping with the Lord and with one another.

2:18–29 The Antichrist: He Who Denies Christ

In this final section of 1 John 2, the point of direct conflict between those who stand for the truth and those who oppose focuses on the identity of Jesus. Is he or is he not the Christ? This christological question signals the eschatological moment of crisis.

The author then announces in 2:18 that the last hour has arrived signalling the coming of the antichrist. In fact, many antichrists have come. The time expression "last hour" is unique to 1 John and does not occur in the Gospel. The Gospel instead features several time expressions. The first alludes to Jesus' crucifixion and appears in one of the following forms: "my hour" (John 2:4), "his hour" (7:30; 8:20; 13:1), "the hour" (12:23; 17:1), and "this hour" (12:27). The second refers to a coming hour that has arrived in which true worshippers worship the Father in spirit and truth (4:21, 23). The third expression has four different referents: (a) a coming hour of the resurrection that has arrived (5:25, 28); (b) a coming hour when the disciples will be persecuted after Jesus' departure (16:2); (c) a coming hour when Jesus speaks plainly and no longer in figurative language (16:25); and (d) a coming hour that has arrived when the disciples scatter and abandon Jesus (16:32). Another expression speaks of the "last day" when the dead are raised (6:39–40, 44, 54; 11:24) or when judgment is executed (12:48). This last expression appears to be eschatological.[98]

Of all the time expressions in the Gospel listed above, a coming hour when the disciples will be persecuted after Jesus' departure (16:2) comes closest to correlating with the coming of the antichrist and the arrival of many antichrists in 1 John.[99] Then the sequence implied by lining up the Gospel

---

98. A. W. Pink regards the "last hour" to be an eschatological reference (*An Exposition of the First Epistle of John* [eBook edition], 95–97. Online: http://www.chapellibrary.org/files/2213/7547/5526/1joh.pdf (accessed May 11, 2015). Pink only covered 1 John 1:1–3:1 before passing away. Constable interprets "last hour/days" as the inter-advent period before the Lord's return (*Notes on 1 John*, 37). Similarly, D. Edmond Hiebert, "An Exposition of 1 John 2:18–28," *BSac* 146 (1989): 77–79.

99. Marshall expands the scope of his discussion on the "last hour" to include Christ's return and concludes that the time-scale cannot be ascertained but that the sense of urgency emerges as a primary emphasis (*Epistles*, 148–151).

narrative and extrapolating to the later narrative of 1 John allows us to superimpose the advent of the antichrists with Jesus' prediction of persecution targeting the disciples. The presence and activity of the antichrists confirm the arrival of the last hour.

This verse serves as confirmation of an earlier warning. The author states: "as you have heard."[100] The comparative "as" recalls a similar but unidentified statement the author must have made about the antichrist earlier. We do not know how long ago or how frequently he may have foretold his readers. But the important point on which they must focus is that many antichrists have arrived. The temporal adverb "now" and the verb "have come" emphasize fulfillment of the warning.[101] The contrast of the singular "antichrist" and the plural "many antichrists" implies a distinction between the two. There may be an eschatological reference in the singular referent.[102] But with the arrival of many antichrists, the prophecy of the coming antichrist finds fulfillment in the sense that they oppose Christ or the teaching about Christ and his adherents.[103] The presence of the antichrists confirms without doubt that the "last hour" has arrived.

Continuing, the author comments that a number of former church members left, thereby revealing their true identity: "They did not really belong to us.[104] For if[105] they belonged to us, they would have remained" (2:19). A contingent that used to be part of the congregation departed and by their

---

100. In the present tense, the verb "is coming" depicts an ongoing process that may have been in the works for some indeterminate time before the antichrist makes his eventual appearance. The overall thrust points to a future event with present build up that culminates in that predicted event.

101. In the perfect tense, the verb "have come" depicts a state of being or condition which, for this verse, speaks of the presence of the predicted antichrists. But given the earlier verb "is coming" the readers are prepared to expect the appearance of the antichrists. Their presence is no surprise.

102. Brown reviews some Jewish conceptions of this figure that spans both history and end times (*Epistles*, 332–337). Smalley remains open to the figure being mythological or eschatological (*1, 2, 3 John*, 98–100).

103. Grayston, *Epistles*, 77. More specifically, Rensberger identifies them as opponents within the Christian community (*Epistles*, 37). However, 2:19 indicates that for a time they were within the church but have now left.

104. The prepositional phrase "to us," literally "of/from us," functions as a partitive genitive depicting the separatists as former members of the community denoted by "us." Being members of a community requires sharing a common trait. But the separation represents the inevitable departure because of the lack of a common ground.

105. The particle "if" introduces a contrary-to-fact (second class) conditional statement where the author views the protasis as false but presents the condition as though it is true for the sake of argument. The conditional marker *an* in the apodosis confirms the conditional classification, although the protasis is obviously false in view of the context.

separation confirmed that they had nothing in common with those who remained behind. Their spiritual status or identity meant that that they could not continue in alliance with the church.

The immediate concern focuses on the identity of those who departed. Given the proximity of the two adjacent verses (2:18–19), the many antichrists of 2:18 are the very ones who left the church.[106] Then in view of the larger context of 1:6—2:17 we can characterize the antichrists. They walk in darkness and do not practice the truth (1:6), and are not cleansed by Jesus' blood (1:7). Deceived in thinking that they have no sin (1:8), they do not confess their sins (1:9), boasting of being sinless (1:10). They spurned Jesus' propitiatory activity and so face God's wrath (2:1–2). Disobedient to the Lord's commands, they falsely claim to know him (2:3–4) and so fail to experience God's love perfected in them (2:5). They hate others and remain in darkness, being thereby blinded (2:9, 11). Unforgiven (2:12) and not knowing Jesus (2:13–14) nor the Father (2:14), they have succumbed to the evil one (2:13–14). They love the world and not the Father (2:15). They are consumed by the desires of the flesh and eyes and marked by pride (2:16). As part of the world, they too will pass away for failing to do the will of God (2:17).

But why call those separatists antichrists? The characterization so far would justify labelling them sinners, unforgiven and uncleansed, deluded, blind for walking in darkness, and having succumbed to love for the world. But the moniker "antichrist" takes them to a deeper level of villainy where the author accuses them of aggressively opposing and denying Christ.[107]

Then the author turns his attention back to those who remain. He affirms their ability to discern truth from falsehood because of their anointing from the holy one (2:20–21). The referent of "the holy one" may allude to the Father, the Son, or the Holy Spirit. Clearly the source is divine. But it seems best to identify Jesus as the holy one because of the parallel in 2:27–28.[108] Only here does the author employ the expression. That the referent cannot be the Holy Spirit can be confirmed by clear references in this letter that simply feature "Spirit" (3:24; 4:2, 13; 5:6, 8).[109]

---

106. Kysar, *I, II, III John*, 59–60.
107. Jobes views them as heretics with "aberrant Christian behavior" (*Letters*, 416). Hence, a wrong christological understanding results in wrong morality.
108. Johnson, *1, 2, and 3 John*, 58. Johnson finds other occurrences of Jesus as "the holy one" in Mark 1:24; Luke 4:34; John 6:69; Acts 3:14; Rev 3:7 and in the apostolic fathers (1 Clem 23:5; Dign 9:2), (63).
109. In 4:6, "the spirit of truth" may not be referring to the Holy Spirit given its opposition to "the spirit of error." There the author may be contrasting truth and error as mutually

Amazingly, the author affirms that all his readers "know the truth" which implies that they have all received the anointing.[110] Then, receiving the anointing marks a person as a true disciple. Given the evident contrast between those who left (2:19) and those who stayed (2:20), the anointing serves to highlight the difference as one of discernment. True disciples stayed because they were not deceived.

Rhetorically, the writer appears to encourage his readers. Any schism in the church inflicts emotional and spiritual wounds. Having endured a church split years ago, I can still recall the related events rather clearly. It is not something easily forgotten. Lessons can be learned; but scars may also remain. One leader was so traumatized that he never resumed leadership again, even after a couple of decades. Others were grimly determined to prevent the seeds of division from being sown again. There are no winners and losers; and the danger of tainting Christ's name lurks to undermine the church's witness and effectiveness.

But the situation the writer portrays suggests that separation was not only inevitable but highly desirable.[111] How can a church thrive if a portion walks in the light and enjoys fellowship with one another and with the Lord while, at the same time, another portion walks in darkness and hates others? There can be no fellowship when there is no common bond. Hatred sows seeds of discord; and falsehood threatens to compromise truth. By permitting those who love the world to remain in fellowship, the church would invite the world in to exert a powerful, compromising influence within. Consequently, the church cannot remain pure. Eventually all will walk in darkness and hatred will supplant love.

---

exclusive concepts.

110. In 2:20, the second conjunction "and" bears a consecutive nuance "so" or "hence." Anderson labels the conjunction's function as introducing result (*Exegetical Summary*, 76). Semantically, there is no significant difference between the consecutive or the resultative use of the conjunction. Liturgically, Lieu ponders whether "anointing" might not refer to "baptism" as an initiation rite of the church (*I, II, & III John*, 103).

111. Church discipline where a member, due to unrepentant sin, is excommunicated differs from biblical separation because of apostasy. For the former, see R. Bruce Compton, "Church Discipline: Separation from a Believer or Excommunication of an Unbeliever? Comparing Matthew 18:15–17, 1 Corinthians 5:1–13, and 2 Thessalonians 3:6–15." Online: http://www.dbts.edu/pdf/macp/2009/Compton%20Church%20Discipline%20and%20 Excommunication.pdf (accessed May 12, 2015). In the first two passages of the title, an unrepentant excommunicant is regarded as an unbeliever. This mirrors the situation in 1 John. For the latter case, see Ernest Pickering with Myron Houghton, *Biblical Separation: The Struggle for a Pure Church*, 2d ed. (Schaumburg, IL: Regular Baptist, 2008).

1 John

The writer does not record the circumstances surrounding the separation. The omission seems to invite us to see different scenarios that could result in a split.[112] We can read our own story into the text by way of application. The interpretation is unequivocal – there can be no fellowship between light and darkness, truth and falsehood, love and hatred. But the mention of antichrists narrows the possibilities because the conflict was specifically christological.

Anointed to discern and not needing instruction, the readers exercised mature discernment. We infer that the readers took an active rather than a passive role in the separation, that is, they may have initiated and facilitated the separation. In contemporary parlance, the readers may have kicked out the deviant contingent. Rather than tolerate their unhealthy presence the readers forced them out in order to preserve the truth and protect the church.

However, we want to be as specific as possible – what particular aspect of the truth required preservation and what specific threat posed a danger to the church? For the answer we move to the next subsection (2:22–23).

The writer directs his attention to the departed contingent and describes them in terms related to Christ. He begins with a rhetorical question: "Who is the liar? It is whoever denies[113] that Jesus is the Christ" (2:22a). This categorical denial attacks Jesus' very identity, his relationship to OT messianic prophecies, and the proclamation of the canonical Gospels. The Gospel of Matthew, for example, portrays Jesus as the Son of God and the Christ.[114] To deny Jesus as the Christ goes against the weight of divine testimony and incurs certain judgment. It is a most serious sin that effectively calls God a liar (blasphemy) and rejects the only means of redemption. This error rejects Jesus' deity; and the repercussions are seismic.

The author adds: "Such a person is the antichrist – denying the Father and the Son" (2:22b). Denying one person of the Godhead leads to denial of all persons of the Godhead.[115] Even though the Spirit is not explicitly named, the implications are clear. One cannot revere the Father only. All persons of

---

112. For a discussion on narrative gaps or omissions, see Meir Sternberg, *The Poetics of Biblical Narrative: Ideological Literature and the Drama of Reading* (Bloomington, IN: Indiana University Press, 1985), 186–190. Also Adele Berlin, *Poetics and Interpretation of Biblical Narrative* (Winona Lake, IN: Eisenbrauns, 1994), 137–139.
113. In the present tense, the substantive participle "whoever denies" portrays continued, steadfast, obstinate denial.
114. Donald Senior, *Invitation to Matthew* in *Invitation to the Gospels* (New York: Paulist, 2002), 47–48.
115. This is an implication of the doctrine of the Trinity. From a biblical studies perspective, see, for example, Richard Mayhue, "One God – Three Persons," *Master's Seminary Journal* 24 (2013): 161–165, and Thomas A. Keiser, "The Divine Plural: A Literary-Contextual

the Godhead must be revered. Either all are worshiped or none are. Then this christological heresy features a strong theological element. It represents a primary doctrine of major importance. To deny Jesus is to deny the Father and inevitably the Spirit. The implications are far-reaching and cannot be localized to the person of Jesus only. This heretical challenge cannot be left unanswered by the church. It must act decisively, for its very existence hangs in the balance.[116] The church in 1 John did so and the church today must follow suit.

In view of some churches today splitting off or being planted because of perceived differences over doctrinal, ecclesiastical, or personal issues, we need to ascertain the nature of the separation documented in 1 John.[117] The specific case focuses on whether Jesus is the Christ or not. The broader ramifications affect his deity and dual nature, the efficaciousness of his blood and his propitiatory activity, the necessity of obeying his commands, and the basis on which disciples may have fellowship with the Lord and with one another. Hence, separation in 1 John involves Christology, soteriology and, to some extent, ecclesiology.[118] So care must be exercised when we seek to adapt the biblical text for modern application. If we face issues with christological implications, we stand on firmer ground when we look to this epistle for guidance about issues of separation.[119]

Argument for Plurality in the Godhead," *JSOT* 34 (2009): 131–146. For a standard evangelical systematic theology, see Wayne Grudem, *Systematic Theology: An Introduction to Biblical Doctrine* (Grand Rapids, MI: Zondervan, 1994), 226–261.

116. Harold O. J. Brown traces church history replete with heresies that threatened orthodoxy and undermined the church (*Heresies: Heresy and Orthodoxy in the History of the Church* [Peabody, MA: Hendrickson, 1984]).

117. For example, Singapore's Bible Presbyterian Church (BPC) movement began when a church broke with the Presbyterian Synod because of perceived liberalism in associating with the Ecumenical Movement and the World Council of Churches. The BPC strongly emphasized a fundamentalist, literal interpretation of the Bible. For a time the BPC recognized only the King James Version, alleging that the Hebrew and Greek texts behind the version stood closest to the original text. Other English versions based on different Hebrew and Greek manuscripts and utilizing dynamic equivalence were unacceptable. So they distanced themselves from churches that used other versions.

118. These three traditional categories in systematic theology cover the person and works of Christ (Christology), the doctrine of salvation (soteriology), and the doctrine of the church (ecclesiology). See, for example, Millard J. Erickson, *Systematic Theology*, 3d ed. (Grand Rapids, MI: Baker Academic, 2013). His book features major sections entitled "The Person of Christ," "The Work of Christ," "Salvation," and "The Church." Another publication, edited by Daniel L. Akin, is *A Theology for the Church* (Nashville, TN: Broadman & Holman, 2007). His major headings are "The Doctrine of Christ," "The Doctrine of Salvation," and "The Doctrine of the Church."

119. Christological controversies punctuated early church history with scribes changing the biblical text to better support their views and thereby to gain greater credibility. Bart D.

1 John

Then 2:23 proclaims that denial of the Son ruins any relationship with the Father but "whoever acknowledges[120] the Son has the Father also." Again, the author emphasizes the inseparability of the Father and the Son. The expression "has [or not] the Father" refers back to the fellowship one may potentially enjoy with the Father and the Son (1:3). To have the Father signifies entering into fellowship with him.[121]

A fundamental principle emerges – fellowship here corresponds to Paul's union with Christ as articulated by the phrase "in Christ" occurring numerous times in Paul's writings. John's Gospel refers to this union in terms of relationally knowing the Father and the Son. To have the Father is to know him which correlates with being in fellowship with him and having eternal life. To not have the Father implies not having eternal life.

The author now looks back to his prologue as he writes (2:24): "See that which you have heard from the beginning remains in you." If so, his readers remain in the Son and in the Father. The referent for "that which" is Jesus himself. But the prologue applies the experience of hearing Jesus to the author and his generation of disciples rather than to the readers as in the present verse. However, the manner of describing the hearing is different and so distinguishes the author and his generation from his readers and their generation.[122] For the author and his contemporaries the encounter with Jesus had a profound effect that prompted them to bear witness for him to the next generation. In fellowship already with the Father and the Son, he wanted his readers to enter into that relationship also. They will enter provided the condition stipulated in 2:24 is satisfied. The author urges them to let what they have heard or experienced with regard to Jesus remain within. This is

---

Ehrman documents three major christological disputes where the text was changed – adoptionism (Christ was a man but not God), docetism (Christ was God but not a man), and separationism (the divine Christ and the man Jesus were two separate persons) in *The Orthodox Corruption of Scripture: The Effect of Early Christological Controversies on the Text of the New Testament* (New York: Oxford University Press, 1993).

120. In the present tense, the two substantive participles "no one who denies" and "whoever acknowledges" showcase steadfast denial or confession that serves to characterize the person.

121. Bultmann observes that the verb "has" connotes relationship (*Epistles*, 39).

122. The prologue features the verb "we heard" in the perfect tense conveying a resultant condition or state of being because of an earlier encounter with Jesus. But in 2:24 the same verb appears in the aorist tense that simply denotes the fact of hearing Jesus without any further implication. Thus, whatever effect the experience has on the readers is not noted and for good reason. The conditional statement in 2:24 indicates that the intended effect of encountering Jesus has not been consummated in the readers as it has in the author and his contemporaries.

equivalent to truth remaining within (1:8; 2:4).[123] Indwelling truth operates as an inner force that guides and directs them to confess sin and to obey Jesus' commands. Then they walk in the light, have fellowship with other disciples and with the Lord, and have all their sins cleansed by Jesus' blood (1:7).

Conceptually, "that which" the readers heard from the beginning can be either Jesus himself (as in the case of the prologue) or the report the author gave to them (1:3). For either possibility the time phrase "from the beginning" alludes to the time of their encounter with Jesus through the author's witness. Hearing the report leads to a spiritual encounter that every generation of disciples may experience. The parallelism with indwelling truth (1:8; 2:4) supports regarding the truth about Jesus reported (rather than Jesus himself) as that which must remain in the disciples in order that they may enter into fellowship with the Son and with the Father. It is a conditional promise that bears fruition when they internalize the truth.[124]

Then the writer recalls the Lord's promise of eternal life (2:25). Thus, 2:24–25 equates having fellowship with the Son and with the Father with possessing eternal life.

Then professing Jesus as the Christ is a non-negotiable. One's eternal destiny and union with the Lord hangs in the balance. Any threat to this truth, Jesus' messianic identity, demands expulsion or the church will cease being the church, the repository of the truth. And so the church of 1 John fulfilled its duty when the contingent that denied Jesus left. The church today must do nothing less than to remain firm and steadfast, ever faithful in defending

---

123. In the context of religious pluralism, such as characterizes Asia, truth means different things to different people. Then no conception of a particular truth can claim absolute superiority over all other truths. Such reasoning poses a difficult challenge for Christians to refute. See, for example, Kevin Schilbrack's evaluation of and response to John Hick's writings on religious pluralism ("Religious Pluralism: A Check-up," *RelSRev* 40 [2014]: 1–7). In advocating pluralism, Hick rejects Christ's two-natures, for example, as a logical contradiction. Schilbrack documents the difficulty Christians have in presenting counter-arguments that are both valid and compelling. Although thoughtful Christians may still engage in theological dialog with those of a different religious orientation, they do well to heed 1 John's irrefutable emphasis on living out the truth. Such an exemplary lifestyle no one can effectively counter.

124. Based on Elliott's classification, the statement here is a probable condition that can be readily fulfilled (*Conditional Sentences*, 129–130). The hypothetical nature of this condition requires the use of the subjunctive mood to convey an indeterminate or contingent condition. The results are not assured. The writer regards his readers as quite able to fulfill the condition but is uncertain as to whether they will. The promise is conveyed by "will abide" in the future tense in the last clause of 2:24. The future may function modally, that is, it expresses permission or ability. See Maximilian Zerwick, *Biblical Greek* (Rome: Editrice Pontificio Istituto Biblico, 1994), 94.

and propagating the truth, and always ready to expel those who reject Jesus as the Christ.

Returning to the threat facing the church, 2:26–27 assures that the anointing received abides within and they have no need to be taught. Their anointing teaches them all things necessary to guard against deception, provided they remain in the Lord. Again, this anointing comes from a divine source as 2:20 affirms.[125] Through these verses the author warns and assures his readers. They need to be alerted to the deceptive threat posed by the antichrists (2:18) who came out from their midst (2:19). Yet, at the same time he assures them of their anointing that enables them to discern the christological error being promoted. Further, he assures them that the anointing abiding within will continue to teach them.[126] But the anointing remains effective only as long as the disciple abides in the Lord.

We readily see complementary activities, one divine and the other human. A mutual dependency seems to be at work. The disciple depends on the Lord's anointing in order to maintain the truth. And the anointing depends on the disciple being in fellowship with the Lord to help expose error. This collaborative effort flourishes with the divine-human relationship.

At the same time, we infer the horizontal relationship between disciples through the author's use of the plural "you" when he refers to his readers. What may be suggested here is a collaborative discernment in the fellowship of believers (1:3d). The picture presented showcases a corporate anointing and exercise of discernment to defend the truth and to oppose falsehood. Undoubtedly, collaboration implies a coming together to pray, discuss, and query the Scriptures. Fellowship involves accountability as we discussed earlier and also working together to oppose the antichrist threat. Mutual encouragement and exhortation compels the church to close ranks upon the departure of the antichrists. They are in the world and the world is a threat

---

125. Smalley identifies the anointing to be the Spirit and the word of God (*1, 2, 3 John*, 123).
126. The verb "to teach" with his anointing as the subject is in the present tense depicting the ever active function of the anointing. Anytime a potential error surfaces, the indwelling anointing responds by alerting the disciple about the error and identifying the corresponding truth. Lieu notes the ambiguity of this verse where the possible indwelling agents that teach may be the anointing itself or God or Jesus (*I, II, & III John*, 113). Also the final clause may be a simple statement of fact or a command and the final preposition phrase could be "in it (anointing)" or "in him." Lieu observes that such ambiguity characterizes the author and whichever way we choose to interpret does not make much difference. Kysar concurs (*I, II, III John*, 66). David Smith, however, unequivocally views the final clause as an imperative (*The Epistles of John* in *The Expositor's Greek Testament*, Vol. 5 [Peabody, MA: Hendrickson, 2002], 181).

from without (2:15–16). Moreover, there is no indication that another antichrist will not emerge again from within the church in the future. Vigilance requires constancy and faithfulness to the truth. The church must continue to be spiritually alert and not grow complacent.

Coming to the end of this section, the writer urges his readers to remain in the Lord so that "when he is revealed"[127] they can be confident and not ashamed, and then adds: "If you know that he is righteous, you know that everyone who does what is right has been born of him" (2:28–29). With this eschatological reference to Christ's coming, the idea of accountability emerges especially with the need to be confident before the Lord. He is just and upholds justice. Present stewardship calls for abiding in him. Remaining faithful confirms personal righteousness that further substantiates that one is begotten from him.

In 2:29, the writer emphasizes knowing certain truths. First, he crafts a conditional statement – if his readers know that Jesus is just; a divine characterization. The writer introduces a degree of uncertainty. The situation cannot be that the readers may or may not know. Earlier he acknowledges that they know all things because of their anointing (2:20). Now he hesitates in his confidence in them. Or so it appears. Rather, he challenges them to live in a manner that ensures their confidence at Jesus' coming (2:28).[128] In that day, Jesus will manifest his justice toward the disciples. And depending on their present manner of life, they may be confident or ashamed as he judges their stewardship. Only those who consistently practice[129] righteousness will prove that they are born of the Lord.

Practicing righteousness based on 1 John 2 involves obeying the Lord's commands, loving others, discerning truth from falsehood, and defending and proclaiming the truth that Jesus is the Christ. Also, righteousness compels them to identify the antichrist and expel him from their midst. They must practice sanctifying separation. This righteousness refers to the individual disciple and the corporate gathering of disciples.

---

127. The three successive verbs "is revealed," "would have," and "be unashamed" are all in the subjunctive mood. The reason for their assuming this mood rests in the first verb forming the protasis with "when" (*ean*, normally "if") and the next two verbs forming the apodosis but nestled in the purpose clause ("in order that"). The entire construction serves to express the author's hope for his readers when the Lord returns.
128. Lewis translates "know" as "consider" which serves to place responsibility on the readers to apply what they already know about Jesus' righteousness (*John and the Johannine Letters*, 116).
129. In the present tense, the substantive participle "the one who practices (literally, "does")" expresses the norm or consistent conduct as a general rule.

1 John

In view of the multiplicity of religions in Asia, we interpret and apply 1 John 2. Any and all religious confessionals that fail to recognize Jesus as the Christ, that is, Jesus as the sole object of worship, devotion, and allegiance, fits 1 John's label of "antichrist," a rather harsh assessment. Unique to 1 John, the term "antichrist" in the singular and plural forms appears to represent the author's unequivocal polemic against the separatists. He highlights the threat they pose to the church as strongly as possible to ensure that his readers do not dismiss the deadly danger. With apostolic authority and insight, he labels the separatists' denial of Jesus.

In the white-and-black world of 1 John, people acknowledge Jesus as the Christ or they do not. Even if they ascribe to Jesus a position of honor, unless he occupies first place, then they have aligned with the world. Islam and Hinduism grant Jesus a place of honor, as prophet or guru, respectively, and may recognize that his death has significance (for Hindus his resurrection may be interpreted as reincarnation). But such "esteem" fails to accord Jesus the status of being the unique Son of the Father.

Religious plurality undergirds a postmodern respect for other religions in addition to one's own. This respect recognizes the legitimacy of all religions as vehicles of truth that can carry their adherents to the desired *nirvana* for Buddhists, *moksha* (liberation) for many Hindus, virtuous life for Confucianists, or union with the *Tao* for Taoists. Religious Asians may even ascribe to Jesus a metaphorical rather than a literal divinity in explaining why Christians are compelled to be less self-centered and more loving of their neighbors.

We cannot simply discard 1 John, or at least the term "antichrist(s)," from the biblical canon because we find it inflammatory in our Asian world. A reading of 1 John must be made in view of a christological reading of the rest of Scripture. When we do that, we find confirmation that Jesus is "the way and the truth and the life. No one comes to the Father except through [him]" (John 14:6); "Salvation is found in no one else for there is no other name under heaven given to mankind by which we may be saved" (Acts 4:12); and "this righteousness is given through faith in Jesus Christ to all who believe" (Rom 3:22). It is beyond the scope of this commentary to develop in detail an Asian hermeneutic for this letter.

But how does the Asian church respond? Or perhaps more to the point, can the Asian church be an effective witness for Christ within religious pluralism? There are no simple and straightforward answers or solutions. To claim otherwise is to ignore the enormous and complex challenge. We Christians cannot out-argue our neighbors nor can we claim a longer history, with Christianity arriving long after the other major religions had become entrenched. A minority presence, we find ourselves disadvantaged economically, politically, and socially. Another question then surfaces – will the church survive in Asia? Sustainability and viability are two big goals seemingly out of reach. Sustainability asks, can the church last? Viability asks, can Christianity be seen as a legitimate contender for people's faith and devotion among the many other contenders?

1 John 2 issues a key command – abide in the Father and the Son. That implies a community marked by fellowship with the Lord. With the departure or expulsion from the church of those who deny Jesus as the Christ and with the prohibition of not loving the world, does that mean that Asian churches maintain their purity of faith and fellowship by isolation?

But isolation is not the answer. Why? We live in a fast-paced and globally connected world, exciting and potentially dangerous. Jesus articulated the age-old dilemma facing disciples when he prayed: "They are still in the world . . . [yet] they are not of the world" (John 17:11b, 14c). Immersed and constantly exposed to the world's allurement and philosophy, disciples may gravitate toward the world without even being aware as they adopt seemingly innocuous ideas, practices, and values. Reduced sensitivity to things marginal can numb the senses and undermine discernment. What once may have been scandalous no longer seems so evil. After all, "everyone is doing it."

1 John 2 supplies the solution – the anointing from the Lord abides within each of us. We must continually and vigilantly monitor and discern teachings, beliefs, and values being propagated in our Asian world. We achieve sustainability and viability through obeying the teachings of 1 John 2. The text does not promise that we will win the world for Christ. It says that the world is passing away.

But what is our role in the world? We must read further in 1 John to find out.

1 John

1 JOHN 3

In Asia, urbanization, ethnic tension, war, the lack of social status for women and children, and corruption lead to widespread poverty and exploitation. To have a meaningful role in society, the church must respond to these challenges in concrete ways. This concern motivated the author to pen 1 John 3, issuing a charge to love others by laying down our lives. The immediate context indicates he probably meant fellow believers. But he broadens the scope of our compassion by telling us of the Father's compassion for the world (2:2; 4:14), of our using the world's goods to help others (3:17), and of our overcoming the world by faith (5:4–5). I believe that overcoming the world means more than resisting its allurement and retaining the truth without compromise. It also means overcoming the evils of suffering and hopelessness that mark our Asian world.

1 John 3 characterizes two kinds of people, one affiliated with the Father and the other with the devil. We affirm our affiliation by actions motivated by love or hate. We can. 3:2–3 urges us to grow in Christlikeness now and promises that when Christ returns we shall reflect his character perfectly. So we strive to love others by ministering to them in their affliction. This is what our Lord did and we ought to follow his example.

3:1–3 Children of God: Becoming Like Him

Being designated a child of someone signifies our possessing the defining characteristics of that person.[130] A child of God, then, manifests godly qualities.

1 John 3:1 affirms the readers' identity as children of God, the object of the Father's great[131] love but, at the same time, their relational distance from the world. Significantly, the writer uses "Father" here.[132] The designation prepares us to read the purpose of the gift: "that we should be called children of God." Love prompts the Father to give the gift of adoption. The short clause immediately following, "and that is what we are," serves to reinforce the preceding description of the Father's love.[133] The Father's intended gift

---

130. Bradley R. Trick, "Sons, Seed, and Children of Promise in Galatians: Discerning the Coherence in Paul's Model of Abrahamic Descent" (PhD diss., Duke University, 2010), 55, 68. Also, Caroline Johnson Hodge, *If Sons, Then Heirs: A Study of Kinship and Ethnicity in the Letters of Paul* (Oxford: Oxford University Press, 2007), 19–42.
131. Robert W. Yarbrough translates the adjective as "how great" to describe the Father's love (*1–3 John* [Grand Rapids, MI: Baker Academic, 2008], 175–176).
132. The designation "Father" appears 13 times in 1 John.
133. The shift from subjunctive for "should be called" to indicative "are" delimits the scope of the clause defining the magnitude of the Father's love. The following indicative "are" makes an

achieves his purpose. Consistently, "to know" someone speaks of having a relationship. The world has no relationship with the children of God nor can it. An unbridgeable gulf separates the two. The reason why the world does not know God's children is because it does not know the Father.

The Father births a disciple as a love-act to become his child. Intentional and transformational, his love comes as a gift unmerited, fully a testament of his gracious initiative. The form of the verb "has lavished" depicts a nuanced portrait.[134] The child's identity is a settled reality, once determined it remains unchanged since the birth is strictly a divine act. The Father's love, as evidenced by the birth, highlights a divine benevolence that seeks a permanent relationship. Any and all blessings come through the relationship.

The writer again affirms his readers' identity as children of God even though what they shall become in the future remains unknown and concludes: "We know that when[135] Christ appears, we shall be like him, for we shall see him as he is." An eschatological expectation characterizes children of God. They will experience two states of being – a present state as the object of the Father's love and a future state when they become like Christ.[136] The final state remains a mystery in that we do not know the specifics. Only at Jesus' return will we see him and thus see ourselves as a reflection of his character.[137]

Through this timeline we see two transformations mapped in our lives. The first transformation resulted in our becoming the children of God and being distinct from the world. We now dwell in the light and have the indwelling truth as an operative principle governing our choices and actions. The adverb "now" emphasizes the immediacy of our transformation. We live in fellowship with the Father and the Son and with one another. Still in the world, we do not affiliate with it in any compromising way. At the present time we should be growing in Christlikeness; but when Jesus returns we become like him perfectly.

---

assertion that the author views as true.
134. The perfect tense suggests the resultant identity of someone loved and birthed by the Father. His love implies election and sovereign favor by incorporation into a family relationship of intimacy. The verb pictures a prior action with continuing ramifications. Believers have a new and permanent identity.
135. The word is normally translated "if" to introduce a conditional statement implying contingency. However, here no contingency is envisioned but a definite future event is anticipated. This is tantamount to a promise.
136. According to Talbert, it was a common belief among early believers (*Reading John*, 29).
137. Schnackenburg draws a distinction between deification (becoming God) and Christlikeness (*Epistles*, 158–160).

An implied contrast emerges when we compare our personal development with the unchanging character of Christ.[138] We need to change; he does not.

The next verse states that all[139] who have this hope purify themselves, with Christ as the measure of purity (3:3). Anticipation breeds hope. Hope is more than mere expectation of the future. Hope expresses an eagerness and desire to be ready, to do whatever is necessary in order to usher in a future reality. Purifying oneself connotes an active and purposeful participation.[140] Sanctification represents the only proper response to God's election and love.

3:4–10 Habits Good and Bad[141]

Continuing on this moral/ethical line of thought, 3:4 offers a proverb: "Everyone who sins[142] breaks the law; in fact, sin is lawlessness." A major motif threading 1 John correlates sin and lawlessness. The word "command" appears 14 times (2:3–4, 7 [3x], 8; 3:22, 23 [2x], 24; 4:21; 5:2–3 [3x]). The frequency of use clues us to the importance of divine authority and human submission as seen in right ethical behavior.[143] Regarding the Lord's commands as law and disobedience as lawlessness, we agree with the writer equating sin with lawlessness. Righteousness, then, reveals itself through willing conformance with the law of God.

Informed by the previous verse depicting hope in the Lord's return, we contrast the disciple spurred by sanctifying hope with the one marked by lawlessness.[144] The latter harbor no hope in transformation to be like Christ and foster no relationship with the Father. We rightfully doubt their identity

---

138. "Is" changes from the present to the future as it describes the disciple, conveying a change in character or nature between that of the present and that in the future. However, the verb remains in the present when describing Christ.
139. The indefinite adjective "all/everyone" generalizes the referent to a broader spectrum. There is no special privileging of a smaller select group (Brooke, *Epistles*, 83).
140. The present tense of "purify" connotes a lifestyle of righteousness. See Bultmann, *Epistles*, 49.
141. Anderson includes 3:3 with 3:4–10 as a unit (*Exegetical Summary*, 100). However, as even he admits, 3:3 depicts the outworking of the hope specified in 3:1–2. It would be better, then, to divide this passage as 3:1–3 and 3:4–10.
142. In the present tense, the substantive participle "who sins" and verb "breaks (literally 'practices lawlessness')" signify a practice, norm, or pattern of behavior that reveals an inner attitude or state of mind predisposed to sin.
143. Jobes regards 1 John as rhetorical writing that urges readers to adhere to principles, convictions, and values they already embrace, technically epideictic rhetoric (*Letters*, 413). A prominent theme is truth "as the ethical standards that God has established" (*Letters*, 414).
144. Smalley views "lawlessness" accompanied by the definite article as something more pernicious than general sin, more akin to arrogant rebellion against God (*1, 2, 3 John*, 155). Then this term applies only to those who have left the church and not to anyone remaining behind.

as children of God since they lack any indication of an inner compulsion for holiness. They focus on this life (2:15–16) and desire nothing that lasts (2:17). Impacted by the love of the Father, the child of God instead seeks permanence; that which will endure beyond the confines of this world and life.

Then 3:5 recognizes that the readers know[145] the Lord's salvific mission at his first coming. We might think that the writer recalls 3:2 but in fact the temporal markers differ. The expression "he appeared" seems to correlate with "when Christ appears" (3:2). The statement of 3:5, however, refers to a past event as depicted in the Gospel that details Jesus' first advent.[146] The orientation of 3:2 is futuristic and anticipates Jesus' second advent when his disciples will become like him.

Sanctifying oneself pertains primarily to practicing righteousness and avoiding habitual sin. Anyone characterized by a sinful lifestyle denies Jesus' redemptive ministry in practice regardless of verbal profession to the contrary. A major feature of righteousness, according to 1 John, centers on obeying the Lord's command to love one another.[147] Such love would nurture the fellowship disciples have with one another. Hatred, in contrast, would create rifts in the fellowship and severely weaken the church. At the same time, the church needs to maintain unity in its members' understanding of and commitment to the messianic truth in order to withstand the threat of the antichrist in its midst. There should be unanimity among church members in their understanding of truths concerning Christ; otherwise a portion may be deceived (2:26).

Significantly, the writer pens another propositional truth: "And in him is no sin" (3:5c). This truth contrasts with the lie of 1:10 by which we would blaspheme God by calling him a liar if we should claim sinlessness. Then we see the correlation between Jesus taking away our sins and his personal sinlessness.[148] He must be without sin in order to deal with ours redemptively.

---

145. In the perfect tense, "know" portrays a condition, that is, a person is knowledgeable.
146. Anderson notes that the aorist "appears" implies a "once and for all in history" (*Exegetical Summary*, 103). Although the event is non-repeatable, the aorist does not necessarily imply that. Only context can confirm that.
147. Collins emphasizes that the command to love is not even the most important but obedience to this command signals true knowledge of God and being a member of the believing community ("New Commandment," 244).
148. Lieu does not regard this clause as conveying an explicit doctrine of Jesus' sinlessness (*I, II, & III John*, 130). This is true as seen in John E. McKinley's review of the sophisticated patristic models of Christ's impeccability and temptation ("Four Patristic Models of Jesus Christ's Impeccability and Temptation," *Perichoresis* 9 [2011]: 29–66).

1 John

This trait does not disqualify him from being fully human, but it does set him apart as unique. Only he can secure our salvation and does.

Moreover, the writer points out two opposing truths: "No one who lives in him keeps on sinning. No one who continues to sin has either seen him or known him" (3:6). Again, we see a familiar dualism, two possible lifestyles diametrically opposite to one another and mutually exclusive. A cause-and-effect relationship exists that can be restructured as an equivalent conditional statement – if they abide in him, that is, Jesus, they would not practice sin.[149] Abiding in Jesus depicts a relationship in which the disciple submits to his lordship by obeying his commands, consistent with what the writer has been emphasizing in the first two chapters of this letter. A corollary brings to the surface an underlying life principle – so long as disciples abide in Jesus they will not succumb to a life marked by sin. The form of the descriptive ("he who abides") portrays an active and intentional abiding in Jesus.[150] The universalizing "no one" reduces all possible factors down to one that may influence the kind of life lived. The only factor necessary for living life free from chronic moral failure and staying on the path of uprightness is abiding in him. So a new believer and a Christian leader have equal potential of abiding in Jesus and living a virtuous life.

Negatively, anyone plagued by habitual sin cannot see or know Christ or the Father. The forms of the two verbs "see" and "know" connote a condition, state, or status.[151] Such a description applies to the world (3:1e). The parallelism of 3:1e and 3:6b reveals one of the defining characteristics of the world as living in sin and hence not able to know Christ or the Father. Then anyone so marked belongs more to the world than to the fellowship of disciples.

The context of 1:6–3:6 contends that sin, unconfessed (1:8, 10), hypocritical (1:6, 8, 10; 2:4, 9), denying Christ and the Father (3:22–23), hating believers (2:9, 11), loving the world and its allurements (2:15–16), and disturbingly normative (3:4, 6), marks someone who failed to appropriate the

---

149. Schnackenburg affirms that the believer is immune from sin as a consequence of fellowship with Christ (*Epistles*, 173). Schnackenburg clarifies that immunity does not imply sinlessness but that the believer, as a rule, does not sin.
150. The descriptive is a substantive present participle that connotes normative behavior. Disciples make decisions and conscious choices that align their lives with the will of the Lord. The other substantive present participle "who sins" depict people habitually making decisions and choices that oppose God's will.
151. Being in the perfect tense, both verbs describe people's inability to see and know Christ. This inability stems from the resultant spiritual/moral condition of habitual, willful sin. Yarbrough understands this knowledge to feature doctrinal, ethical, and relational aspects of the true knowledge of Christ that transforms (*1–3 John*, 184–185).

Christ who took away sins (3:5) and who became the propitiation for the sins of the whole world (2:1–2).[152] Rejection of Jesus as the Christ is rejection of redemption available only through him. Rejecters walk in darkness and do not practice the truth (1:6). They will pass away along with the world (2:17) and have no hope in Jesus' return to spur self-sanctification (3:3).

Dare the church preach and teach these truths and demand that its members take their sanctification and relationship with the Father and the Son seriously? Dare it take a clear and firm stand for Jesus as the Christ even in the midst of many antichrists?

The writer admonishes his readers not to be led astray and to do righteous deeds as a reflection of Jesus (3:7). The propositional statement about Jesus being righteous occurs four times (1:9; 2:1, 29; 3:7). As children of God, they would already bear the trait of righteousness (2:29) and reflect the character of the Lord. So why continue to admonish them to be righteous?

Being righteous is both a status and a process. It is a status as the mark of children of God; but it is a process in that disciples must continually sanctify themselves (3:3) and be ever on the lookout for deception.[153] They must actively maintain their status lest it slip away in an unguarded moment.

The children of God share in the Lord's righteous character, thereby confirming their birth and identification with the Lord. Both the Lord and his children share in the simple statement "he is righteous." Fellowship, then, requires a shared trait that facilitates intimacy.

The form of the prohibition "do not let anyone lead you astray" indicates inherent ability.[154] Even though the author does not specify the source of deception, those who departed from the church represent the most likely candidates.[155]

The following verse (3:8) declares that those who habitually sin are of the devil, because he has sinned from the beginning. The Son of God came

---

152. For 1:5–3:10, Lewis proposes the overriding theme to be "God as light" (*Gospel According to John and the Johannine Letters*, 112–117). Light symbolizes moral uprightness, including love for others.
153. The verb "do [not] let [anyone] lead [you] astray" is in the present tense depicting an ongoing vigil where even a momentary dropping of the guard makes one vulnerable. The child of God must be constantly vigilant.
154. The present imperative depicts steadfast resistance to deception. Recalling the anointing every disciple received (2:20, 27), successful resistance depends on the individual. God supplied all necessary resources but the decision in every situation belongs to the believer.
155. Brooke allows for the possibility of a particular opponent without narrowing the options (*Epistles*, 87). Johnson, however, identifies the culprits as "the secessionist false teachers" (*1, 2, and 3 John*, 72).

to destroy the devil's work. Placed in juxtaposition, the two verses (3:7–8) contrast the person begotten of God and the one associated with the devil. The contrast is not perfect in that only the disciple is said to be born of God (2:29), whereas the sinner is simply "of the devil."[156] Yet, the difference between Jesus and the devil stands out – the former is righteous and the latter sins from the beginning.[157] The phrase "from the beginning" alludes undoubtedly to before the fall (Gen 3:1–19).[158] 1 John portrays the devil as the primary influence for evil among humanity. Then he is humanity's archenemy.[159] As a consequence, the Son of God appeared to destroy his works.[160] These works include the sins he commits and also the influence he exerts in provoking people to sin. Precisely what destroying the devil's works entails can be ascertained by referring back to 2:2. Jesus' propitiation appeases God's wrath against the sins of the world. In doing so, Jesus removed the consequences of the world's sins through securing forgiveness and cleansing (1:9).

Then 3:9 repeats 2:29c, but conversely, that the children of God do not continue in sin because his seed remains in them. Although parallel with 2:29c, the writer adds important new information. Disciples born of God possess God's seed within, preventing them from practicing sin. To "continue to sin" signifies a life marked by habitual sin.[161] The cause-and-effect relationship views the seed as an operative principle within the disciple much like indwelling truth (1:8; 2:4). In fact, indwelling truth may well be the seed

---

156. Commenting on the phrase "of the devil," D. Edmond Hiebert writes that the expression denotes the source of the evil prevalent in a sinner's life ("An Exposition of 1 John 2:29–3:12," *BSac* 146 [1989]: 211). Yet, sinners are still held responsible because they rejected God's word.
157. The verb "sins" is in the present tense to portray uninterrupted practice of sin. Thus, the devil always sins since the beginning. Practicing sin approximates the devil's character but in a limited way (not "from the beginning").
158. Twice Scripture ascribes the devil as "from the beginning" (1 John 3:8 and John 8:44). Brown regards the devil's duplicity in Cain killing Abel as the primary reference and the sin of Adam and Eve as background (*Epistles*, 405–406). According to Sidney Page, the concept of "Satan" is not well defined in the OT and depends heavily on Job's depiction ("Satan: God's Servant," *JETS* 50 [2007]: 449–465). "Satan" can allude to non-supernatural adversaries.
159. F. F. Bruce portrays the conflict as between the families of God and the devil (*The Epistles of John: Introduction, Exposition and Notes* [London: Pickering & Inglis Ltd., 1970], 91). The world opposes God and his people, yet the real culprit is the devil who rules the whole world (5:19).
160. The conjunction "in order that" expresses purpose. The NIV simply features "to destroy." The following clause gives the purpose or reason for the Son being sent. The "big picture" encompassing the Gospel and 1 John supports the contention that the Father is the implied but unidentified sender in 1 John 3:8.
161. In the present tense, the verb "continue" (literally "does") depicts continuous, repetitive, or normative conduct.

within.¹⁶² Surprisingly, the writer proclaims that the disciple with God's seed cannot sin because he is born of God. This "inability" is more a protective hedge surrounding disciples that prevents them from habitual or chronic sin or moral failure. But precisely what this hedge may be or how the disciple is prevented from sinning as normative behavior is not explained.¹⁶³

In 1 John, the Scriptures and the indwelling Holy Spirit may be equivalent to indwelling truth (1:8; 2:4). 1 John also explicitly references Christ as advocate (2:1–2), the fellowship of disciples (1:3), and the giving of the Holy Spirit (3:24; 4:13).¹⁶⁴ These provisions may well be the hedge that safeguards believers.

The writer offers two traits that help distinguish the children of God and the children of the devil (3:10): doing what is right and loving brothers and sisters. Only two different kinds of children exist.¹⁶⁵ The tension between the two groups comes from the opposition between God and the devil. The only significant advance in thought from this verse is a clarification of the world's denial of Jesus as the Christ, brought out in 1 John 2. The point at which the church encounters the world represents the battleground between two cosmic forces, God and the devil who opposes God by denying Jesus. The conflict takes place along two fronts – in the life of disciples who must decide to pursue righteousness and fellowship with God and their fellow disciples, and in the church which must insure that the antichrist leaves or is expelled from its midst. Righteousness and love for others mark those who are born of God and walk in the light with indwelling truth.¹⁶⁶ Both traits are important aspects of discipleship. Righteousness results from obedience to Jesus' commands, confessing and being forgiven of and cleansed from sins, loving the Father rather than the world and its things, and confessing that

---

162. Schnackenburg prefers identifying the referent as the Holy Spirit rather than God's word (*Epistles*, 175). Although Schnackenburg cites the context to justify his preference, the immediate context remains ambivalent.

163. The Johannine literature does not address issues of the "flesh" in the same way that Paul does. For a treatment of Paul on this topic, see Steven L. Porter, "The Gradual Nature of Sanctification: Σάρξ as Habituated, Relational Resistance to the Spirit," *Them* 39 (2014): 470–483. The protective hedge in 1 John is indwelling truth and the work of the Spirit. But this hedge can be compromised if the believer loves the world and is consumed by its lusts (2:15–216). In 2:16, "flesh" represents that which opposes the Father's will.

164. The actual expression in 3:24 is literally "out of the Spirit which he gave to us" and similarly "out of his Spirit he gave to us" in 4:13, the two incidences being essentially identical.

165. B. F. Westcott, *The Epistles of St. John: The Greek Text with Notes*, 4th ed. (Grand Rapids, MI: Eerdmans, 1966), 108. The author distinguishes between church members and those in the world, including the separatists (2:19).

166. Yarbrough, *1–3 John*, 186–191.

Jesus is the Christ. Love for others, likewise, demonstrates obedience to Jesus' commands and also pursues fellowship with one another and with the Father and the Son.[167] The first manifests personal virtue and morality; the second addresses relationships within the believing and confessing community.

One's identity and affiliation rest on a core truth, the messianic identity of Jesus. This truth marks the dividing line between two kinds of children and defines the battle line of the conflict between God and the devil.[168] If people acknowledge Jesus as the Christ, they will assume the defining characteristics of the children of God. But if they reject Jesus' messianic identity, they will be children of the devil. Then 1 John views Jesus' messianic identity as an authority figure to be obeyed, an advocate to be trusted in, an advent to be hoped for through self-sanctification, and the Son to fellowship with. Through these defining activities disciples walk in the light and avoid the darkness that permeates the world.

3:11–18 Love and Hate, Life and Death

In 3:11–18, the contrastive pair of love and hate reveals which of the two corresponding destinies a person may expect; love leads to life while hate results in death.[169] This sharp dichotomy moves readers to a decision with no acceptable middle ground. They must choose to love or to hate.[170] Indecision would nudge them toward hate because love can only be intentional. More fundamentally, the decision really centers on Jesus' messianic identity. To love others requires choosing to love God and not the world but only if we acknowledge Jesus as the Christ. If we do not, we join the world full of antichrists and so hate God and his people. Alerted to these two options, the church must take action to equip its members to make the right decision.

For guidance in applying these either-or declarations and imperatives, we look to the wisdom literature. Proverbs tend toward "stable or conservative" wisdom sayings where the norm is the rule and applies to particular

---

167. Smalley observes that a believer's love for others is a response to the love of God (*1, 2, 3 John*, 181).
168. John R. W. Stott writes of the world's antagonism to Christ in persecuting the church (*The Epistles of John: An Introduction and Commentary*, TNTC [Grand Rapids, MI: Eerdmans, 1964], 141).
169. Steven P. Vitrano discusses "mortal sin" leading to death and sin that is "not mortal" ("The Doctrine of Sin in 1 John," *Andrews University Seminary Studies* 25 [1987]: 123–131). I will discuss this issue when I address "the sin that leads to death" (5:16).
170. Marshall carefully points out that love for others "is the evidence, not the basis, for spiritual life" (*Epistles*, 191).

situations.[171] As a rule the righteous are blessed and the wicked are punished. But Job, for example, represents "subversive or radical" wisdom where the norm does not apply and the exception does.[172] Righteous Job still suffered and for the rest of the book he does not understand why. In this life, things do not always accord with the moral norm but, in the end eschatologically, the righteous and the wicked will receive their due.

As we read and meditate on 1 John, then, the norm depicted may not always accord with our experience. Rather than becoming discouraged, disillusioned, and worst, cynical, we must recognize the kind of wisdom latent in this epistle. It addresses the moral norm that captures the divine will and does not factor in the exception. But even with the exception we can be confident that the eschatological end of both the righteous and wicked allows no exceptions.[173]

The writer begins with the message his readers heard from the beginning: "We should love one another" (3:11). The conjunction "for" that starts this verse links with the previous verse (3:10) and indicates that the writer offers a reason for his preceding statement. In 3:10, he equates not practicing righteousness with not loving others. According to the many allusions to the Lord's commands (2:3–4, 7–8; 3:22–24; 4:21; 5:2–3), the term "message" seems to be either a softened reference to the Lord's directives or a broader concept. The critical qualifier is "from the beginning." Only in 2:7 what was received from the beginning refers specifically to the Lord's command (John 13:34). In 1:1 and 2:24, however, what was heard from the beginning remains general and unspecified. That the message in 3:11 alludes more narrowly to a command finds confirmation with the explanatory clause "we should love one another" in this verse.

Then the writer warns against committing Cain's sin of murder because his own actions were shown to be evil compared to his brother's actions (3:12).[174] In characterizing Cain's actions as evil and that of his brother as righteous, the writer infers divine evaluation. But what either man did remains unspecified. However, the immediate context offers a clue. The comparative

---

171. Marcus Borg, *Meeting Jesus Again for the First Time: The Historical Jesus and the Heart of Contemporary Faith* (New York: HarperCollins, 1995), 69–70.
172. Ibid.
173. Terry L. Smith, "A Crisis in Faith: An Exegesis of Psalm 73," *ResQ* 17 (1974): 184. Job seems to lend support to this truth. See R. Laird Harris, "The Book of Job and Its Doctrine of God," *Grace Theological Journal* 13 (1972): 32–33.
174. Culy points out that the choice of verb implies violence and mercilessness and so can be translated "slaughter" (*I, II, III John*, 81).

"like" defines this OT story as a relevant illustration to the command to love one another in the previous verse. Then we can surmise that "actions" refer to loving others. Cain failed to love his brother.[175]

A principle governs the relational dynamics of the church. Love heals and gives life. Hatred kills and fragments. Love builds strong churches. Hatred tears down churches and makes them dysfunctional. No intermediate state is envisioned. One does not withdraw love and not hate. Even inaction in response to the plight of others expresses hate in that it is not love (see 3:17–18).

An implied motive seems to be behind Cain's murder of his brother. The writer asks the rhetorical question, "Why did he murder him?", and supplies the answer, "Because his own actions were evil and his brothers were righteous." The comparison clearly highlights the evil of Cain's works and character.[176] This disparity proved too glaring for Cain to ignore or accept.[177]

We draw two conclusions from the writer's use of Cain. First, Cain had a choice to do right or not. Secondly, his actual choice led to sinning against his brother.[178] For the readers of 1 John, choosing to do right meant loving one another. Withholding that love leads to sin and harm to others.

As members of a church, we obey God by loving others. If we fail to love proactively, we sin and "commit murder," thereby sabotaging the church. Our fundamental motive to love must be submission to the Father's will and care for others.

The subject of hate dominates 3:13–15. The writer issues a warning: "Do not be surprised if the world hates you" (3:13). In other words, expect it. In 1 John, hate typifies those who walk in darkness, lost because they cannot see and hate others (2:9, 11). By contrast, love characterizes God (3:1, 16–17; 4:7–12) and those who walk in the light and obey his commands (3:10–11, 14, 17–18, 23). Hate identifies those who may profess knowing God and

---

175. Kysar suggests a subtle but pointed reference to Abel representing the faithful who remained in the church and Cain the separatists who left (*I, II, III John*, 83).
176. 1 John clearly distinguishes the two brothers. The nature of the two offerings and why God preferred one over the other cannot be ascertained from Genesis. But for a survey of interpretations, see Jack P. Lewis, "The Offering of Abel (Gen 4:4): A History of Interpretation," *JETS* 37 (1994): 481–496. However, Karolien Vermeulen extracts meaning from the gaps in the narrative ("Mind the Gap: Ambiguity in the Story of Cain and Abel," *JBL* 133 [2014]: 29–42).
177. As Glenn W. Barker observes, righteousness triggers hatred from the devil, the children of the devil, and darkness because the light of the righteous exposes evil (*1 John* in *Hebrews through Revelation*, EBC [Grand Rapids, MI: Zondervan, 1981], 12: 335).
178. As John Byron emphasizes, Cain killing Abel was fratricide, killing a family member ("Slaughter, Fratricide and Sacrilege: Cain and Abel Traditions in 1 John 3," *Biblica* 88 [2007]: 526–535). Byron declares (526): "The figure of Cain stands in direct contrast to Christ."

loving others but whose actions disprove their claim. Hate separates one from the light of God to dwell in darkness. Since the world hates the disciples, then the world does not know God (3:1), nor does the one who does not keep the Lord's commands (2:3–4).[179] Then the one who hates disobeys the Lord's commands and does not know God, identifies with the world, and assimilates into it.

Specifically, the writer depicts the world's hatred as directed at the disciples. Even though the statement is conditional, the writer views the condition reflective of reality. Two realms, then, stand in opposition to one another mutually exclusive – the realm in which Jesus rules as the Christ and the world that is full of antichrists (2:18–19) denying both the Father and the Son (2:22). This verse echoes Jesus' warning to his disciples in John 15:18–25. The world will hate them because they do not belong to the world.[180] As it first persecuted Jesus, so it will persecute his disciples because of his name.

The writer assures his readers that they have passed[181] from death to life because of their love for each other, but those who fail to love remain in death (3:14). This verse hints at a migration or journey that we make provided we obey and love others. Our starting point is death, the realm of darkness where the world resides. We all find our origin there. We were all part of the world once. But because of our response to the message by the disciples (1:1–3) that centers on Jesus as the propitiation for our sins, we enter into fellowship with the Father and the Son and with other disciples (1:3) by walking in the light (1:6) and being forgiven of our sins (2:12). The transfer must be a complete break from the past. Any lingering in the world through loving the world compromises our move (2:15–16).

Concurrently, we require confirmation that the transfer in fact has taken place. The indication of movement is love. If we love, we are assured that we are now in the light and no longer in the darkness. But if we do not love,

---

179. Narrowly, Kysar identifies the "world" as exclusively the separatists (*I, II, III John*, 83). Johnson, however, broadens the reference to include false teachers and their devotees and others who persecute the church (*1, 2, and 3 John*, 81). But Anderson goes further to include the wicked of the world (*Exegetical Summary*, 116). The same verb "go out" describing the many antichrists (2:18–19) and the many false prophets (4:1) supports Kysar's position.
180. "World" in the gospel finds representatives in Jesus' opponents who will oppose his disciples after his departure back to the Father (15:18–25). But in 1 John, former members of the church serve as the chief persecutors.
181. In the perfect, "have passed" denotes a state of being or status. The author notes that "we" have a different status as a result of moving from the realm of death to that of life. The move distinguishes them from the world.

we remain[182] in darkness and death. Action or, more accurately, lifestyle and practice provide the only infallible proof of the move.

The writer then charges anyone who hates[183] a brother or sister as a murderer who lacks eternal life (3:15). With Cain as the template, anyone who hates others is called a murderer without exception. Unequivocal and unapologetic, the writer presses home his point forcefully. He affirms that his readers already know that murderers do not possess eternal life. The reminder serves as strong inducement not to hate but to love. He need not persuade them further. Lacking eternal life leads to the idea of judgment and eschatological consequences.

The form of the verbals depicts a settled state of being, norm, or character rather than an occasional symptom.[184] Thus, 3:15 portrays those lacking eternal life and having failed to appropriate Jesus as their advocate and propitiation.

The term "murderer" is metaphorical and not necessarily literal. Yet, the effect of their hatred destroys relationships and poisons others even if they are not the primary target. Hate tears down and does not build up because a hate-filled person wants to hurt and kill.

In church many interactions between members harbor the potential for misunderstanding, disagreement, friction, personality clashes, and the like. Tempers and irritation flare. In an Asian context, members typically avoid direct confrontation and may display passive-aggressive behavior instead.[185] The anger can simmer just below the surface for a long time. Genuine dislike forms a barrier between members and they may barely tolerate one another. Others caught in the crossfire may be forced to take sides and so division in the church forms. In practice, someone invariably becomes an intermediary between the two conflicting parties in an attempt to "negotiate." The indirect approach helps both sides save face. Yet, the "hate" of 1 John is categorically

---

182. The present-tense verb "remain" as an intransitive signifies a continuation in a current situation or state. Lack of love substantiates the sad truth that no movement or transfer has occurred

183. In the present tense, the substantive participle depicts normative conduct that marks a person's defining trait.

184. The verb "has" and the adjectival participle "residing," in the present tense, characterize the attribute. Such a person is not a believer.

185. Catherine Tien-Lun Sun writes about implicit or indirect communication by the Chinese who avoid direct ways of stating emotions and opinions (*Themes in Chinese Psychology* [Singapore: Cengage Learning, 2008], 125). The indirect approach leaves room to make adjustments in case a message is rejected so that honor ("face") and harmonious relations are preserved.

different than the ill-will that surfaces in church. Hate signals the lack of eternal life.

The implications for hating seem extreme because we have all experienced anger and perhaps hatred. Does that mean we stand in danger of losing our salvation? But we must realize that the writer speaks of a settled state or condition, not the spontaneous emotional response to a situation. This characteristic within the dualism of 1 John categorizes a person as belonging to the world which hates the fellowship of disciples who love one another.[186] The dichotomy implies possession of eternal life or not. The correlation finds its grounding in God's character – "God is love" (4:8) and "love is from God" (4:7). Having God indwelling within implies receiving his life principle. Because God is love and loves his children, his children bear his loving image in loving one another. The one who does not love lacks God's image and his indwelling presence. Such a person lacks the life that God imparts to his own.

A definition for love now flows from the writer's pen: Jesus laid down[187] his life for his disciples (3:16a). They in turn ought to lay down their lives for one another (3:16b). In following the example of the Lord, disciples love by laying down their lives for one another. The writer echoes Jesus' very words (John 13:34; 15:12). He called his disciples friends because he had revealed to them what he heard from the Father (John 15:13–15). Jesus held nothing back from them by giving to them all he received from the Father. In a similar fashion, they in turn ought to hold nothing back from one another.

What might such love look like in the Asian church? For an authoritative answer, I cite a 2001 guidebook by the Federation of Asian Bishops' Conferences (FABC) which sought to challenge the Asian church to address the particular needs of Asians. The guidebook stated:

> The Church in Asia, then, with its multitude of poor and oppressed people, is called to live a communion of life which shows itself particularly in loving service to the poor and defenceless. The Church's Magisterium in the recent past has insisted on the

---

186. The concept of church may require contextualized reformulation to be viable in Asia. Based on the Federation of Asian Bishops' Conferences, Jonathan Yun-Ka Tan proposes "a uniquely Asian ecclesiology" featuring six traits for the church of Asia ("A New Way of Being Church in Asia: The Federation of Asian Bishops' Conferences [FABC] at the Service of Life in Pluralistic Asia," *Missiology: An International Review* 33 [2005]: 72–94). I mention two traits: responsiveness to the diversity and pluralism of Asia, and dialoging with Asian cultures, religions, and the poor.
187. The verb "laid down" (literally, "placed") conveys a sacrificial sense of giving of one's life for others.

need to promote the authentic and integral development of the human person.[188]

With a clearly articulated mandate, the Asian church must "focus on the hungry, the needy, the homeless, those without medical care and, above all, those without hope of a better future."[189] In order to be an effective presence, the church must first excel in loving one another so that, with unanimity of purpose in mobilizing available resources for the common good, it may compellingly preach Christ by treating everyone, regardless of ethnicity, economic and social status, level of education, and even religious background, with dignity as befitting humans created in the image of God. True, the government and technology have their roles to play in alleviating suffering among the people. But only the church can help restore human dignity in recognizing the image of God in every person. The church follows Christ who, as depicted in the gospels, treated everyone, the powerful or the outcast, with compassion, for everyone was the object of the Father's love.

"Laying down" one's life in the case of Jesus meant the cross – something literal and figurative. Literal in that he actually died; figurative in that his death redeemed humanity. With Barnabas as representative, his laying the proceeds from the sale of his property at the feet of the apostles signals a metaphorical meaning. The very verb "to lay down" (trans. mine) in Acts 4:37 is the same verb in John 15:13 and 1 John 3:16. To lay our lives down for one another connotes giving of ourselves in whatever manner and extent possible in order to meet the needs of others. Sometimes that calls for significant sacrifice.[190] Paul expresses this same concept in his metaphoric body of Christ imagery, without division in the body as members care for one another (1 Cor 12:25). In 1 John 3:16, the plural "we ought to lay down our lives" implies the same principle. Only when we all love in this manner will the church be unified, strong, and corporately walking in the light as a repository of the truth.

1 John 3:17 poses a question – those having the provisions of the world and seeing others in need but harden their hearts, how can God's love flow through them? The verse addresses opportunity and ability. The rhetorical

---

188. *The Church in Asia in the 3rd Millennium: A Guidebook to the Apostolic Exhortation, The Church in Asia, Ecclesia in Asia* (FABC Papers 98), 34. Online: http://www.fabc.org/fabc%20papers/fabc_paper_98.pdf (accessed June 5, 2015).
189. Ibid., 35–36.
190. Schnackenburg notes that the actual "laying down of one's life remains the exception" but more normally the sharing of earthly goods is the primary intent (*Epistles*, 182).

question challenges, confronts, probes the conscience. It indicts for failure to show compassion when the need can be met. It opens the eyes to survey within the church for anyone in need. The presupposition is that the need is real. We have all heard alarming stories of people taking advantage of a church's kindness and generosity. But the writer presupposes a genuine need. Within the context of 1 John, the person in need would be a church member, someone from within the fellowship of disciples. Although this verse does not explicitly preclude an outsider, the primary thrust points to a believer in need.[191]

Beginning the verse, the construction "whoever has" encompasses every believer capable of helping a brother to do so.[192] The verse does not imply that only one person should attempt to cover the need. Any number of church members may come together and corporately address the situation. Such unanimity of purpose and mutual interdependence speak more powerfully of the church in action than simply one individual offering to help as can be traced in Acts.

The clause "the love of God abide[s] in him" pictures love as a personal attribute or trait that manifests itself consistently and not just occasionally.[193] It confirms one's identity and claim to be born of God (4:7).

Significantly, "the provisions of the world" translates the term "life" to refer to provisions essential for sustaining life in this world, that is, the basic necessities. This term contrasts with the other word the author regularly uses to indicate eternal life.[194] The purview of this love appears to focus on life-threatening situations of dire need. Hence, needs of a less desperate nature may not be the primary focus. However, that does not exempt meeting less severe needs.

In Asia, the specter of "life and death" is unfortunately the norm in many regions.[195] The phenomena of urbanization; migration due to poverty, war, or

---

191. Culy, *I, II, III John*, 88.
192. Smalley, *1, 2, 3 John*, 196. Smalley qualifies the situation as what "occurs generally" and is repeated. Culy, however, regards the present tense as implying a process (*I, II, III John*, 88). Although the tense can support both ideas, the context suggests a contemporaneous idea – when a need arises, the believer who can help ought to help. Vigilance primes believers for timely response. Marshall hints at this readiness (*Epistles*, 195).
193. The verb in the present tense portrays a defining characteristic that emerges in specific acts of kindness and compassion as normative. The source of the acts is within and only seizes external opportunities to emerge.
194. The first term for "life" is the progenitor for "bio" that becomes biology, the study of living things. The second term "zoa" regularly alludes to eternal life. However, there are a few incidences in which "zoa" is comparable to "bio" in referring to the life of this world (Acts 17:25; Rom 8:38; Jas 4:14). See Smalley, *1, 2, 3 John*, 196.
195. *The Church in Asia in the 3rd Millennium*, 11–12.

ethnic conflict; industrialization; and the negative impact of tourism and the mass media contribute to an erosion of Asian cultural traditions, to poverty and to exploitation. The marginalization of women is another major blight affecting millions. If ever a time exists for the church to make a difference in material and tangible ways, it is now. James 1:27 defines true religion before the Father as care for the orphan and widow in their affliction, and personal righteousness. Compassion for the afflicted has a direct correlation with personal purity. Our compassion moves us to assume a certain perspective, adopt values and priorities, and to live a particular way that results in purity. We guard ourselves against the threat of materialism and secularism.[196] We strive to simplify our lives in order to free up our resources to help meet felt needs. Or as Mahatma Gandhi once proclaimed: "Live simply so that others may simply live."

In picturesque language, "to close the heart" (3:17c)[197] connotes shutting or excluding others from the compassion they so desperately need. What should have been a natural expression of care is forcefully curbed and becomes unnatural.

A rhetorical question concludes the verse: "How can the love of God abide in him?" In asking, the author is not seeking information but a mental response that leads to desired action.[198] Questions can stimulate thought by applying the issue to the reader ("How can the love of God abide in me if I do not show compassion?").[199] They can lead to personal conviction that motivates one to pursue the prescribed course of action.

Proceeding to the next verse, the writer exhorts his readers to "love in action and in truth" (3:18c). Again, he calls them "children" thereby softening the tone set in the previous verse. Their relationship remains intimate even

---

196. Ibid., 11.
197. Lewis's rendering of "refuses compassion" does not quite capture the intensity of thought (*John and the Johannine Letters*, 118). The term "heart" literally means "bowels/inward parts" signifying the "seat of the emotions" capable of "heart-felt emotions."
198. Richard E. Petty, John T. Cacioppo, and Martin Heesacker investigate the persuasive power of questions ("Effects of Rhetorical Questions on Persuasion: A Cognitive Response Analysis," *Journal of Personality and Social Psychology* 40 [1981]: 432–440). Under certain conditions questions can add persuasiveness to a message.
199. George A. Kennedy categorizes rhetorical questions as figures of thought that draw attention (*New Testament Interpretation through Rhetorical Criticism* [Chapel Hill, NC: University of North Carolina Press, 1984], 27). 3:17 is deliberative rhetoric, what Aristotle calls "political" oratory (*Rhetoric*, book 1 ch. 3 [trans. W. Rhys Roberts]), 15. Online: http://www.bocc.ubi.pt/pag/Aristotle-rhetoric.pdf (accessed June 6, 2015).

as the writer shares with them confrontationally. Direct and to the point, he hones in on the essentials of the faith.

He describes two kinds of love, one to be avoided and the other to be practiced. Admonishing, he urges his readers not to be content with artificial love that lacks any impact on others. To love by word and tongue is not really love but deceives the one who professes it.[200] And those who hear such profession find it a mockery that leaves their predicament unabated.

The compound expression "in action and in truth" describes a single concept – "sincere action."[201] It represents a sincere inner desire to do something pragmatic and concrete.

Genuine love addresses each need by inquiring into the nature and extent of the need, and the proper manner and necessary resources to satisfy the deficiency. No one approach is necessarily superior to other approaches. But in an Asian culture, the church must protect the care-receiver's "face" (dignity).[202]

3:19–24 Right Knowledge Assures

In this final section, we find that right knowledge in providing the proper perspective on life and our duty to God gives us strong assurance of our standing before him. This undergirds our confidence when we approach him in prayer.

Continuing his discussion from 3:18, the writer assures his readers that they can know[203] that they are from the truth and can persuade their hearts before the Lord (3:19). Only when we love others in practical ways in meeting needs can we be certain that the love of God abides within us – both our

---

200. Kysar sees no difference in meaning between "word" and "tongue" (*I, II, III John*, 85). This is not a case of a hendiadys where the two terms form a single concept with one modifying the other as Culy notes (*I, II, III John*, 90). Perhaps using two synonymous terms provides emphasis through repetition.
201. The construction appears to be a hendiadys. See Schnackenburg, *Epistles*, 184, and Lieu, *I, II, & III John*, 152, although neither identifies the expression as a hendiadys. Kysar states that "truth" is the revelation of God in Christ (*I, II, III John*, 85), but this idea is too ambiguous. Lieu rightly alludes to 1:6, 8 that describe one practicing truth.
202. See Young Gweon You, "Shame and Guilt Mechanisms in East Asian Culture," *The Journal of Pastoral Care* 51 (1997): 57–64. Confucianism undergirds the belief that human dignity is found in relationships. A fundamental relationship in 1 John is that between two successive generations of disciples whereby the next generation respect the previous in heeding their instruction and guidance.
203. In the future tense, "to know" and "to persuade" have a modal function (one of the possible functions the future tense can perform) in expressing ability or potential. We "can" know/persuade for certain about something.

love for God in obeying him and God's love that has its intended effect in loving others.

A survey of 1 John informs us that "truth" indicates one's status or condition and the operative principle in our lives. As disciples walk in the truth they may enjoy fellowship with the Father and the Son (1:6). Under the influence of the truth disciples freely acknowledge sin, confess (1:8–9), and also keep the commands. They love others by meeting needs (3:17–18). Their actions confirm an inner reality, that the truth determines their whole orientation in life.

The second assurance centers on being confident before the Lord. Because of love for others, disciples' consciences are clear (heart persuaded) and they confidently know that they satisfy the condition for fellowship with the Father and the Son.

Then 3:20 states that should our hearts condemn us, God is greater than our hearts and knows all things. In order to understand this verse, we need to read 3:19–20 together. The writer attempts to allay possible misgivings in his readers. Offering assurance about their standing before God, he strives to neutralize the possible negative verdict of their heart. The basis of his assurance and their confidence before the Lord rests in their love for those in need (3:16–18). So even if their conscience condemns them, they ought not succumb to feelings of guilt or shame.[204]

God's witness and judgment supersede the inner witness of the heart or conscience. Having a grasp of good theology means realizing that God knows all things and occupies a superior position to judge accurately and fairly. The writer does not imply that his readers must undergo some kind of mystical experience. Rather, the theology of 1 John supplies the needed truth that should inform their appraisal of their situation and condition. The more acquainted they are with God and his nature, the more assurance they may obtain to silence their accusing hearts.[205] In knowing all things, God possesses all the information necessary to reach an informed judgment. By fulfilling the mandate of 3:16–18, disciples may maintain every confidence that they can approach the Lord and not be rejected. God's love is perfected in them in that his purpose gets fulfilled in and through his disciples.

Our emotions (heart) constitute a significant aspect of our being human. We ought not to deny them. But unsound theology and an unhealthy sense

---

204. This inner shame or guilt may be akin to You's private shame of internalizing the fear of losing face ("Shame and Guilt," 60).
205. Bultmann writes of confidence in God's grace (*Epistles*, 56 n. 59).

of self can lead to wrongful behavior and undermine our ability to harbor legitimate emotions. Kellemen offers a helpful analysis of the interplay between our presuppositions and our emotions.[206] Beginning with a working definition, he declares: "Emotions are our God-given capacity to connect our inner and outer world by experiencing our world and responding to those experiences. Our emotional capacity includes the ability to internally experience and respond to a full range of both positive (pleasant) and negative (painful) inner feelings."[207]

In 3:19–20, the heart's reaction corresponds to Kellemen's emotional response. Different situations arise, over some of which we have no control. The writer, however, emphasizes right knowledge (internal perception conditioned by correct biblical belief) by which disciples may control their heart (persuade) or emotional response. Theology, the all-important knowledge, concerns knowing and being confident in God who alone is capable of executing correct judgment. Armed with this knowledge, disciples can live life confidently and fruitfully.

The writer then promises that if their hearts do not condemn them, they may confidently ask God and can expect a favorable response, because they please him by their obedience (3:21–22). Again, he offers a word of endearment, "beloved," to encourage his readers. Through the author, God affirms his affection and benevolence toward them. The promise of answered prayer supposes that a condition is satisfied ("if our heart does not condemn us"). Based on 3:19–20, however, this condition is automatically met if disciples stand firm in their identity ("of the truth" 3:19) and steady their heart with right theology. That realization, an internal perception, produces confidence before God in prayer. This assurance of a favorable response to whatever is requested recalls John 15:16. There Jesus stipulated the condition of bearing fruit as the necessary precursor to answered prayer.

The scope of what can be asked and answered appears unbounded given the expression "whatever." But the context eliminates whimsical or immoral requests. Characterized by obedience, disciples would ask according to God's will and purpose.[208] Their entire orientation and perspective are conditioned

---

206. Robert Kellemen, "Emotions: Why We Feel What We Feel?" Online: http://www.rpm-ministries.org/2014/03/emotions-why-do-we-feel-what-we-feel/ (accessed August 6, 2014).
207. Ibid., n.p.
208. In the present tense, the verbs "to keep" and "to do" in 3:22 convey normative conduct. Submissive to and respectful of the Lord, such disciples would ask in accord with their character.

and they would not ask for something that is inconsistent with their life pattern. Then, presumably, the Lord would be pleased to answer the request, whatever it may entail. Significantly, the expression "whatever we should ask we receive" suggests concurrent activity that substantiates a vibrant relationship between the disciple and the Lord.[209] Marked by consistent, regular prayerful dependence and divine favor and faithfulness, the relationship showcases the fellowship the author mentions in the prologue of this letter.

But another condition needs to be met for answered prayer. A clear conscience instills confidence, even boldness, in coming to God. If they stand condemned, by their heart but not necessarily by God, they are still handicapped. False guilt debilitates. Shame, a sense of worthlessness, erects barriers to God. The gospel truth proclaims that we who are in Christ no longer face condemnation (Rom 8:1). Favorably inclined toward us (Rom 8:31),[210] God did not withhold his Son to redeem (Rom 8:32) and justify us (Rom 8:33). Even if our Asian culture attempts to shame us, we hold on to the truth that the elect are justified by God (Rom 8:33).[211]

Continuing, 1 John 3:23 commands us to believe in the name of his Son, Jesus Christ, and to love one another. The command to love recalls 3:11, 16–18. However, the command to believe in the name of the Son adds a new element. Here both elements are linked together to form one compound command, implying that both aspects must be obeyed together for the whole command to be fully honored. Listed first, the command to believe in Jesus' name signifies the proper foundation by which and context in which a disciple may be able to love others.[212] Belief brings people into fellowship

---

209. "Should ask" and "receive" in the present tense depict a tandem that works together in unison whereby as disciples ask they receive. It manifests a relationship between disciple and Lord, dynamic, intimate, and functional.

210. Brent Kruger observes that the protasis of "if God is for us, who can be against us?" (Rom 8:31b) is not a question but part of a conditional statement viewed as true ("If God Is for Us: A Study of Pauline Theodicy in Rom 8:18–39" [PhD diss., The Catholic University of America, 2013], 163). Thus, it affirms God's favor to us.

211. Writers discuss theodicy in Rom 8:18–39, "defense of the justice or goodness of God in the face of doubts or objections arising from the phenomena of evil in the world" (Kruger, "If God Is for Us," 2–3). Kruger quotes Robert Audi, "Theodicy," in *The Cambridge Dictionary of Philosophy* (Cambridge; New York: Cambridge University Press, 1999), 794–795. Asians who wrestle with shame and face hardships prevalent in many regions of Asia, may find theodicy a personal faith-issue. The aspect of theodicy Paul addresses concerns God's faithfulness in view of Israel's unfaithfulness (Kruger, "If God Is for Us," 4). Paul answers in Romans 9–11.

212. Brooke Foss Westcott, *The Epistles of St John: The Greek Text with Notes*, (repr. Grand Rapids, MI: Eerdmans, 1976), 120.

with the Father and the Son and into fellowship with other disciples.[213] The relationship they foster with the Son forms them into a loving person for the command implies ability to comply.[214] That inherent capacity further implies a new nature. Those who belong to the world lack this capacity because they have a different nature. The writer implies this change of nature by recognizing the transition from death to life (3:14).

Concluding the chapter, 3:24 assures readers that their obedience to God's commands enables the mutual indwelling of God in them and they in him. The Spirit facilitates that mutual indwelling. Here is the first mention of the Spirit. The Spirit is mentioned also in 4:2, 13; 5:6, 8.

Consistent with its immediate context (3:21–24), we find the author assuring his readers of their standing before God. In 3:24, however, the author focuses on mutual indwelling.[215] Their obedience assures disciples that they have the Father. Responsibility and expectations qualify the relationship – the Father expects obedience and trust on the part of the disciple, whereas the disciple expects fellowship, eternal life, forgiveness and cleansing, and answers to prayers.

1 John 3 answers two fundamental questions: "Who can I be?" and "What can I achieve?" The first question implies the power of choice. According to this letter, I can choose to act in a manner consistent with being a child of God or a child of the devil. These are mutually exclusive lifestyles. Proof of our identity comes primarily from our manner of life.

A child of God is someone chosen and called by God himself to enter an intimate relationship maintained by personal righteousness. Collectively, the children of God form a community characterized chiefly by love for one another shown in practical ways.

---

213. The compound command, "we should believe in the name of his Son Jesus Christ and we should love one another," consists of two subjunctive verbs. The verb "should believe" is aorist and "should love" is present tense. If a distinction is to be pressed about the tense shift, the aorist functions as background to "should love." Thus, we can render the command as "believe in the name of his Son Jesus Christ and, on that basis, love one another."
214. As Paul A. Rainbow notes, "Only people who know and believe in God can love him" (*Johannine Theology: The Gospel, The Epistles and the Apocalypse* [Downers Grove, IL: InterVarsity Academic, 2014], 311).
215. A potential ambiguity exists where the identity of "he" can potentially allude to God himself or to Christ. The immediate context supports God as "he." See Brooke, *Epistles*, 105–106.

1 JOHN

1 JOHN 4

Wouldn't it be great to have diagnostic tools by which to determine whether our members subscribe to the truth and pursue loving relationships, two key characteristics that mark true disciples? Simply attending church or serving, while good, do not give us an accurate read on their spiritual condition. These activities may indicate spirituality or may be ritualistic. Truth deals with inner beliefs, convictions, and worldview, whereas love reflects a fundamental aspect of God's character. As we read 1 John 4, we will uncover those tools to diagnose our people.

To help us in examining this chapter, we observe that the address "beloved" appears three times (4:1, 7, 11), each occurrence marking the start of a subdivision of the chapter.[216] So we can see a clear transition from a discussion on truth (4:1–6) to love at 4:7 that continues through the rest of the chapter. Then a diagnostic tool emerges from each of the two major sections – one tool helps us to evaluate our members' grasp of the truth and the other tool enables us to assess their love for others.

4:1–3 Discerning and Overcoming False Spirits[217]

The admonition to test the spirits claiming "truth" (4:1) takes special significance in Asia. We are constantly bombarded by various "truths" and in our daily activities associate with many who embrace those "truths." Disciples face two opposing spirits, both claiming "truth"; but they cannot both be true. Implicit in this is the fact that the readers have the ability to distinguish truth from falsehood. Indeed, 4:1 commands them to critically assess each spirit's teaching to see whether it is from God or not.[218] With his warning about false prophets, the author refers to human prophets proclaiming a false message reputed to be from God but which instead is prompted by spirits

---

216. Kysar marks off the passage into two major sections, 4:1–6 on the spirit of truth and the spirit of error and 4:7–5:5 on God's love and the believers' love (*I, II, III John*, 90–106). Johnson agrees with Kysar, differing only at the perceived end point (*1, 2, and 3 John*, 93–122). Whereas the idea of love continues in 1 John 5, I discern a shift at 5:1 back to recognizing that Jesus is the Christ with attendant authority.
217. Although 4:1–6 forms a subsection, I divide into separate discussions 4:1, 4:2–3, and 4:4–6 for heuristic reasons.
218. The present imperatives, "do not believe" and "examine," represent coordinated actions. See Kenneth L. McKay, "Aspect in Imperatival Constructions in New Testament Greek," *NovT* 27 (1985): 206–207. The negated present imperative does not connote "stop believing every spirit" as some older grammars teach. See Douglas S. Huffman for examples (*The Handy Guide to New Testament Greek: Grammar, Syntax, and Diagramming* [Grand Rapids, MI: Kregel, 2012], 72).

not sent by the Lord and hence, lack authority to speak in his behalf. Thus, disciples must examine the spirits.[219] But how do they discern? What is the specific diagnostic tool that facilitates distinguishing truth from falsehood?

First, we note the expression "many false prophets have gone out into the world" echoes the earlier statement about the many antichrists who have come out of the fellowship of disciples (2:18–19). The parallel suggests that the labels "antichrists" and "false prophets" refer to the same group of individuals who used to be part of the church but departed because they did not belong to the faith.[220] Viewing the separation as a past event (2:19) implies that the present admonition to discern the spirits requires constant vigilance to protect the church from the threat of the false prophets. They deny that Jesus is the Christ and, as a consequence, deny the Father (2:22–23a). Such denial rejects Jesus' advocacy and the necessity of his redemptive activities (2:1–2; 4:14) and shows a lack of eternal life (5:11–12).

But what precisely are these spirits, whether from God or not? Even though the first occurrence in the current verse is singular, the expression "every spirit"[221] and the plural form ("the spirits") later suggests a large number and so cannot refer to the Holy Spirit (see 5:6, 8). This reference to a multitude of spirits parallels the widespread recognition of spirits having a significant role in people's everyday lives in Asia. A recent study traced the rise of religiosity and the accompanying influence of spirits in Southeast Asia as various countries have enjoyed economic growth over the last several

---

219. Alfred Plummer observes the NT using two words that mean "test, prove" (*The Epistles of St. John* [Cambridge: Cambridge University Press, 1886; repr., Grand Rapids, MI: Baker, 1980], 94). In Matthew 4:1–11, the first word depicts temptation (Andrew Schmutzer, "Jesus' Temptation: A Reflection on Matthew's Use of Old Testament Theology and Imagery," *Ashland Theological Journal* 40 [2008]: 19). The second word (e.g. in Rom 12:2) alludes to discerning God's will. The former term has a sinister objective and the latter a good objective. In 1 John 4:1, the latter term appears.

220. J. L. Houlden supports this identification but hesitates making an exclusive one-for-one correspondence between the false prophets of 4:1 and those who left the church in 2:19 (*A Commentary on the Johannine Epistles* [London: Adam & Charles Black, 1973; repr., London: Adam & Charles Black, 1976], 109). Kysar, however, has no hesitancy (*I, II, III John*, 91).

221. The negative particle "not" immediately precedes "every spirit" which in turn precedes "believe." Then the particle may be more associated with "every spirit" than with the verb in which case the author is saying, "not every spirit believes" rather than "do not believe every spirit." Although the semantics of the two versions appear quite similar, the first version appears to emphasize that a disciple may believe some spirits but not others. See Hiebert, "1 John 4:1–6," 421. He cites A. T. Robertson, *A Grammar of the Greek New Testament in the Light of Historical Research*, 5th ed. (New York: Richard R. Smith, n.d.), 752.

decades.[222] Many Asians who take these spirits seriously are not primitive people from backwater communities but are educated, cosmopolitan, and well-to-do. They may strive to appease the vengeful spirits of the dead in order to avoid harm, or seek good fortune in love, family well-being, financial success, and career advancement. Vietnam, for example, has witnessed a resurgence of the cult of mother goddesses, a form of the prosperity religion common to other regions in Southeast Asia. Although many Asians profess not to believe in these spirits, they feel compelled to honor them for pragmatic reasons – securing protection or blessings.[223] The means for interacting with these spirits are the mediums, shamans, and "ghost seekers" who proliferate in much of Asia. They potentially serve as a modern parallel to the false prophets in 1 John.[224]

For us Asian Christians, should we believe in the spirits? If real, do they pose a threat to us? How should we view the mediums? 4:2–3 acknowledges the spirits and the threat they pose. Given the pervasive interaction with spirits in Asia, we need to take them seriously. Identifying their potential for good or harm depends on our ability to recognize them. In these two verses, the author presents a diagnostic tool to distinguish between the spirits, whether from God or not. If the spirit acknowledges Jesus Christ has come in the flesh, then it is from God. Otherwise, it is the spirit of the antichrist. The term "antichrist" here signifies rejection of Jesus as the Christ and as advocate (2:1), propitiation (2:2; 4:10), and Savior (4:14). The term occurs four times (three times in the singular [2:18, 22; 4:3] and once in the plural [2:18]). In the singular form, the word alludes to the spirit, milieu, teaching, or influence of the antichrist, used in 1 John to connote any teaching or belief that denies Jesus' true identity and authority. Unique to 1 John, this label ("antichrist") characterizes the world's opposition to Jesus and hence the church. Clearly the point of concern focuses on whether we will be drawn closer to the Lord through the ministry of the spirits God has sent or we will pull away from him through the spirit of the antichrist.

---

222. Peter J. Bräunlein, "Spirits in and of Southeast Asia's Modernity: An Overview" *Dorisea Working Paper* Issue 1 (2013): 1–17. Online: http://www.academia.edu/4072136/Spirits_in_and_of_Southeast_Asias_Modernity (accessed January 15, 2016). Dorisea stands for "Dynamics of Religion in Southeast Asia."
223. Ibid., 12.
224. Matthijs J. De Jong makes an important distinction between two kinds of prophets: "characterization of the prophets as loyal servants of Yahweh and the characterization of the prophets as deceivers" ("The Fallacy of 'True and False' in Prophecy Illustrated by Jer 28:8–9," *Journal of Hebrew Scriptures* 12 [2012]: 28). The difference is one of association, either prophets are loyal servants of God or they are not.

The spirits at work may be the thoughts in our minds or the voices of others. We weigh the thoughts and voices and ask are these from God or not? We want God's will and purpose to prevail. We must overcome the evil one (2:13–14) through the anointing of the Holy One (2:20, 27). The anointing gives us the ability to discern truth and falsehood.

Hence, we realize that the spirits our Asian neighbors strive to placate or to invoke for favor belong to our Asian world. With Christ as our Savior, we fear nothing, not even coming judgment (4:17) and we seek no other favor than what the Father and the Son grants. Overcoming our Asian world means that we overcome evil forces by refusing to interact with the spirit of the antichrist. Then we must refuse any reliance on mediums and shamans.

4:4–6 From God or from the World

Encouragingly, in 4:4 the author affirms three truths about his readers' identity: (1) they are children of God; (2) they have overcome the spirits speaking through the false prophets; and (3) they possess a greater power within than what dwells in the world.

Identity implies association.[225] By virtue of their identity, they do not belong to the world but to fellowship with the Father and the Son and with one another (1:3), characterized by joy (1:4). Then they will abide forever and not pass away along with the world (2:17).

This affiliation, however, implies tension with the world. The root cause centers on the world's alienation from God. It does not know him (3:1) in that it cannot relate to him. The precondition for knowing God is obedience to his commands (2:3). But those who belong to the world do not keep his commands and, as a consequence, do not possess indwelling truth (2:4). They walk in darkness (1:6) whereas God dwells in light (1:7) and is light (1:5).

The immediate and logical implication calls for God's children to avoid involvement with the world that poses a potential compromise or danger to their relationship with the Lord. This, of course, requires discernment. Asian Christians immerse in the daily activities associated with family, tribe,

---

225. The statement "you are from God" affirms a condition, serves to describe the subject, or provides identification. In the present case, "you" refers to the readers as identified with God. The identification is a current possession.

neighborhood, or cultural identity.[226] They face a double challenge – preserving the purity of their Christian identity and being a witness to their community.[227]

The concept of overcoming involves more than not being deceived by false prophets and their teachings, and implies more than isolated individual believers being triumphant. Victory over darkness is a corporate enterprise involving the whole church. If a portion remains steadfast and another portion becomes deceived, schism results and undermines the entire community. Something of this disunity must have been the case just prior to a contingent leaving the church in 2:19. So purification by repentance of those in error or by separation from those persistent in error represents the only acceptable solution. An overcoming church strives to clarify the error and dangers of false teaching and beliefs for the sake of its members.

The conjunction joining "you are from God" and "you have overcome them" may define a logical relationship between the two clauses.[228] The first clause specifies the condition that results in the second clause. Since the readers are born of God, they acquire the characteristic of overcomers. Although this verse does not specify additional conditions to be an overcomer other than being a believer, the broader context of 1 John voices several admonitions – for example, walking in the light (1:7), confessing sins (1:9), not loving the world (2:15), and loving one another (3:11, 16–18) – which, if obeyed, will enable the believer to achieve victory.

---

226. For a Muslim context, Jim Leffel ponders how to establish a sustainable Christian witness ("Contextualization: Building Bridges to the Muslim Community." Online: http://www.xenos.org/sites/default/files/essay-pdfs/Contextualization.%20Building%20Bridges%20to%20the%20Muslim%20Community%20%28Leffel%2C%20Jim%29.pdf [accessed June 14, 2015]). Of the six models of contextualization (C1 – C6), he favors C4 where Christians adopt features of Muslim worship, diet, dress, and terms. But neighbors do not see them as Muslims.

227. Richard Engle defines contextualization as "showing the whole Bible relevant to the total individual in all his relationships of life" ("Contextualization in Missions: A Biblical and Theological Appraisal," *Grace Theological Journal* 4 [1983]: 100). Christians do not compromise their faith but must also be compelling witnesses. Their identity encompasses affiliation with Christ and familial, social, and cultural affiliations. See Don Fanning, "Contextualization," *Trends and Issues in Missions* (2009): 1–28. Online: http://digitalcommons.liberty.edu/cgi/viewcontent.cgi?article=1004&context=cgm_missions (accessed June 14, 2015).

228. The conjunction "and" usually links two items together as part of a list. However, here in 4:4 it seems to convey a logical relationship whereby the second clause represents a logical consequence of the first clause. This nuance is called "consecutive." See James H. Moulton, W. F. Howard, and Nigel Turner, *A Grammar of New Testament Greek: Volume II: Accidence and Word Formation* (London, New York: T & T Clark, 1963; repr., Edinburgh: T & T Clark, 1976), 422.

But the primary reason for victory lies in the following statement that concludes 4:4 – "Because the one who is in you is greater than the one who is in the world." Believers possess a greater power within than what dwells in the world, ensuring certain victory. They have the indwelling Holy Spirit (3:24). The Spirit within believers is greater than "the one who is in the world" (4:4). The verse identifies this entity in the world as the spirit of the antichrist. The author envisions any number of spirits denying Jesus' identity and affiliation. But they all share a common trait – they are identified with and empowered by the activity of the antichrist. 1 John correlates the devil and the antichrist in terms of activity and influence which oppose God, his people, and the truth. But the Spirit indwelling believers is greater than the adversary and, as a result, they can discern the spirits and not be deceived.

Then the author clarifies that these false prophets speak from the world's perspective and so the world listens to them (4:5). They have gone out into the world (4:1), a reference to former church members who departed (2:19). Their separation from the fellowship of disciples exposed their true nature and doctrinal stand and, at the same time, purified the church of their defilement. The term "world" signifies the system of thought or ideology, priorities, and values that oppose God and the truth.

Because of the inherent tension between God and the world, advocates of one would meet resistance from the other. However, the reaction of each toward the other is not a mirror image of each other. The world responds with hostility and hatred to God and those who align with him (3:13). In fact, hatred marks someone not belonging to God (2:9, 11; 3:15; 4:20). No similar hostility or hatred characterizes believers. At most, the author admonishes his readers not to love the world (2:15). He does not exhort them to hate the world. An adversarial regard toward the world, however, emerges from the author's acknowledgment of his readers overcoming the evil one (2:13–14), overcoming the deceiving spirits empowering the false prophets (4:4), and overcoming the world (5:4). The three separate adversaries vanquished, the evil one, deceiving spirits working through false prophets, and the world, may connote different things but they can be catalogued under the rubric "world" being the more frequent term.[229] The world lies in the evil one (5:19) in the sense of being under its control. Hence, the evil one rules the world. The world's doctrine and teachings stem from the evil one, a probable

---

[229]. "Evil one" occurs twice (2:13–14), "spirits" as in worldly or evil spirits three times (in 4:3 as a spirit that does not confess Jesus and the spirit of the antichrist [the term "spirit" is not explicit but implicit]; in 4:6 as the spirit of error or deception), "false prophets" once (4:1),

reference to Satan. Then ultimately the conflict pits God and Satan against each other, and those belonging to either master are likewise in conflict with each other.

Given the positive regard God has toward the world as the object of redemption (2:2; 4:9, 14), his disciples ought also to have a redemptive interest in the world. This interest results in greater complexity in how believers interact with the world to mirror God's multifaceted relationship with the world.[230] The Gospel declares God's love for the world (John 3:16) and yet 1 John warns his children not to love the world (2:15). Clearly the concept of "world" in the two passages differs. In the first incidence, "world" signifies the object of God's love and redemptive interests (1 John 2:2; 4:9, 14), referring to people living in the world who can be forgiven of their sins, be reconciled with God, and be incorporated into the fellowship comprising of the Father and the Son and other believers. But believers must abstain from the world that prohibits love for the Father (2:15) and denies that Jesus is the Christ (2:22). At the very least, "world" in the second sense includes the false prophets, all the things in the world (the lust of the flesh and of the eyes and the boastful pride of possessions, 2:16), and whatever opposes Jesus' true identity. Thus, believers ought to make a careful distinction that God makes with regard to the world.

A Thai Christian, for example, summarized her discovery of an important truth: "Now that I . . . have discovered how the gospel relates to culture, I am realizing that I can be both Christian and Thai."[231] In Thailand there is a prevailing mantra that states: "To be Thai is to be Buddhist."[232] This Thai believer felt compelled to renounce her Buddhist family and culture because of a misconception that a westernized gospel was the only legitimate expression of the truth. Certain aspects of Thai culture, for example the virtue of

---

and "world" in a negative sense 18 times (three times in 2:15; twice in 2:16, 2:17; 3:1, 13; 4:1, 3–4; three times in 4:5; twice in 5:4, 5:5, 19). But "world" occurs as a neutral or even in a positive light being the object of God's love and redemption (2:2; 4:9, 14, 17).

230. Darrell L. Whiteman explains that contextualization strives to: "communicate the Gospel in word and deed and to establish the church in ways that make sense to people within their local cultural context, presenting Christianity in such a way that it meets people's deepest needs and penetrates their worldview, thus allowing them to follow Christ and remain within their own culture" ("Contextualization: The Theory, the Gap, the Challenge," *International Bulletin of Missionary Research* 21.1 [January 1997]: 2). Although 1 John primarily challenges Christians to take a victorious stand in the world, the redemptive theme threads the letter (2:2; 4:9–10, 14 and possibly 5:6–9) and so encourages readers to consider their intercessory role toward outsiders as suggested in 4:6b and 5:16.

231. Whiteman, "Contextualization," 2.

232. Ibid.

meekness (a Buddhist principle), may be honored as a means to acknowledge Christ "in the Thai way."[233] Love for one's Buddhist family does not necessarily compromise one's devotion to Christ.

In 4:6 the author affirms that shared identity and association paves the way to mutual understanding and acceptance. All those associated with God recognize each other as sharing the same perspective on the truth. A common bond undergirds the relationship. As one of them speaks, the others recognize the spirit of truth speaking. Any deviation from the truth exposes the spirit of falsehood. True disciples know[234] God and so hear and accept the truth about Jesus. They know God through fellowship with him and other true disciples (1:3). But such a relationship is only possible if they practice the truth (1:6), that is, they obey the Lord's word or commands (2:5) which implies that they love others (2:10; 3:11–18). They also subscribe to Jesus' true identity (2:23b) and possess eternal life (2:25). And because they practice the truth, they are capable of discerning and embracing the truth when they hear it proclaimed.[235] Hearing the truth signifies not only understanding it but also practicing it.

Those who do not submit to the truth proclaimed and showcased by the lifestyle of true disciples reveal their true identity as being affiliated with the world. Even if they understand intellectually the truth, they cannot practice it because they lack the Holy Spirit (3:24; 4:13). They are incapable of fellowship with the Lord and his disciples. Characterized by darkness (1:6; 2:9, 11), they lack the abiding word of God within (1:10).

4:7–10 Love or Its Absence Reveals Identity and Association

In this subsection, the author begins with the admonition to love one another to confirm that one is born of God and knows him (4:7). He repeats his earlier statement "we ought to love one another" (3:11b). Following immediately the preceding declaration about the spirit of truth and the spirit of error (4:6), the admonition to mutual love must come from the spirit of truth. A defining trait of God, "love comes from God," ought to define his child.

---

233. Ibid.
234. The verb "know" [*ginwskw*] occurs at least 15 times in 1 John and generally specifies experiential or relational knowledge resulting in confidence (2:3, 5, 29 [twice]; 3:1 negatively, 3:24; 4:2, 6 [twice], 7, 13; 5:2, 20). But in 2:18, "know" refers to recognizing the signs of the times and, in 3:20, God is depicted as knowing all things. Another term for "know" [*oida*] alludes to ability to discern (2:11, 20, 21 [twice]) or objective knowledge (3:2, 5, 14–15; 5:13, 18–20). In 2:29 and 5:15 [twice], however, this second term approaches the first term in meaning.
235. Jesus declared a similar principle (John 7:16–17).

1 John

A shared trait provides undeniable proof of association and so serves as our second diagnostic tool to assess our members. Do they love fellow members?

The admonition[236] to love one another may at first sight appears superfluous given that children of God by nature ought to love. So why does the author bother with the command? The overall structure of the verse points to an appeal to his readers to confirm their identity and affiliation.[237] He does not question their status but urges them to live in view of their status and to showcase that fact. Then follow two reasons that substantiate the appeal.[238] In answer to an implied question ("why should we love one another?"), the author offers the first reason: "love is from God." Twice the author states a propositional truth: "God is love" (4:8, 16). Love is a fundamental attribute of God. The second reason highlights two truths. First, children of God share in God's character and also love. Loving others confirms their claim to being God's children. As a consequence, they know God, the second truth.[239] Given the particular thrust of "and" that appears twice in 4:7, we can render the author's reason as "because love is from God, then everyone who loves is begotten from God and, as a consequence, knows God." God's love enables his children to love, resulting in them knowing him relationally. The form of the two verbal words ("who loves" and "knows") depicts normative or characteristic behavior.[240] Love confirms a person's identity as a child of God.

With a new identity in Christ, we gain a new ability – we can know God. Experientially, we know him through a familial relationship, suggesting intimacy and belonging. God has included us by birth into fellowship with

---

236. The author uses the present hortatory subjunctive to express his admonition. In the first person plural, the verb includes both the author and his readers to give heed to the command. The inclusiveness reinforces the idea that every believer, not just the readers, ought to love fellow believers. The present tense conveys the idea that compliance is an ongoing process where the focus is on development, that is, growth in loving others. See McKay, "Aspect in Imperatival Constructions," 204.
237. Schnackenburg hints at this by writing, "only those who prove themselves by loving . . . share the divine nature and have fellowship with God" (*Epistles*, 207).
238. The conjunction "because" introduces two reasons. Even though there are three verbs, there are only two distinct subjects, "love" and "everyone who loves." The second reason, then, consists of a compound verb clause: "everyone who loves is begotten from God and knows God."
239. As in 4:4, the conjunction "and," appearing twice in 4:7, exhibits the consecutive use, where the second clause represents the logical consequence of the action depicted in the first clause. Both conjunctions bear this nuance.
240. Both the participle ("who loves") and the verb ("knows") are in the present tense, portraying ongoing activity that is in the process of unfolding. If the idea of progress or development is intended, then the author implies that the children of God are growing in their love for others and deepening in their knowledge of God.

the Father and the Son and with other children of God. We can grow in our knowledge of God – a practical, relational theology. He pours his love into our lives. His love serves as the active agent in our lives, empowering us to love others sacrificially and to preserve the vitality of the fellowship.

A contrast comes in 4:8 with the declaration that failure to love leads to failure to know God. Since a defining trait for children of God centers on love, inability or refusal to love indicates unequivocally that such people are most likely not believers and hence have no relationship with the Lord. And so they cannot possibly know God.[241]

Next, 4:9 states that God showed his love by sending his "one and only Son" into the world to give the gift of life. The unique Son of God embodies divine love.[242] This love represents God's salvific purpose and plan – "that we may live through him."

What surprises us about God's love is his determination to love and bless with eternal life those who naturally hate him.[243] The world hates his disciples (3:13) because it hates him (John 15:18). Condemnation of the world, however, does not imply God's hatred but a righteous response to sin and willful disobedience, rejection, and unbelief (John 15:22–24; 16:8–11).[244]

Through his Son, God takes the initiative to bridge the distance between himself and those in the world who respond to his love by believing in his Son.[245] Sending the Son into the world speaks of a sanctifying presence in the world.[246] Whereas Jesus was physically present for the first disciples, he

---

241. In the aorist tense, the verb "know" simply describes the fact of knowing without consideration for how the knowledge is gained. The present participle "the one who loves" being negated portrays a person who, as a practice or norm, does not love. It is this kind of person who cannot relate to God.

242. I understand "one and only" to signify the uniqueness of the Son to distinguish him from the children of God. In contrast to the children who must be given eternal life (5:11), the Son is life (1:1–2). I derive this equivalence from the construction "the word of life" (1:1f), appositionally "the word which is life." See Plummer, *Epistles*, 102.

243. The conjunction "that" expresses God's redemptive intent in sending his Son. Johnson, *1, 2, and 3 John*, 103.

244. Scripture elsewhere speaks of God's hatred toward sinners, in particular the violent, prideful, and those oppressing others (Ps 11:5; Prov 6:16–19). He hates abominable conduct (Deut 12:31; 16:22). But our author consistently contrasts God's love and the world's hatred, which are mutually exclusive. Hence, he does not ascribe hatred to God.

245. The final clause of 4:9, "that we may live through him," features the subjunctive "may live." The subjunctive conveys the idea of projection or visualization. See Stanley E. Porter, *Idioms of the Greek New Testament* (reprint ed.; London: Continuum, 2007), 56–57. The verb captures God's intention of giving life through his Son.

246. In 4:9, "world" refers to humanity, the object of God's love and the Son's mission. Elsewhere in 1 John "world" assumes a pejorative sense as in 2:15 and 4:1, 3–5. Only context determines which sense "world" carries.

is no longer present for later generations, including those living at the time of writing 1 John. Yet, the Son is present through the proclamation of one generation to the next and so later disciples may encounter him and experience God's love (1:2–3).

Unless the church speaks with one unified voice of a common encounter with Jesus, those in the world cannot experience Christ transformationally. A loving community of believers represents a powerful witness to the world for they manifest God's love in and for the world.[247] The witness must be perceptible for the world to see – hence the requirement to love in tangible ways to meet real needs (3:16–18).

Living in a pluralistic and multi-religious society in Asia, many faiths compete for the inhabitants' allegiance. What sets Christianity apart from other religions? C. S. Lewis once famously declared that grace makes the Christian faith distinct.[248] It requires grace for the Christian in an Asian culture to make inroads for Christ. In some regions, locals view Christianity as a foreign religion and to convert means giving up one's native identity and becoming a foreigner.[249] The other extreme lies in "cultural syncretism, which results from mixing elements from different cultures."[250] Whether native-born or foreign missionary, the believer must contextualize without syncretism. The example of Roberto de Nobili, an Italian Jesuit who carved a niche for himself in South India at the beginning of the seventeenth century, provides a guideline for us today.[251] His chief virtue was his cross-cultural sensitivity. He learned the local languages and customs, even gaining a working knowledge of Sanskrit to study the ancient Vedas and other Hindu scriptures. He became a *sannyasi* (akin to a holy man, an ascetic devoted to the study of his scriptures and to his gods) who was respected by all castes, including

---

247. Thompson sees the manifestation of God's love by two means – sending of the Son and love of believers for others (*1–3 John*, 121–122). A third manifestation is the gift of life to believers. Refer to Grayston, *Epistles*, 125–126.
248. See http://www.christianity.co.nz/grace-13.htm (accessed September 6, 2014).
249. Edmund Chia, "Asian Christianity: The Postcolonial Challenge of Identity and Theology," *Compass* 4 (2012): 9–13. Online: http://compassreview.org/autumn12/3.pdf (accessed September 8, 2014).
250. Rick Brown, "Contextualization without Syncretism," *International Journal of Frontier Missions* 23 (2006): 128. The other kind of syncretism is mixing worldviews. The classic example of the first kind of syncretism is where converts must adopt Western clothing. An example of the second kind is seen in C6 contextualization where Christians in a Muslim society pray the *salat*, reciting "There is no God but God, and Muhammad is his prophet." Central to the Islamic faith, the *salat* is an act of worship. See Leffel, "Contextualization: Building Bridges to the Muslim Community," 8.
251. Fanning offers a brief sketch of Nobili's approach ("Contextualization," 25–27).

the Brahmins. Over the course of many years, he was able to understand the Hindu mind and how religion impacted all aspects of life, thought, and practice. His innate kindness and enculturation of things Hindu without compromising his Christian faith eventually won the respect of all and, as a result, he introduced many to Christ. Even though his knowledge of Hinduism was impressive, it was his character that the Indians cared about. According to Fanning, Nobili contextualized the gospel in three ways:[252]

1) He took on an identity that was genuine and one which the Indians could understand and respect. He placed himself within the caste system where he could gain a hearing.
2) He studied the religion of the people he was trying to reach and used his understanding of Hinduism to enhance his presentation of the gospel.
3) He did not alienate his converts from the church at large. He never spoke evil of the *Parangis* [a lower caste by which the Hindus labelled the foreigners including other Jesuits] but rather allowed his converts to worship in the way that was natural to them and then made them understand that the *Parangis* were their brothers and sisters.

Then 4:10 defines love in terms of God sending his Son as an atoning sacrifice for sins. Two incidences of the conjunction "that" frame the definition, stating first what love is not and then stating what love is. Only God's love proves sufficient as it stems from his character (2:5; 3:1, 16–17; 4:7–9). The sending of his Son and our receiving life testify to his love (4:9). Concrete and tangible, his love atones (propitiates) our sins through his Son. God's love means that he took the initiative to send his Son to secure the forgiveness of our sins.[253]

Love must be defined in terms of God's intentions and corresponding activities. Because he is love by nature, he acts according to that character. The more fully we know God the more confident we can be in anticipating how he will act in our lives. We presume on his faithfulness, that he remains true to his character.

---

252. Ibid., 27.
253. Smalley notes that the absence of the definite article before "atoning sacrifice" signifies a qualitative idea and not "*the* sacrifice for our sins (to the exclusion of all other sacrifices)" (*1, 2, 3 John*, 244). But Smalley's assessment runs counter to the verse and context. God's love and the giving of life are fully demonstrated and carried out by the sending of his Son. No other sacrifice is necessary.

Love defines and makes possible fellowship with the Father and the Son and with one another. As love has a redemptive effect on our relationship with God, so in a similar fashion our relationship with one another may have redemptive implications – forgiveness, reconciliation, and restoration. We forbear and forgive one another. We seek reconciliation, to mend broken relationships within the church. We desire to restore a wayward believer back into fellowship. The end result is a functional and healthy church, harmonious and loving.

4:11–14 Loving Testimony for the Son

In 4:11 the author urges his readers to love one another because God loved them. The construction "so . . . also" supports more explicitly believers' ability to follow God's example of love. This was implied in the previous verse. The object of love in both cases is the same – fellow believers.

The little word "so" in the clause "God so loved us" conveys a lot of meaning. Indeed, the whole verse depends on our handling the word properly. It can be rendered "in this manner" signifying that believers must examine the manner and purpose of God's love. Why and how he loves becomes the pattern by which believers are to love one another. In 4:9–10, the author describes God's love as a proactive gesture as seen in his sending his unique Son into the world as a propitiation that results in believers being forgiven their sins and gaining life eternal.[254] But believers must exercise restraint in not thinking that their love will be redemptive in the same sense as God's love. Their love will not send the Son nor result in forgiveness of sins.[255] But their love is to be proactive and intentional as God's. And their love is the fruit of God's love in forming the community of believers, redeemed and loving.[256]

Then the author promises his readers that, if they love one another, God dwells within and his love is perfected in them even though no one has ever[257]

---

254. The verse does not specify "eternal," only "life" (zōa). But the overall message of 1 John supports the insertion. The term "eternal life" occurs in 1:2; 2:25; 3:15; 5:11, 13, 20. "Life" by itself can connote eternal life. In 1:1–2, "life" appears three times, once with "eternal" appended. The tight syntax supports taking all three occurrences as referring to "eternal life." Likewise, the tight syntax of 3:14–15 where both "life" and "eternal life" imply "eternal life." Also in the tight syntax of 5:11–13 where "life" occurs five times with the adjective "eternal" appended to the first and last occurrence forms an *inclusio*. Hence, all five incidences connote "eternal life."
255. In the next chapter, I will discuss 5:16 where, I believe, we come closest to participating in another person's salvation and forgiveness of sins.
256. Lieu, *I, II, & III John*, 184–186.
257. The construction "no one ever" underscores the fact that there is no exception. It is a timeless truth.

seen God (4:12). Our desire and ability to love others exceeds our natural inclination and capacity. Loving others confirms God's presence and activity in us individually and collectively. His love transforms and empowers.

Two immediate ramifications come to the fore if disciples love one another.[258] First, God's presence resides in the church.[259] His presence sanctifies, encourages, and empowers. Holiness demands that we all be like-minded, wholeheartedly devoted, and kindred spirits. There can be no deviation. Any failure to love defiles the church.

The second ramification is his love being perfected in the church.[260] The author depicts an enduring state or condition.[261] And the passive form suggests that God is the active agent working in the midst of believers in fulfilling the intent of his love among them.

As a follow up to the previous verse, the author explains that the gift of God's Spirit assures believers of their living in him and him in them (4:13). "This" refers to the gift of the Holy Spirit.[262] Believers have two assurances of God's presence: the mutual love disciples have for each other (4:12), and the gift of the Spirit (4:13). The form of the verb "has given" depicts a characterization.[263] Then the Spirit serves as the active divine agent prompting each disciple to love others. An advance in concept progresses as one reads 4:12 and then 4:13. First, the author states God dwelling in his disciples. Then a mutual indwelling of God in them and them in him characterizes the

---

258. The clause "if we love one another" is classified as "the probable condition" by Elliott and denotes an anticipated or expected future condition that has some probability of occurrence (*Conditional Sentences in the New Testament*, 148, 151–164). This probable condition (labelled "third-class condition" by some grammarians) expresses "a potential future reality" (164). The author uses the condition to express hope that readers fulfill the condition.

259. In the apodosis (the "then" clause), the verb "lives" depicts a durative, ongoing process that is timeless as depicted by the present tense and context. God's presence is permanent not momentary.

260. The compound apodosis consists of two clauses, each conveying a ramification. The periphrastic construction in the second clause (second ramification), "made complete," may emphasize continuing action. See James L. Boyer, "The Classification of Participles: A Statistical Study," *Grace Theological Journal* 5 (1984): 173. If a progressive element is present, then the author portrays God's love as steadily being more fulfilled over time.

261. The participle within the periphrastic construction is in the perfect tense, conveying the state of being or condition of God's love in the believer or, more accurately, in the company of believers characterized as loving one another.

262. "Holy" is presumed given "his spirit" where the possessive pronoun "his" particularizes spirit.

263. In the perfect tense, "has given" reflects a stative aspect that serves to describe believers now in possession of the gift. The focus is not on the giving of the gift but on its permanent possession.

relationship. Believers may enjoy strong confidence in the fact that God is ever with and in them.[264]

Both parties have an active role. Then this reciprocity reflects the mutual indwelling found in the Triune Godhead.[265] However, the dynamic found in the church is but a rough analogy. The mystery of the One God and three distinct Persons cannot be comprehended nor explained in earthly terms or analogies. Finitely, we can share some of God's qualities like mercy and justice, wisdom and knowledge. We need the Spirit in order to love. We cannot say that any Person within the Godhead needs the Other in a similar fashion since each is fully God.

The plural in "we live in him and he in us" indicates that this mutual indwelling operates at the corporate level. God lives in the church and the church lives in God. Then they can and will love one another. This is the picture of the functional church.

The leadership can insure that members pursue a vibrant relationship with the Lord through the spiritual disciplines by way of modeling, instruction, discipleship, and accountability. Many churches find small groups to be an effective means to accomplish this goal.[266] Other churches make intentional discipleship a key strategy.[267] The methodology may vary so long as the vision and goals are clear and pursued.

The author, along with his generation, testifies to the Father sending his Son to be the Savior of the world (4:14). The forms of the first two verbs characterize the witnesses.[268] Their testimony about the Son blesses others.

---

264. The verb "know" signifies assurance or confidence. Believers may be assured that God is with and in them because of the gift of the Spirit. See Brooke, *Epistles*, 120–121, and Marshall, *Epistles*, 219.

265. See, for example, http://www.cprf.co.uk/articles/mutualindwelling.htm#.VA7GVıwcTmI (accessed September 9, 2014) and Ng Kam Weng "T. F. Torrance on Perichoresis (Mutual Indwelling of Persons within the Trinity)." Online: http://www.krisispraxis.com/archives/2006/05/t-f-torrance-on-perichoresis-mutual-indwelling-of-persons-within-the-trinity/ (accessed September 9, 2014). Ng cites Torrance on the mutual indwelling as a "mutual movement of loving self-communication between the Father, the Son and the Holy Spirit, an intensely personal Communion, an ever-living ever-loving Being."

266. For a balanced, critical assessment of the small-group phenomenon in churches in both Asia and the West, see Peter Koh, "The Cell Group Church Structure: An Evaluation," *Church and Society in Asia Today* 6 (2003): 40–53. Online: http://www.ttc.edu.sg/csca/CS/2003-Apr/CELL%20GROUP%20CHURCH%20STRUCTURE.pdf (accessed September 9, 2014). Note his appeal for contextualization (47–48).

267. See, for example, the website of Covenant Evangelical Free Church in Singapore. Online: http://www.cefc.org.sg/index.php/training-resources/idt (accessed September 9, 2014).

268. The verb "have seen" in the perfect tense characterizes the eyewitnesses. And the second verb "testify" in the present tense pictures the witnesses as regularly performing this activity.

Implicit, the target of the testimony may well include the world so that a new generation of disciples may emerge. Hence, a chronology of generations extends the encounter of the original generation so that each new generation may experience the Son anew, thereby fulfilling Jesus' intention (John 10:16) and prayer (John 17:20).

Now we come to the third verb "has sent."[269] The author alludes to the first advent of Christ. From the vantage point of 1 John, Jesus' coming is a historical event. He came as the Savior of the world as the gospels record. This event continues to have significance for the world although several generations removed and will be meaningful to yet future generations. Jesus as Savior does not go out of vogue, at least not until the second advent. Now is the age of grace and invitation. Does the church understand its mandate to be witnesses?

4:15–16 Confessing What We Know and Believe

This subsection begins with a requirement for the mutual abiding of God in believers and them in him – "if anyone acknowledges that Jesus is the Son of God" (4:15). In recognition of God sending his Son as the ultimate expression of his love, the author appeals to his readers to acknowledge Jesus' true identity. God affirmed his Son by sending him and believers are to confess that affirmation.

The confession of Jesus as Son of God is equivalent to other confessions – "Jesus is the Christ" (see 2:22–23) and "Jesus Christ has come in the flesh" (4:2). All three confessions complement each other.

Our challenge takes the form of a question: "Are our lives making a clear confession about Jesus?" Two corollaries emerge: (1) "Do we have sufficient faith to confess as God intends?" and (2) "Is the Spirit free to perform his functions in us?"

The explicit presence of the first-person plural pronoun "we" is emphatic and includes the author's generation of disciples as those who have experienced the Son, recalling the prologue (1:1–5). Kysar also includes the readers as part of "we" (*I, II, III John*, 99).

269. The perfect-tense verb depicts a past event that continues to reverberate in subsequent history. But perhaps more importantly, God as the subject of the verb is characterized as the sender of the Son to be Savior. In view of 4:10, God as the sender points to him as the one who loves believers redeemed by the Son. So the perfect tense serves to portray God as the one who initiates and decrees salvation.

1 John

The thrust of the confession is that Jesus' presence in the world represents God's presence, for Jesus is the full revelation of God (John 1:18 and 14:9–11).[270]

At the corporate level we ask: "Is our church clearly confessing Jesus as Christ who came in the flesh to be Savior of the world?" Loving one another makes our confession authentic and powerful. The world cannot deny that we are Jesus' disciples for we bear his loving character and our presence invites all to experience him in a potentially life-transforming way.

Cautious, we unpack what it means to confess Jesus and his incarnation. It cannot mean that we pursue "incarnational ministry" as many have presumed.[271] If by being incarnational, we mean "to identify with another culture rather than to testify to the life, death, and resurrection of Jesus . . . [where there is no] need to bear witness to Christ," then we stand in danger of substituting our life and presence for Christ's.[272] If we misappropriate the concept of witness to mean "being Christ" to society, then we have neglected the Holy Spirit who alone can make Christ present in our lives and ministry (John 15:26–27). Only one incarnation conveys redemptive significance and that belongs to Christ.

We may immerse ourselves in society hoping to make a difference through our corporate compassion in meeting felt needs. But our mandate features both the evangelistic mandate and social mandate maintained in proper balance – not overemphasizing one to the neglect of the other. To confess Christ, then, must entail proclamation and objectively verifiable compassion.

1 John 4:16 reiterates confidence in God's love for two reasons – (1) God is love, and (2) being a loving person ensures mutual abiding. The forms of the first two verbs suggest a foreground-background composite picture: knowing and relying on God's love forms the foreground and confessing (4:15) provides the background.[273] Knowing God's love through experienc-

---

270. Westcott, *Epistles*, 154. Thompson interprets Jesus as the manifestation of God's love in the world and the confession of Jesus expresses trust in God (*1–3 John*, 125).
271. For a critique of "incarnational ministry" even among evangelicals, see J. Todd Billings, "The Problem with 'Incarnational Ministry': What if our mission is not to 'be Jesus' to other cultures, but to join with the Holy Spirit?" *Christianity Today* 56 no. 7 (July/August 2012): 58–63. Online: http://www.christianitytoday.com/ct/2012/july-august/the-problem-with-incarnational-ministry.html?start=6 (accessed September 10, 2014).
272. Ibid., 58.
273. The verbs "know" and "rely" are in the perfect tense. The contrast between this tense and the aorist of the subjunctive "acknowledge" in the previous verse suggests that the author emphasizes the condition of believers which enables them to confess Jesus. The confession is the outward confirmation of the all-important inner reality of the confessor. Supporting this

ing his compassion in redeeming and incorporating us into fellowship with him and other disciples constitutes the basis for faith in him. God's love invokes a desire to obey his word and love one another. He desires that they cultivate faith in him and rely on his love for them.

An immediate outgrowth of faith in his love results in mutual abiding. This phenomenon appeared earlier in 4:13 and John 15:4 explicitly and was suggested in 1 John 1:3 and 2:24, 27–28, and in John 15:7, 9–10; 17:21, 23. The author draws a correlation between faith and love – God's love spurs faith in him and love for him and others. His love transforms.

4:17–21 Love Perfected as We Love Others

The author now explains what perfected love signifies for disciples in 4:17. They will have confidence on the day of judgment;[274] and at present they can be like Jesus. A number of recent verses begin with "this" (4:2, 9-10, 13), all of which point to something ahead in the later portion of the given verse. So it is natural to presume that it would also be a forward reference here as well.[275] However, the flow of thought in 4:16–17 would be logically disrupted unless "this" looks back at what has just been stated in 4:16. The author focuses attention on believers having confidence when anticipating future judgment.[276] This is the key thought of the verse. The purpose for perfected love is for believers to be confident and even bold. "This" alludes to the means by which love can be fulfilled in them. But the means is not specified in 4:17. Instead, the means is found at the end of 4:16 ("and the one who lives in love lives in God and God lives in him"). Thus, mutual indwelling represents the means by which love is perfected, thereby giving believers boldness at the judgment.[277]

---

correlation, "and" ties 4:15 and 4:16 into one single statement. Schnackenburg states that the perfect tense "shows that the knowledge of God's love is an abiding and unshakable conviction" (*Epistles*, 221). Bultmann also explains that this knowledge involves acknowledgment (*Epistles*, 71 n. 9).

274. In the OT, a comparable phrase, "day of the Lord," occurs and signals coming end-time judgment of the wicked. For example, Isa 13:6, 9; Ezek 30:3; Joel 1:15; 2:1, 11, 31; 3:14; Amos 5:18, 20.

275. Brooke makes such an argument (*Epistles*, 123). Bultmann follows suit without explanation (*Epistles*, 72 n. 1). However, Westcott opts for a backward reference noting that the author is making an argument to support a consequence (*Epistles*, 157). Interestingly, Smalley advocates a dual reference of both looking back and forward whereby "by this" serves as a bridge between 4:16 and 4:17 (*1, 2, 3 John*, 256–257).

276. The word "confidence" may also be rendered "boldness" or "courage." In view of the natural fear mankind may harbor toward judgment, granting the word a stronger nuance sharpens the contrast between believers and the world.

277. In the perfect tense, "perfected" characterizes believers as fulfilling the intent of God's love for them. There is no thought of them progressing toward greater fulfillment as if they

1 John

The final clause of 4:17 offers the reason why believers may be bold – "in this world we can be like Jesus."[278] Both Jesus and believers share a number of things in common at present.[279] First, Jesus warns his disciples that the world will hate and persecute them just as it hated and persecuted him because of association with his name (John 15:18–21). Secondly, Jesus notes that they both are "not from the world" (John 17:14). Thirdly, just as the Father sent Jesus into the world so also Jesus sent his disciples into the world (John 17:18). Jesus' mission was to reveal the Father (John 1:18) and theirs is to testify in behalf of Jesus (John 17:21). Although the two missions bear fundamental differences, yet both have a revelatory element. Fourth, there is a mutual indwelling between the Father and the Son and the disciples in them (John 17:21), thereby attaining unity (John 17:21–23). Therefore, the disciples have every reason to be fearless with regard to coming judgment because judgment is reserved for the world and its ruler (John 16:11).[280]

The subject of fear receives fuller treatment when 4:18 observes that perfect love drives out fear, because fear inflicts[281] punishment and, as a result,[282] fearful people cannot be perfected in love. Being mutually exclusive, love and fear cannot characterize someone simultaneously.[283] Either fear consumes people or love drives out fear and fills them with confidence. Fear prevents love from fully forming and God's purpose from being accomplished. "Perfect love" understands that they will not face punishment because Jesus

---

have not yet achieved God's purpose. It is accomplished. Then they have every right to anticipate coming judgment fearlessly.
278. The future tense bears a modal sense here, indicating capability and potential. Disciples are able to be like Jesus.
279. Believers are to lay down their lives as Jesus did. But this commonality between Jesus and believers seems to contradict the statement in 3:2 that anticipates believers being like him only when he returns. To resolve this apparent contradiction, I follow Smalley in my discussion (*1, 2, 3 John*, 258–259).
280. Lieu explains that fear results from uncertainty of outcome and expectation of punishment (*I, II, & III John*, 195).
281. Literally, the verb "has" renders the clause as "fear has punishment," rather awkward. Culy translates it: "fear stems from an expectation of judgment" (*I, II, III John*, 117). Similarly, Grayston, *Epistles*, 131. But Bultmann seems closer to the author's intent with "fear contains its own punishment" (*Epistles*, 74). He historicizes the eschatological punishment, that is, fear inflicts inner turmoil now. Hence, I translate "fear inflicts punishment."
282. Usually the conjunction "and" gathers a list of items as a group. However, here it appears to have a consecutive nuance in conveying a logical sequence between the two clauses. The condition of the first clause ("fear inflicts punishment") leads to the condition of the second ("the one who fears is not perfected in love").
283. Since confidence is associated with love, Houlden declares "fear is the antithesis of confidence" (*Epistles*, 119).

is their advocate whose propitiatory activity appeases God (2:1–2).[284] Indeed, perfect love casts out fear.[285]

This verse, however, does not exclude all fear, only what relates to God's condemnation. Hence, it does not cover fear of heights, for example, or closed spaces, or fear for one's safety.

The final clause, "the one who fears is not perfected in love," pictures those who failed to cast out fear. Consequently, fear inflicts them with punishment or inner turmoil that affects the emotions and may manifest itself outwardly in poisoned relationships and witness, and prevents them from achieving the purpose of God's love in their lives. Thus, an ongoing tension between love and fear threatens to prevent either from reaching its full potential.

A brief statement follows: "Let us love,[286] because he first loved us" (4:19). The admonition to love implies responsibility. Accountable, we will answer to him about opportunities seized or missed.

Continuing, we read that if[287] people[288] claim to love God but hate a brother or sister, they are liars (4:20). They cannot love an invisible God if they fail to love brothers and sisters. The author presents a truism. It is much more difficult to love an invisible God than to love those more accessible. But if we fail to love others, we cannot love God.

The author presents a hypothetical but realistic situation of those who claim to love God and yet show hatred for others.[289] The incongruence be-

---

284. The adjective "perfect" that describes "perfect love" in 4:18 is a cognate of the verb "is perfected" in 4:17. The two expressions "perfect love" and "love is perfected with us" are interchangeable, both describing a state or condition marking believers. They are secure in God's love and in their resultant state through that love.
285. The adverb-verb combination "cast out" pictures a rather violent dismissal of fear from one's life and thoughts.
286. "Love" can be indicative "we love" or a hortatory subjunctive "let us love." I regard the verb in 4:19 a hortatory subjunctive as in 4:7 because that better facilitates the contrast between the previous verse and the present verse. The end of 4:18 portrays those afflicted with fear. Then 4:19 repeats the thought of 4:7–12, 16 – God loves us. An indicative in 4:19 creates a logical disconnect. How can we love if gripped with fear as 4:18 implies? Those described in 4:18 know God's love and still fear. Rendering the beginning of 4:19 as exhortation serves to plead with fearful readers to love. They lack faith not knowledge. They need encouragement not information.
287. The form of "if" and accompanying verb in the subjunctive indicate a probable conditional statement that anticipates an event with some degree of certainty. Then this statement functions like a warning: "don't do it."
288. "People" is actually "someone," an indefinite pronoun that generalizes with no particular person in mind. Although no specific reader is in view, yet all the readers are potential referents, prompting each to self-evaluation.
289. Lieu regards "brother" as a reference to the community of readers (*I, II, & III John*, 197). With the earlier vocatives, "beloved" in 4:1, 7, and 11, clearly the author views his readers as

tween their words and their behavior labels them liars. This very strong charge implies that they may not be believers (see John 8:44).

The author depicts a mutually exclusive dualism within the church. Either members love others or they hate them. The inevitable conclusion is that failure to love is equivalent to hate. 1 John imposes a moral obligation on believers. They must be characterized by love; otherwise their spiritual status comes under question.

The form of the verb "sees" conveys a condition that describes people's character and situation.[290] The positive and negated forms of the verb marks their abilities and boundaries. The positive form indicates their capability; the negated form their inability.

What would love look like in an Asian church? In many regions, the plurality of cultures, languages, socio-economic status, ethnicities, and educational achievement create tension that may, on occasion, escalate to conflict. The marginalization of women and poverty is normative. Love breaks down barriers, eliminates prejudice, respects the innate dignity of every person regardless of gender and socio-economic status, and addresses felt needs, especially the needs of the poor within the church. If the church reflects the pluralism of society through its diverse membership who love one another, then it can drive out fear and continue in the path toward being perfected in love. The church can foster Jesus' presence in its world.

The final verse of this subsection refers to God's command (4:21): "Anyone who loves God must also love their brother or sister." The author reinforces his previous verse with this one repeating essentially the same thought.[291] Whereas 4:20 provides a natural argument (disciples cannot love an invisible God if they cannot love visible brothers and sisters), 4:21 strengthens the appeal with an explicit command. It now becomes an issue of obedience.

Because the command comes from God directly through the agency of the author, it bears full divine authority and demands unquestioned compliance. The verb at the heart of the command, "must love," demands moral responsibility and accountability. Its form carries the weight of divine

---

disciples. Hence, the discussion deals with interpersonal relationships within the church.
290. The perfect tense characterizes people and their situation. They are confined to this world, limited to the physical senses. They can only relate with a fellow human. An implicit gulf separates them from God.
291. At the beginning of 4:21, the conjunction "and" serves to link 4:20 and 4:21 together as one linguistic unit.

expectation.[292] The adverb "also" brings together two conjoined realities. Loving God and loving others go hand in hand and cannot be separated. To do one implies doing the other. By the same token, failure to do one implies failure to do the other. Disciples substantiate love for God by loving others, and loving others is the chief means of loving God. Love, then, is two-dimensional. And the use of the first person plural "we" situates obedience within the corporate realm of the church. Unity and reciprocity ought to portray the church. There should be unity of devotion to the Lord and his command; and there should be reciprocity as each member loves the other and receives love from the other.

Based on their identity as children of God, the author exhorts his readers passionately and repeatedly to love one another in 4:7–21. Thus, as God is love so his children are to excel in love. With love as a fundamental characteristic, its absence challenges any claim to belonging to God.

A church proves its pedigree if its members love one another. Because God loves his disciples, they in turn can and ought to love (4:11, 19–21). Love empowers. By loving one another with God's love, church members invoke God's active presence.

How does the Asian church comply with 1 John 4 then? It can be Asian in featuring the pluralism of Asia within its membership by welcoming all ethnicities and cultures to come and become an integral part of the life and ministry of the church. No partiality should be shown to one kind of person to the disadvantage or disrespect of another kind. All are treated alike, respected, accepted, and loved. The church strives for unity in the midst of the diversity. Likely some members live in dehumanizing poverty. Then the church addresses felt needs compassionately in order to alleviate affliction, although total elimination of the effects of poverty may not be possible. With sensitivity, it seeks to restore some measure of personal dignity to the poor in its midst. It may consider specialized ministries to marginalized female members and to victimized children.

The Asian church needs wisdom to be peacemaker and reconciler when different ethnicities and cultures enter into membership. Natural tension and

---

292. "The subjunctive form is used to grammaticalize a projected realm which may at some time exist and may even now exist, but which is held up for examination simply as a projection of the writer or speaker's mind for consideration" (Porter, *Idioms*, 56–57). The subjunctive projects in clear terms the desired outcome of obedience to his word. In the present tense, the verb focuses on the process of loving others with regard to what demonstrable love entails. See Buist Fanning, *Verbal Aspect in New Testament Greek* (Oxford: Clarendon, 1990), 390–391.

traditional prejudices may arise, requiring a patient yet firm hand in guiding them to embrace one another. Facilitating different languages requires innovation and perhaps the judicious use of technology if available. Should the leadership reflect the rich diversity of membership? Having representation on the leadership team of each significant cultural or ethnic component of the church can go a long way to assure that all will be understood and recognized.

In some regions, socio-economic status and something akin to the caste system pose challenges. How does the church promote love for one another between members of different socio-economic, educational, and possibly caste levels? The leadership must understand the nuances of these differences in order to help members differentiate between what the world deems important and what promotes God's purpose in and through the church. These differences, however, are deeply ingrained and to go against long-held traditions may also challenge one's family practice.

Our author presents a clear non-negotiable when he discusses the church's responsibility of testing the spirits of the age. These spirits make truth-claims. When confronted with a plethora of "truths" where each of many beliefs that typify Asia tout its veracity, even the wisest among us struggle to exercise spiritual discernment between truth and falsehood. Taoism, for example, advocates that opposites exist in nature and humans. The Taiji Diagram, consisting of a circle divided by a curve into two parts, the Yang and Yin, colored white and black, respectively, represents opposites. Each part features a dot of the opposite color indicating the possibility that a given condition may change into its opposite. Misfortune can become a fortune. Taoists strive for a harmonious society where people treat each other with kindness and fairness. We can find truth in Taoism even if we do not embrace all of its beliefs. We subscribe to the possibility that conditions can change for better or worse and that peace between neighbors is a noble pursuit. But we stop short of accepting that the Qi, reputed to be an essential element in all things, constitutes gods, spirits, and humans.

Upholding the truth through teaching represents the most effective strategy. Our author sets the example. He encapsulates three important truths in 4:4: (1) disciples are children of God and that identity cannot be taken away; (2) they are characterized as overcomers, victory is assured; and (3) greater is the Holy Spirit within them than the spirit of the antichrist in the world. As long as they remain vigilant in testing the spirits, faithful to the truth, and obedient to the command to love one another, they as the church will overcome and God will accomplish his purpose in and through them (4:12, 17).

TALE OF TWO REALMS – STANDING ON THE TRUTH

Two contrastive realms, one characterized by light and the other by darkness, form the universe depicted in the Gospel of John and 1, 2, and 3 John. The Gospel prologue briefly sketches the two. The light takes the initiative and shines in the darkness. Metaphorically, shining connotes an invitation to receive life. But the darkness rejects the proffered gift. Yet it is not total rejection as some do accept the gift and become children of God.

As children of God, Christians become part of a sanctified community in the world. This community constitutes the church, associated with God's kingdom while living in the world.

The ubiquity of the internet, social media, music, and the arts, however, can threaten the church trying to remain untainted by the world. But the world intrudes into our homes and ultimately into our minds and hearts when we view and interact with the ideologies and values proffered through cyberspace. Tech-savvy and quick to adapt to new technology, young people, Asian or not, are especially vulnerable. Moreover, our interaction with schoolmates, colleagues at work, and neighbors exposes us to the beliefs, values, and practices of the world.

The world's invasive challenge to the church as it strives to proclaim Jesus as the Christ and Savior demands that Christians balance between contextualization and syncretism.[1] Contextualization is to communicate the gospel in word and deed and to establish the church in ways that make sense to people within their local cultural context, presenting Christianity in such a way that it meets people's deepest needs and penetrates their worldview, thus allowing them to follow Christ and remain within their own culture.[2] Scripture shapes Christians' worldview which manifests itself in their life choices, values, and beliefs. Their biggest threat is syncretism, "the replacement or dilution of the essential truths of the gospel through the incorporation of non-Christian elements."[3] The most effective means to guard against the encroachment of non-Christian elements is the authoritative truth of Scripture. Understanding this, the author of these epistles repeatedly emphasized the importance of the truth.[4] But he focused on one particular aspect of the truth

---

1. Rick Brown, "Contextualization without Syncretism," *International Journal of Frontier Missions* 23 (2006): 128–129.
2. Darrell L. Whiteman, "Contextualization: The Theory, the Gap, the Challenge," *International Bulletin of Missionary Research* 21 (1997): 2.
3. Michael Pocok, Gailyn van Rheenen, and Douglas McConnell, *The Changing Face of World Missions: Engaging Contemporary Issues and Trends* (Grand Rapids, MI: Baker Academic, 2005), 331.
4. 1 John 1:6, 8; 2:4, 21; 3:18–19; 4:6; 5:6; 2 John 1:1–4; 3 John 1:1, 3–4, 8, 12.

1 JOHN

related to Jesus as the Christ and labelled any deviation as antichrist, not in the eschatological sense but doctrinal.

This is the world's challenge. Can the church be Asian and still affirm Jesus as the Christ?

1 JOHN 5

C. S. Lewis once wrote: "You never know how much you really believe anything until its truth or falsehood becomes a matter of life and death to you."[293] That sentiment captures the tenor of 1 John 5. A number of factors, if present, assure people that they possess eternal life. And a certain condition, if it exists, may mean death, a very disturbing prospect.

The author avows as irrefutable the divine proofs from the water, blood, and Spirit that attest to Jesus Christ as the means of eternal life (5:6–12), the assurance of efficacious prayer, and the righteous lives of believers that affirm their profession of faith. Faith overcomes the world (5:4) and enables us to believe that Jesus is the Son of God (5:5). That very faith is a matter of life and death.

A key term appears a number of times in 1 John 5, "know," confirming that knowledge of the truth proves critical to faith and victory over the world. We know (are assured) of our love for others by our obedience to God (5:2). The author wrote 1 John that his readers may know (be assured) that they have eternal life (5:13). Praying according to God's will, we know (are assured) that our prayers will be answered (5:15). We know (are assured) that everyone born of God does not practice sin and is protected from the evil one (5:18). We know (are confident) that we belong to God and not to the world (5:19). And we know (believe) that the Son of God has given us the understanding to know (relate to) him (5:20).

5:1–5 Characteristics of the Children of God

Once again the children of God and their defining characteristics take center stage, not that they left, but the spotlight returns. Nothing really new but the repetition serves as a strong reminder to readers to stay focused on these fundamental attributes and to insure that these traits continue to describe them.[294]

The subjects of truth and love continue from the previous chapter by affirming that belief in Jesus as the Christ establishes one's status as a Christian and loving the Father requires love for his children (5:1). Thus, two traits mark the disciple – belief in Jesus' messianic identity and love for God and

---

293. *A Grief Observed* (London, UK: Faber and Faber, 1961; repr., Goshen, CT: Crosswicks Ltd., 1989), 20.
294. Bultmann notes corresponding sentences with 5:1 in 2:29; 3:9; 4:7, and also 5:4a and surmises that the author used a source (*Epistles*, 76). Likewise, Lieu conjectures the existence of a source (*I, II, & III John*, 199). However, even if the author used a source, it does not explain why he repeatedly inserted the same material into his letter.

fellow disciples. The two go together in that belief in Jesus spawns the capacity to love God and his children. The birth occurs first then the ability to believe.

In 5:2 the author states that if we love God and keep his commands, we can be certain of our love for fellow believers. The form of the verbs depict normative action or behavior and serves to characterize the subject "we" which, being in the first person plural, includes the author and his readers and their respective generation of disciples.[295]

The two clauses – "we love God" and "keep his commands" – represent complementary actions. The conjunction "and" that joins these clauses can be rendered "namely" or "that is."[296] Then they would read: "when we love God, that is, keep his commands." The author affirms that whenever believers love God through obedience, they know that they love his children. With the verb forms specifying customary practice, their loving obedience must be normative. Then they have full assurance of loving fellow believers.

1 John 5:3 clarifies what the love of God entails – obedience and not regarding his commands as burdensome. The expression "love of God" can connote God's love for us or our love for him. Likely both nuances are present with the primary emphasis on our love for him.[297]

This verse provides the reason or basis for 5:2.[298] Keeping his commands without thinking them burdensome showcases love for God. Although God's love serves as the initiator, it fades a bit into the background in order to highlight the children's love for their Lord through willing obedience.

The new thought added, "his commands are not burdensome," depicts willing disciples who submit to God's authority without complaint or resentment. An eagerness to comply describes true children of God. Thomas á Kempis wrote: "Love is a mighty power, a great and complete good. Love

---

295. All four verbs being in the present tense convey action in progress. As events unfold in the lives of believers, their self-knowledge and conduct go hand-in-hand. Conduct affirms the veracity of their knowledge and knowledge provides understanding of the implications of their actions.
296. This is the epexegetical use of "and" that introduces an explanation to the preceding clause.
297. Kysar also arguing from context acknowledges only the objective genitive, that is, love for God (*I, II, III John*, 105). That is a major thrust in this section. But God's love (subjective genitive) is not, I believe, totally absent.
298. Anderson, *1, 2, & 3 John*, 169. Westcott, however, regards 5:3 as an explanation for the latter part of 5:2 (*Epistles*, 179). Discerning which nuance is present depends on whether the author is continuing to develop his argument further or now wants to expound more. Substituting the word "because" in place of "for" makes sense and even brings into sharper focus the argumentation.

alone lightens every burden, and makes the rough places smooth. It bears every hardship as though it was nothing, and renders all bitterness sweet and acceptable."[299]

Continuing, the author notes that every disciple overcomes the world through faith (5:4). This verse presents the reason or basis for the statement in the previous verse, in particular "his commands are not burdensome."[300] Faith describes every child of God, a rather bold statement.[301] The author defines overcoming the world in terms of keeping God's commands with the proper attitude. The form of the verb "overcomes" indicates normative action that characterizes the child of God.[302] Such a bold declaration encourages and emboldens readers to take stock of their identity in Christ and then to face the world and its challenges with confident expectation of overcoming.[303] Victory is available to every believer. We infer that the world poses a threat but not an insurmountable one.

But what does overcoming faith look like? In a multi-religious environment where Jesus may be respected but not seen as Savior of the world, maintaining that truth-claim as a minority adherent can result in being isolated and ostracized. Victory can be measured by one's faithfulness to Christ and love for fellow believers that, in a negative sense, resists the external pressure to conform to the world and, in a positive sense, attract one's neighbors to Christ.

---

299. Thomas á Kempis, *The Imitation of Christ*, ch. 42 "On the Wonderful Effect of Divine Love." Online: http://www.worldinvisible.com/library/akempis/imitation/chapter%2042.htm (accessed September 16, 2014).
300. Yarbrough sees the conjunction beginning the verse as signaling a shift from love for God (5:1–3) to victorious faith in Christ (5:4–5) (*1–3 John*, 275).
301. The opening clause of 5:4, "everyone born of God overcomes the world" forms a parallel with the comparable clause, "everyone who believes that Jesus is the Christ is born of God" (5:1). Two words common to both clauses serve key roles in facilitating the parallel – the adjective "all" and "born" as a perfect passive verb (5:1) and a perfect passive substantive participle (5:4). The passive in both incidences suggests that the divine agent played an active role. The perfect tense of both verbal forms depicts a state of being that functions as an identifier – child of God possessing faith in Christ. The parallel brings faith and victory together where faith leads to victory.
302. In the present tense, the verb describes a process or ongoing activity, regular, habitual, normative. In the indicative mood the verb makes an assertion, in this case a bold assertion.
303. According to classical rhetoric, this declaration is epideictic with the aim of "strengthening of audience adherence to some value, as the basis for a general policy of action" (Kennedy, *Rhetorical Criticism*, 74–75). The readers are urged to exercise faith as children of God to overcome the world. They have the capacity to achieve victory.

1 John

The author raises a question ("who overcomes[304] the world?") and then gives the answer – only the one who believes that Jesus is the Son of God (5:5). The title "Son of God" connotes God's redemptive purpose for the world (3:8; 4:9; 5:12). Belief acknowledges God's redemptive purpose for the world. It submits to his authority and participates in the fellowship with the Father and the Son and with other disciples (1:3). Belief separates from the world (see 2:15–16) and confesses Jesus' true identity, thereby placing the confessor in direct conflict with the world (3:13).[305] As such, a disciple must vigilantly test the spirits to be forearmed against false prophets and to take a stand for the truth (4:1–6).

The only ones who can overcome must have faith in the Son of God.[306] Faith features two components – a vigilant defense against false teaching and an offense that propagates the truth. However, propagating the truth in an Asian culture can be challenging. Aristotle Dy, for example, advocates that only a Chinese theologian can develop a Chinese Christology that would prove meaningful to the Chinese.[307] A Chinese theologian can understand biblical teaching and Chinese history, culture, and language to present Christ effectively to the Chinese.[308]

Asia has a history of exploiting the poor and underprivileged. Also commercialism, greed, and the spirit of competition are on the rise. Overcoming our Asian world means that we combat cultural exploitative habits and discrimination against the weaker elements of our society. Christians in many Asian societies come from the weaker minorities. According to one survey, for example, 70 percent of the Christians in India are Dalits, the lowest caste, who face double discrimination from the government and the church.[309]

---

304. In the present tense, the substantive participle portrays normative, customary conduct that regularly overcomes.
305. Schnackenburg regards faith in Jesus' true identity as resistance against the heretical teaching of the world (*Epistles*, 231). He elaborates that "Son of God" is not given a metaphysical interpretation by the text but "is akin to the title 'Christ'" as Savior of the world (232). Bultmann finds a confession of the historical Jesus (*Epistles*, 79).
306. Brooke sees the equivalence of "Christ" (5:1) and "Son of God" (5:5) but argues that the use of "Son of God" provides greater polemical force against false teachers (*Epistles*, 131). Also Marshall, *Epistles*, 231.
307. Aristotle Dy, "Towards a Chinese Christology: Inculturation and Christology in the Chinese Context," *Landas* 15 (2001): 57.
308. According to Dy, however, an acceptable Christology has yet to be fully developed and nuanced, one for the mainland Chinese and one for those in the Diaspora (Dy, "Chinese Christology," 59–61).
309. "Caste Identity within the Church: Twice Alienation." Online: http://www.dalitchristians.com/html/castechurch.htm (accessed July 5, 2015). Also, Sobin George, "Dalit Christians in India: Discrimination, Development Deficit and the Question for Group-Specific Policies."

What realistic hope do Dalits have of overcoming their world or prejudice within their church? If the church of which they may be members fails to accept them, what hope can they have in facing the world outside?

In the Islamic context of many Asian countries, Christians face many questions in regard to their belief in Jesus as the Son of God. They have an opportunity to prove their belief but not with theological arguments. Rather, their life-witness can demonstrate the divinity and Sonship of Jesus. Unity among Christians is a manifestation of this belief leading to sacrificial living. Overcoming the spirit of disunity, malice and deceit, believers manifest the truth of what they believe. Abstaining from corruption, cheating and other social evils is a sign of overcoming the world. The church's involvement in the emancipation of deprived communities is a generally recognized virtue. This is a way of overcoming the world.

The refrain of an old hymn written by John Yates, entitled "Faith is the Victory," captures the spirit of the passage: "Faith is the victory! Faith is the victory! O glorious victory that overcomes the world."[310]

5:6–12 Supernatural Witnesses

1 John 5:6 declares that the Spirit testifies to Jesus Christ coming by water and blood.[311] The metaphorical language of "water" and "blood" presents a challenge in interpretation.[312] But given the emphasis on Jesus' works of redemption, water appears to signify cleansing, salvation, and eternal life. In the OT, Isaiah 12:3 associates water with salvation. Jeremiah 17:13 identifies the Lord as the fountain of living water. Ezekiel 16:4 regards water for cleansing. In the Gospel, water is associated with purification (John 2:6) and eternal life as living water (4:10–11, 14–15; 7:38). Then "water" in 1 John 5:6 appears to symbolize cleansing and the source or fountain of eternal life.

Working Papers of the Indian Institute of Dalit Studies 6 (2012): 12. Online: http://www.academia.edu/6819127/Dalit_Christians_in_India_Discrimination_Development_Deficit_and_the_Question_for_Group-Specific_Policies (accessed July 5, 2015).
310. See http://www.hymnpod.com/2009/05/16/faith-is-the-victory/ (accessed October 18, 2014).
311. The designation "Jesus Christ" stands in apposition to "the one who came by water and blood" and emphasizes Christ's incarnation. Smalley finds a polemical thrust against two heresies – Jesus was not fully human (so reference to his baptism and crucifixion) and he was not fully God (so full designation as "Jesus Christ") (*1, 2, 3 John*, 279).
312. Lieu surveys the approaches proposed and identifies three major categories: christological, soteriological, and sacramental (*I, II & III John*, 209–213). I chose the soteriological approach based on John 5:36; 10:25, and 1 John 1:7–8; 2:1–2; 3:8, 16; 4:9–10, 14. The reversal of "blood and water" in the gospel by 1 John signals a shift in focus from the power of Jesus' human life to "human appropriation of the gift" (Westcott, *Epistles*, 183).

1 JOHN

And in the OT, blood represents life (Gen 9:4; Lev 17:14) and as such is used to make atonement (Lev 6:30; 16:27; 17:11). In the Gospel, Jesus' blood results in eternal life for those who partake of it in faith (John 6:53–56) and represents his death (19:34). And in this letter, Jesus' blood cleanses from all sin (1:7).

The present verse (1 John 5:6) looks back to Jesus being sent into the world and depicts the means by which and the circumstances in which Jesus' mission as Savior is accomplished.[313] He completes his objective through cleansing all who believe in him of their sins and granting them eternal life through his sacrificial death.

The caveat "not in water alone but in water and blood" seems emphatic to insure that no one inadvertently dismisses the blood when considering the water.[314] The gift of cleansing and eternal life comes at a price, the very life of Jesus Christ.

The statement "the Spirit is the truth" echoes John 15:26. But in the Gospel Jesus looks forward to the Spirit's advent after his departure, whereas 1 John looks back to a past event.

The author proceeds to highlight the agreement of the three witnesses, the Spirit, the water, and the blood.[315] Any one of the three provides a powerful testimony; but when agreeing as one witness,[316] they represent an undeniable force that confronts the world. The world resists. Only faith enables a person to receive the witness.

The reference to the water and the blood as witnesses recalls their mention earlier in 5:6.[317] The water, symbolizing cleansing and the source of

---

313. Culy draws a distinction between two prepositions used here, *dia* and *en* and notes that *dia* focuses on instrumentality whereas *en* looks at the attendant circumstances (*I, II, III John*, 126). Hence, the author refers to both the means and circumstances of Jesus' mission.
314. Tom Thatcher argues that "not in water alone" represents the position of the antichrists where "water" symbolizes the Spirit ("'Water and Blood' in AntiChrist Christianity (1 John 5:6)," *Stone Campbell Journal* 4 [2001]: 235–248). The antichrists' overemphasis on the ministry of the Spirit, to the exclusion of the human Jesus, opened a floodgate for new revelation. The author guarded against that by emphasizing "but in water and blood."
315. Yarbrough discerns 5:7 explaining 5:6 (*1–3 John*, 284). Brooke cites an OT principle of two or three witnesses (*Epistles*, 137). Given Jesus citing independent witnesses for himself (John 5:31–39), it appears that our author is doing the same in 1 John 5:7.
316. All three terms, "spirit," "water," and "blood" are neuter in gender and yet, the substantive participle (witnesses or that which witnesses) in 5:7 and the collective "the three" in 5:8 are both masculine. Smalley suggests that the shift in gender evidences personification (*1, 2, 3 John*, 281).
317. Kysar treats "water" and "blood" in 5:8 as having the same referents as in 5:6, namely Jesus' baptism, his death, and the Spirit's witness in the community (*I, II, III John*, 109). Whereas I agree that the referents do not change between 5:6 and 5:8, I offer a different

eternal life, and the blood, representing Jesus' death that makes atonement for sin, add to the witness of the Spirit. To reject the witnesses is to reject Jesus' redemptive work (the water and the blood) and the Spirit's convicting testimony.

In summary, then, God provides three supernatural witnesses for Jesus' true identity in order to buttress our faith. First, "water" testifies that Jesus cleanses us from all sin and gives us life everlasting. Thus, we maintain distance from the world and its defilement. Secondly, "blood" makes atonement by cleansing us from all sin. And thirdly, the Holy Spirit anoints us so that we may not be deceived by the false prophets of the world. These three witnesses assure us that we have eternal life and that we are children of God.

Continuing, the author presents two truisms: (1) normally people accept human testimony but (2) the witness of God is greater (5:9). He then applies the general principle to the Son. The author does not elaborate on the nature or manner of the divine witness or in what sense it is "greater" than human witness. Likely, God possesses greater credibility.[318]

Whatever strategy the church adopts for evangelism and missions must incorporate the greater witness of God. This certainly implies total dependence on the indwelling Spirit and the use of Scripture. Besides prayer and community outreach (including social action), a loving church serves as a potent witness to the world. The community at large can experience Jesus through the church in its midst.

We next read of a contrast between believers in the Son of God and those who do not believe (5:10). Unbelief calls God a liar by rejecting his witness for his Son. Significantly, the words "the witness in him" imply a divine activity within a person.[319] This letter identifies the agency of the Holy Spirit operating within (3:24; 4:13) testifying on behalf of the Son (5:6, 8).

Then unbelief results from the lack of or resistance to such inner divine activity. As a consequence, unbelief blasphemes God. Apart from the internal divine witness, people cannot respond to God.

---

interpretation as noted in the text above.
318. Brooke notes that since the subject of the testimony is Jesus, then "God alone is fully competent to speak" about his Son (*Epistles*, 138). Lieu states that God's testament equates to or, at least, includes the witness of the Spirit, water, and blood (*I, II, & III John*, 216). D. Edmond Hiebert agrees with Lieu and adds that God's witness "is more reliable and trustworthy" ("An Exposition of 1 John 5:1–12," *BSac* 147 [1990]: 227).
319. The phrase "in him," according to Schnackenburg, alludes to an internalized witness of God that believers accepted and now harbor in their hearts (*Epistles*, 240). Also, Yarbrough, *1–3 John*, 287; and Brooke, *Epistles*, 139.

The form of the verb "does not believe" portrays an established situation or state of affairs.[320] Such people are set and immovable in their conviction. They deny and suppress the inner witness of God.

The concluding phrase "concerning his Son" does not specify what aspect of the Son to which God testifies. Then the focus gravitates to the person of the Son, his identity.[321] Reinforcing this thought, we find the exact same phrase concluding the previous verse, 5:9, and a similar reference to the Son of God in 5:5.

But the very next verse narrows the divine testimony specifically to eternal life in the Son (5:11). He becomes the sole object of hope and faith.[322] The phrase "in his Son" can mean (1) the Son possesses eternal life; or (2) he is the means through which God gives eternal life. The Gospel supports both nuances – he possesses life (John 1:4); and he gives it to humanity (John 5:21; 6:33, 51; 10:10). The requirement to receive life is faith in the Son (John 3:15–16, 36; 5:24; 6:40, 47, 54).

The classification of humanity into two groups now receives explicit attention in 1 John 5:12: (1) those who have[323] the Son have eternal life, and (2) those who do not have the Son of God[324] do not have eternal life (5:12). The key difference is possession of the Son, that is, a relationship with him (see 1:3) or not. Only the former group possesses eternal life. Not having the Son signifies not having the following: the cleansing blood of the Son (1:7), Jesus Christ as advocate (2:1), ability to love others (3:16–18), and victory over the world (5:4–5). This list represents a major loss of benefits for not having the Son. Compounding this loss, additional features of a life in Christ evaporates: fellowship with the Father and the Son and with the disciples (1:3), fullness of joy (1:4), God's love perfected in a person (2:5; 4:12, 17), knowing Christ in an intimate relationship (2:3), and no fear with regard to judgment (4:17–18).

---

320. The perfect tense connotes a fixed attitude. Non-believers harbor a fixed attitude and oppose God's testimony. They have sealed their fate because their condition is permanent (Plummer, *Epistles*, 118).
321. Lieu, *I, II, & III John*, 218.
322. Marshall emphasizes the exclusivity of the Son as the means to eternal life by adding "only" (*Epistles*, 241 n. 43).
323. The present tense connotes an ongoing possession of the Son or lack thereof which, according to Yarbrough, means "to trust him continuously" (*1–3 John*, 290). Alternatively, Lieu suggests that "possession" is tantamount to "relationship" with the Son (*I, II, & III John*, 219).
324. Culy identifies the construction "Son of God" as a genitive of relationship (*I, II, III John*, 131). Possibly, we may also interpret it to be a genitive of source in the sense that God sent his Son (4:9).

Eternal life can be enjoyed now for we do not need to wait for the eschatological future to begin to benefit.[325] Yet, certain things must await the future. The author does not elaborate except for a few brief references – those characterized as doing God's will abide forever (2:17), confidence when Christ returns (2:28), and becoming like him then (3:2–3).

5:13–21 Eternal Destiny: Life or Death

Our author now states the purpose of this letter – his readers who believe in the Son's name may have assurance that they possess eternal life (5:13). The scope delineated by "I write these things" may encompass 5:5-12 or possibly more, up to and including the entire letter.[326] However, the pattern of 1 John, when the author penned "I write these things" (2:1, 26), shows a reference only to the immediate context and hence, most likely, 5:13 refers only to its immediate context.[327] The writer's purpose then would be primarily encouragement and assurance. But why the necessity of assurance? A number of considerations offer a possible answer – the world is temporary (2:17); the spirit of the antichrist pervades (4:1, 3); the world hates the readers (3:13); and the repeated commendation of overcoming the world (2:13–14; 4:4; 5:4–5). The world, ruled by the evil one (5:19), threatens the church. To remain true to its Savior, the church must preserve christological truths by testing the spirits (4:1–3) and overcoming the world's allurement (2:15–16).

5:14–15 Answered prayer

The author directs his readers' attention to the subject of confidence in answered prayer if they request anything according to God's will (5:14). This confidence presupposes knowledge of and submission to his will. The concept of knowledge pervades this letter with the accompanying anointment of the Spirit (2:20; 3:24; 4:13) and objectively verifiable truth (4:1–3, 6; 5:6–8). But simply knowing the truth proves insufficient unless obedience

---

325. Schnackenburg, *Epistles*, 241; and Lieu, *I, II, & III John*, 219.
326. Those favoring the entire letter include Westcott, *Epistles*, 188; Brown, *Epistles*, 608; and Marshall, *Epistles*, 243. They interpret the overall purpose of 1 John as providing readers assurance of eternal life. By contrast, those favoring a more limited reference include Schnackenburg scoping "these things" to 5:5–12 (*Epistles*, 247); and Brooke espousing 5:1–12 (*Epistles*, 142). The former group tends to see a parallel between John 20:31 and 1 John 5:13 as general purpose statements. The latter group favors fellowship as the major theme of 1 John.
327. Gary W. Derickson analyzes both positions and concludes that both have merit ("What Is the Message of 1 John?" *BSac* 150 [1993]: 89–105). But he provides persuasive arguments that limit the scope of "these things" to the immediate context where "eternal life" recalls 5:11–12 and "may know" has forward links to 5:15, 19 (102).

applies that truth. Then praying "according to God's will" means not only knowing his will but obeying his will, expressed by the various admonitions in this letter.

Confidence that the Lord hears our prayers is a blessing. But the author carefully avoids promising answers that conform to our expectations. When and how God answers lies beyond our purview. The only assurance offered is that he is favorably disposed toward us. We exercise faith when we confidently approach the Lord. We recognize that he is the source and authority.[328] Confident prayer characterizes fellowship with the Father and the Son.

If God has given to us both his Son and Spirit, he has given us everything. Then anything else we may ask for would certainly be within his scope of generosity. The apostle Paul makes a similar argument in Romans 8:31–39. God hears us.[329]

A promise now follows: if we know that he hears us – whatever we ask – we can be certain that we will receive our request (5:15). The form of "know" depicts a settled condition and attitude, poised and assured of one's relationship with the Son. This knowledge rests on the certainty of God's promises to his children.

Overall this verse features an "if-then" construction. If the condition proves true, then the consequence will be confirmed. Confidence begets more confidence. Assurance that our Lord regards us with favor leads to further assurance that he will answer our prayer favorably.

If the church teaches this important truth and the leaders model it, we can imagine how vibrant private and corporate prayers will become. Expectancy begets boldness. Testimonies of answered prayer can ignite a prayer movement that will encompass the entire congregation.

5:16–17 Sin that results in death

A statement, intriguing and disturbing, arrests our attention in 5:16. If we see brothers or sisters[330] commit sin that does not result in death, we may intercede for them in hopes that God will give to them eternal life. But for

---

328. The prepositional phrase "according to his will" makes explicit the concept of God's authority.
329. The present tense "hears" portrays a normative pattern that aligns with the present tense "asks" so that, as long as a believer asks in accordance to the divine will, then the divine answer will be correspondingly favorable. The contingency rests with the believer. No uncertainty can be impinged on God. He is absolutely trustworthy.
330. The spiritual status of "brothers or sisters" assumes paramount importance as the theological implications are enormous. If they are true believers and lead a sinful life, they contradict the pattern in 1 John that typifies believers. Irvin A. Busenitz circumvents this problem

sin that results in death, we ought not to intercede. Following on the heels of confidence in answered prayer (5:14–15), the present verse seems out of place. But our confidence depends on praying according to our Lord's will. Then we must conclude that 5:16 expresses his will.

There appears to be two kinds of sin, one resulting in death and the other not. When this letter usually speaks of life, the accompanying adjective "eternal" makes clear that the author has in mind the gift of life from God through Jesus Christ (1:2c; 2:25; 3:15; 5:11, 13, 20). In other usages, "life" is associated with Jesus and implies eternal life (1:1–2a; 5:11–12). In 5:11, two clauses complement one another. The first clause states, "God gave us eternal life," and the second follows with, "this life is in his Son." The second occurrence of "life" lacks the qualifier "eternal" but clearly means that because of the relationship with the earlier clause and the pronoun "this" ("this life") referring back to "eternal life" earlier. Then the close linkage between 5:11 and 5:12 (containing two incidences of "life" unqualified) implies that "life" in 5:12 alludes to eternal life.

Two more incidences of "life" remain for us to examine beside the current verse (5:16) which lacks the adjective "eternal." In 2:16, "life" is a different term.[331] In 3:14 "life" lacks the adjective "eternal" but must connote that because love describes true believers. Then every occurrence of "life" except for one (2:16) and our present verse (5:16) that awaits our further investigation signifies eternal life.

Returning to 5:16, we note that in answer to prayer God will give life. Twice the author describes the object of prayer as "sinning that does not result in death." The form of the word "sinning" depicts characteristic behavior.[332] Given the prevailing pattern in this letter, believers do not have this characteristic. Then the person so described must be a non-believer. Hence, the prayer concerns the granting of eternal life if the sin does not result in death. So "death" must refer to eternal death.[333] Consequently, we must con-

---

by viewing the "brother or sister" as a professing but not true believer ("The Sin Unto Death," *TMSJ* 1 [1990]: 17–33). The pattern proves too great to ignore. The author may hope that the sinner is redeemable and hence a potential brother or sister.

331. The term for "life" in 2:16 is *bios* in contrast to *zōā* in 5:16 and the other passages cited. Whereas *zōā* may signify eternal life, *bios* is confined to life in this world, very temporary.

332. In both incidences the participle in the present tense portrays normative or continuous behavior that characterizes the person.

333. Busenitz, "Sin Unto Death," 30–32. In arguing that "brother" alludes to a sinning believer, Tim Ward ties 5:16 with 2:1–2 that pictures Christ as advocate, thereby suggesting that "not having life" does not refer to spiritual death ("Sin 'Not Unto Death' and Sin 'Unto Death' in 1 John 5:16," *Churchman* 109 [1995]: 230–231).

clude that a certain sin results in eternal death with no chance for eternal life. Identifying that sin becomes paramount because of the enormous ramifications for the church.

The concluding clause of 3:14 assures readers that they transition from death to life because of their love for others. A lack of love indicates death. Then 3:15 reinforces the indictment that whoever hates is a murderer devoid of eternal life. Hatred of others consigns a person to death without any recourse to eternal life. Then 5:11–13 equates possessing the Son with possessing eternal life. Hence, we identify two related statements about people and eternal life. First, they must love others to confirm their possession of eternal life. Secondly, they must possess the Son in order to have eternal life (5:11–12). Possessing the Son implies believing in the name of the Son (5:13).

Conversely, those who do not love cannot know God nor have faith in his Son. They lack the gift of the Spirit. Then we may identify the sin that results in death as failure to obey the command to believe in the Son's name and to accept him as advocate, propitiation, and Savior. It is an obstinate refusal to submit to God and so associates such people with the world that hates believers (3:13) and is passing away (2:17). They failed to overcome the false prophets (see 4:4), the evil one (2:13–14), and the world (5:4–5). The key to overcoming is faith (5:4). Hence, the root problem is a lack of faith in Jesus (2:22–23; 4:15; 5:5). Therefore, the sin of unbelief results in eternal death, a tragic destiny.[334]

This sin is perceptible.[335] When the author confirms that we can "see" the kind of sin being committed, he means that certain characteristics are discernable.[336] Sin that results in death stems from a hardened attitude and willful rebellion against the Father in refusing to recognize the Son. Sadly, we can harbor no hope for such people. And so the author advises us not to intercede for those trapped by sin that results in death. The proverb-like statement utters a general truism. But the author does not elaborate. The verb "should ask" portrays a hypothetical situation that requires a certain course of action.[337] We do not intercede for mortal sin.

---

334. See Brown for a fuller discussion of various interpretations of this verse (*Epistles*, 612–619).
335. Lieu, *I, II, & III John*, 225.
336. However, as Lieu notes, the author did not provide details that differentiate the two kinds of sin (Lieu, *I, II, & III John*, 226).
337. The subjunctive indicates what the writer envisions a possible future situation. As a hypothetical statement, the event has not occurred yet, but remains a possibility. At the same time, the author imposes a moral obligation on the would-be intercessor as to whether to pray or not depending on the situation.

This verse surfaces a thorny issue. In practice, how is the church to distinguish between the two kinds of sin in order to condemn those guilty of the sin that results in eternal death? We readily acknowledge our human limitations since we cannot see the human heart. Do we not pray for such sinners at all?[338] Or do we pray for a certain period of time until it becomes painfully evident that the situation is hopeless?[339] Do we exclude them from Christian fellowship? If they somehow become part of the church, does the church discipline and excommunicate them?

Unfortunately, the author does not provide practical guidelines. However, the separatists of 2:19 may well qualify as those who committed the sin that results in death. Such sinners represent a threat to the church, and so it has no recourse but to expel them.

Two truisms emerge: All unrighteous deeds are sin, and[340] there is sin that does not result in death (5:17). The author starts with a very broad and sweeping declaration concerning every possible unrighteous act as sin necessitating confession in order to secure forgiveness and cleansing (1:9). Then he follows with the more specific statement on non-mortal sin. He seems to invite his readers to confess such sins and to intercede for others who commit such sins.[341] The only real contribution of the present verse to what has already been stated or implied is the recognition that all unrighteous deeds, regardless of type, are sinful and to be condemned. Whether redemption should be sought for the sinning unbeliever is the subject of 5:16. The present

---

338. The syntax features the subjunctive verb "should see" that suggests a hypothetical possibility, and the present adjectival participle "committing [a sin]" portraying habitual, typical sinful conduct. The author does not specify how long one should observe such behavior. Being left unspecified, the author seems to leave the matter to the observer's discretion. Perhaps the author has in mind the believer's anointing (2:20, 27) and responsibility to test the spirits (4:1–3). Then the believer can assess the sin observed as leading to death or not.

339. Randall K. J. Tan suggests that a believer intercedes for sinners regardless of what kind of sin they are committing and leaves the matter to God to decide whether to grant life or not ("Should We Pray for Straying Brethren? John's Confidence in 1 John 5:16–17," *JETS* 45 [2002]: 607–608). The major premise threading through 5:14–17 is the believer's confidence in prayer before God. Then if the sin does not lead to death, God will answer by granting life to the sinner; but if not, then he will respond with the appropriate consequence.

340. Usually the conjunction "and" serves to link similar items together to form a list or to categorize items sharing a common trait. Here, however, the transition from a very general declaration to a more specific and limited statement suggests a slight disjuncture where the author focuses on a particular kind of sin.

341. Marshalls limits the confession and intercession to Christians only, that is, Christians interceding for fellow Christians (*Epistles*, 248–251). I, however, believe Christians ought to confess their sins (presuming Christians cannot commit mortal sins) and to intercede for unbelievers who do not commit mortal sins that God grant them life.

verse charges people to assume personal responsibility for their moral actions. Although the author does not explicitly identify who can commit mortal or non-mortal sin here, the general tenor of the letter points to non-Christians (especially the separatists) as the only ones who can commit mortal sin. However, both Christians and non-Christians can commit non-mortal sin.[342]

The addition of "and there is sin that does not result in death" that recalls 5:16 sounds a note of hope that tempers the first clause of 5:17. To acknowledge one's sin is an expression of remorse, not hopelessness. Apparently any sin not involving unbelief and rejection of Jesus' true identity and redemptive activity finds coverage here. This realization implies a broad spectrum of sins and so highlights the breadth and efficaciousness of God's salvific purpose in Jesus. Propitiation addresses all but one narrowly defined sin that appears comparable to the "unforgivable sin" of Matthew 12:31–32; Mark 3:29; Luke 12:10.

5:18–19 Kept from the evil one

In 5:18 the author repeats a refrain that believers do not practice sin as noted elsewhere. But he adds an important point that God keeps them safe[343] and the evil one cannot harm them. Beginning with "we know," the author aligns his readers with himself in their common knowledge. They recognize their common identity as children of God and a shared lifestyle. Children of God do not continue in sin, a picture of holiness but not perfection. God provides a gracious means to deal with occasional sin through confession and forgiveness (1:9).

Three types of people, then, come before the reader for consideration in 5:16–18. First, the children of God possess life (2:17b; 3:14; 5:11–13). Secondly, pre-believers have not committed a mortal sin and so disciples may pray for them (2:2; 5:15–16). Thirdly, some non-believers have committed a mortal sin and, consequently, cannot be forgiven.

Mindful of this categorization, the church may deliberate over strategy in ministering to each group. Certainly discipleship, training, equipping, and mentoring form the core approach to serving the children of God. Evangelism and missions address pre-believers. The third group is hardened and unrepentant, guilty of unbelief. However, no one can be absolutely certain whether a person belongs to that final category or not. Only God knows

---

342. Smalley specifically regards Christians as capable and, on occasion, guilty of non-mortal sin (*1, 2, 3 John*, 298).
343. The NIV adds "safe" as an interpretation. The following clause supports that rendering.

for certain. Then the church has no choice but to minister to this category as well. However, wisdom and discernment enable the church to prioritize its focus, giving preference to those more receptive.

The challenge of discerning is daunting in much of Asia as, for example, articulated by Leffel:[344]

> The vast majority of people in the world regard personal identity and culture to be fundamentally inseparable from religious tradition and belief. In *their* understanding, conversion to Christianity, *by definition*, implies abandoning one's native culture in exchange for another. Put simply, the dilemma is this: *how can a fellowship of biblical believers grow and witness for Jesus, yet remain authentic, active members of their overtly non-Christian culture?* The relative failure of Christian outreach to Hindus and Muslims illustrates this dilemma and reinforces contextualization as a strategic imperative.

In an Asian context, the question might not simply be "Have people committed a sin that results in death?" but "If the religious tradition of their culture has historically made it very difficult or nearly impossible to respond to the gospel, should we still intercede for them through both prayer and witness?"

The latter portion of 5:18 assures us that Christ[345] keeps us safe and the evil one cannot harm us. Functionally, this portion gives the reason for the preceding pronouncement that believers do not continue to sin.[346] The verb "keeps safe" recalls the same verb Jesus employed in his prayer (John

---

344. Leffel, "Contextualization: Building Bridges to the Muslim Community," 1. The italicized fonts are in the original.
345. Brooke wavers over the identity of the referent in "the one born of God"; a believer or Christ depending on whether the direct object of "keeps" is "him" (*auton*) or "himself" (*eauton*) (*Epistles*, 148–149). Christ is the referent if the pronoun is "him"; but the believer if the referent is "himself." The ancient Greek manuscripts favor "himself" over "him." But Bruce M. Metzger offers a counter (*A Textual Commentary on the Greek New Testament*, 2d ed. [Stuttgart: German Bible Society, 1994], 650). Also, the difference between the perfect substantive participle and the aorist substantive participle (both translated "the one born") may signify a different referent given the pattern of the perfect substantive participle alluding to believers in 1 John. Then I favor reading the referent as Christ.
346. There is a causal relationship between the two major portions of 5:18. A possible reading sees a potential erroneous understanding of believers not continuing in sin that seems to picture a virtuous lifestyle by personal effort alone. Then the following text explains that Christ keeps the believer on track. So the conjunction "but" introduces the corrective.

17:11–12).³⁴⁷ The basic thought is protection from the threat of the world or the evil one. The specific danger may well be the separatists. In spite of the grave threat, believers have overcome the evil one (2:13–14), the many false prophets in the world (4:4), and the world (5:4–5). Although the author identifies these three different threats, all coalesce into one danger.

5:19 offers both assurance to the readers that they are children of God and a sober assessment of the whole world that the evil one rules over it. This sharp contrast highlights two kingdoms, God's and that of the evil one. To lie in someone's domain implies submission to that someone, whether consciously or not.³⁴⁸ Two realms of rule and existence oppose each other. Disciples must always remember their association, under whose rule they live and serve.

This is the second verse in succession that the author starts with "we know" which he will repeat again at the beginning of the next verse (5:20). He affirms what his readers already know and reminds them in order to assure them of their identity in Christ while in the world.³⁴⁹ These two known truths (their identity and the world's plight) taken together highlight a tension. As children of God, the readers cannot suffer what the whole world³⁵⁰ suffers – enslavement to the evil one. Yet, they are in the world. The only possible explanation for their safety and freedom must be Christ's intervention.

5:20–21 Jesus Is God

1 John 5:20 states what the readers already know. First, the Son of God has come.³⁵¹ He is present in the world. Then the verse declares the purpose of his presence – that we may know the true one.

---

347. Jesus also utilized a second verb "guard" (*ephulaksa*) in addition to "keep" (*etāroun* ["I was keeping"] and *tārāson* ["keep" in the imperative]).
348. The preposition in the phrase "in the evil one" assumes a locative sense, denoting the sphere or domain of influence and power of the evil one.
349. John R. W. Stott identifies affirmation and assurance as a major objective of 5:6–21 (*The Letters of John: An Introduction and Commentary*, TNTC 19 [repr., Downers Grove, IL: InterVarsity Academic, 2009], 176–196).
350. Lieu regards "the whole world" as any and all opposition to God (2:15–17) (*I, II, & III John*, 231).
351. Although the verb is in the present tense, the thrust functions like a perfect tense (Smalley, *1, 2, 3 John*, 306). Smalley thinks the verb alludes to Jesus' incarnation and its continuing effects. Similarly, C. Haas, M. De Jonge, and J. L. Swellengrebel, *A Handbook on the Letters of John* (New York: United Bible Societies, 1972), 153. Recognizing the stative aspect of a perfect tense, the verb "come," although present tense, asserts a stative nuance, that is, the Son of God has not just come but is present in the world.

This knowledge, signifying the capacity to know,[352] is not merely cognitive but also relational in that the two parallel phrases – "in the true one" and "in his Son Jesus Christ" – juxtapositioned and in apposition, implies that Jesus Christ the Son is the true one.[353] So then the purpose of his coming is that believers may know him relationally. This relationship is only possible because the Father sent him into the world (4:9).

Then somewhat surprisingly the author declares that Jesus Christ is the true God and eternal life. Having such an explicit confession of Jesus as God[354] in the NT is rare. John's prologue proclaims Jesus' pre-existence (John 1:1–3). In defense of his working on the Sabbath, he affirms that his work reflects the Father working on the Sabbath, which the Jews rightly interpret as a claim to deity (John 5:17–18). Later, Jesus tells Philip, "The one who has seen me has seen the Father" (John 14:9d). And Thomas confesses, "My Lord and my God" (John 20:28).

Finally, 5:21 admonishes the readers to keep themselves from idols. At first reading, the mention of "idols" seems to be totally unrelated to the context.[355] But the term assumes a metaphorical orientation.[356] Then the concept of idolatry, according to 1 John, represents failure to pass the three fundamental tests in this letter – the doctrinal test (confessing Jesus' true identity),

---

352. Two terms can be translated "know." The first term, *ginosko*, appears 22 times to connote knowing someone relationally (2:3 [2x], 4–5, 13, 14 [2x], 29b; 3:1 [2x], 6, 16, 20, 24; 4:2, 6b, 7–8, 13, 16; 5:2, 20d). The second term, *oida*, designates 14 times the knowledge about something (2:11, 20–21 [2x]; 3:2, 5, 14–15; 5:13, 15 [2x], 18–19, 20a). But in 2:18 (*ginosko* refers to the "last hour"), 2:29a (*oida* shows familiarity with the Lord's righteousness), 3:19 (*ginosko* alludes to confirmation of one's identity), and 4:6d (*ginosko* relates to discerning between truth and deception). Hence, in ninety percent of the incidences of the two terms, the categorical distinction holds.
353. Yarbrough regards the adjective "true" as pointing to the divine essence/nature (*1–3 John*, 319 n. 10).
354. Marshall, *Epistles*, 254–255; Lewis, *John and the Johannine Letters*, 124; Thompson, *1–3 John*, 148. Thompson emphasizes the Son's revelatory role, "to know the Son is to know the Father."
355. Benjamin L. Merkle argues that the author did not append 5:21 as a random afterthought but flowed from the letter's overall themes and structure centered on the three tests of righteousness, love, and right belief ("What Is the Meaning of 'Idols' in 1 John 5:21?" *BSac* 169 [2012]: 329–331). In summarizing the argument of his dissertation, Terry Griffith advocates that 5:21 functions to define the limits of the believing community ("'Little Children, Keep Yourselves from Idols': (1 John 5:21)," *TynBul* 48 [1997]: 188).
356. Merkle argues for the metaphorical use of "idols" and correlates the term to the three major tests in the letter where idolatry would be seen in a person worshipping a false Jesus that permitted loose morals, exempted one from loving others, and rejected Jesus' true Messianic identity ("Meaning of 'Idols'," 335–340). Contra Julian Hills who argues for a literal interpretation ("'Little Children, Keep Yourselves from Idols': 1 John 5:21 Reconsidered," *CBQ* 51 [1989]: 285–310).

the moral test (living a life marked by righteousness), and the social test (loving one another).³⁵⁷ All three tests emerge as commands that call for acknowledging God's authority.

At the very core of idolatry lies the heart's rejection of God and his authority in favor of an alternative. This concept pervades 1 John. The admonition not to love the world and the things in it (2:15–16) calls on disciples not to desire an alternative to God. To do so denies their identity in Christ. That is why the author repeats the truth that his readers are the children of God (in this chapter alone: 5:1–2, 4, 18–19). That is also why combating the spirit of the antichrist must be waged with all diligence (2:18–27; 4:1–6) boosted by the undeniable witness to Christ (5:6–15). Idolatry labels God a liar because it leads to an idolatrous lifestyle that denies his truth and witness (1:10; 5:10) and effectively makes the idolater a liar (2:4, 22; 4:20). Idolatry fails to love God. In this letter, love for God must be seen in love for others (4:20–21; 5:1–2) and represents obedience to his commands (2:5; 3:23; 4:21; 5:2). And obedience manifests itself through righteousness (3:10). Finally, idolatry prevents any relationship with God (2:5; 4:7–8, 12, 16) and showcases enslavement to the evil one (5:19b).

This verse (5:21) must be seen as a warning.³⁵⁸ In view of the immediate context of 5:19–20 and the two realms depicted, people's location depends on whether they succumb to idolatry or remain faithful to Christ. Then idolatry means being associated with the world.³⁵⁹

In Asia, filial piety is an integral aspect of culture and in the three major "religions" of China.³⁶⁰ If conflict arises between our responsibility to parents and devotion to Christ, what should we do? If we choose to honor our parents over Christ, does this act constitute idolatry? But if we sacrifice them for

---

357. Merkle, "Meaning of 'Idols'," 338–340.
358. Lieu, *I, II, & III John*, 237.
359. Ibid. Bruce takes them to be "false conceptions of God" (*Epistles*, 128).
360. Robert J. Reese, "Filial Piety in Chinese Religion." Online: http://www.casawomo.com/essays/filial-piety-in-chinese-religion (accessed October 18, 2014). I have put "religions" between quotation marks because not everyone agrees that Confucianism, Buddhism, and Taoism are religions. According to Judith A. Berling, Confucianism is a "social and ethical philosophy" ("Confucianism," *Focus on Asian Studies,* Vol 2, No 1: *Asian Religions* (1982): 5–7. Online: at http://www2.kenyon.edu/Depts/Religion/Fac/Adler/Reln270/Berling-Confucianism.htm (accessed October 18, 2014). See also Michael McGhee, "Is Buddhism a Religion?" *The Guardian*. Online http://www.theguardian.com/commentisfree/belief/2013/oct/07/is-buddhism-a-religion (accessed October 18, 2014). And refer to http://blog.eteacherchinese.com/china-culture/taoism-a-philosophy-or-a-religion/ and Michael H. Jenkins, "Religious Taoism vs. Philosophical Taoism" at http://people.opposingviews.com /religious-taoism-vs-philosophical-taoism-6900.html (both accessed October 18, 2014).

Christ, being mindful of his admonition (Matt 10:37; Mark 10:29–30; Luke 14:26), we invite guilt feelings that can hinder joy in serving him and worry that we placed a "stumbling block" for our parents coming to Christ. We need to act wisely in how we follow Christ and also honor our parents. For a helpful exposé of Christians' duty to parents without compromising on their faith, see Tan Eng Boo's article.[361]

Religious pluralism in Asia spawns three realities that confront the Asian church.[362] First, Christians form a minority where the majority practices other religions. Secondly, Christians suffer periodic oppression and persecution. And thirdly, mission is bold-yet-humble witness by an often oppressed and yet confident minority.[363] Asian Christians maintain their identity "through clear identification of the community with Jesus Christ . . . Sacramental, liturgical and ethical life is ordered around the life, death and resurrection of Jesus Christ . . . without this center the community takes on a new identity; a Christ-influenced identity, but not a Christian identity."[364] A "Christ-influenced identity" represents another religion or idolatry.

---

361. Tan Eng Boo, "Filial Piety and Burial Customs," *The Burning Bush* 9 (2003). Online: http://www.febc.edu.sg/bbvol9_2d.htm (accessed October 18, 2014).
362. For the following discussion, see Scott W. Sunquist, "Asian Perspectives on Theological Pluralism," *Theology Matters* 5 (1999): 1–7. Online: http://www.theologymatters.com/SepOct991.PDF (accessed June 20, 2015).
363. Ibid., 4.
364. Ibid. In a Hindu environment, if Jesus is reinterpreted mythologically or metaphorically, he can be viewed as an avatar, just one of many incarnations of God but not unique. Without the biblical truth-claim about Jesus as the Christ, the Christian community becomes another Hindu sect.

CHRISTIAN *FURZ* – OUR RELIGIOUS DUTY

The profile of the child of God portrayed by 1 John is analogous to *furz*, a religious must. In an Islamic context, *furz* represents religious duty which Muslims must perform. If they fail, they must find a substitute: if, for example, they miss a fast in the month of Ramadan they can feed a specific number of poor people or keep a certain number of fasts afterwards. A number of duties in Islam – profession of faith, prayer, and almsgiving – comes under *furz*.

Living in the light by reflecting God's truth and moral purity and abstaining from sin (1:5, 7; 2:29; 3:3, 6–7), obeying the Lord's commands, loving fellow disciples in tangible and meaningful ways, and overcoming the evil one (2:13–14) and the world by faith (5:4–5) constitute Christian *furz*.

For the church to reinforce this *furz*, it must redefine the powerful honor-shame dichotomy pervasive in Asia from a biblical perspective. First, it ought to ascribe honor to members who fulfill Christian *furz*. They walk in the truth, obey the Lord's commands and sanctify themselves in hope. Obedience is perceptible in acts of love. By honoring such members, the church encourages them to continue and others to do likewise.

Shame, however, assumes different nuances in the NT. One kind of shame Paul mentions takes on a judgmental slant where God shames the wise and strong of the world (1 Cor 1:27). A second kind means embarrassment or humiliation which Paul carefully avoids inflicting on his readers (1 Cor 4:14 in the context of 1 Cor 3:18–4:21). Later, he rebukes them for abusing the communion where the well-to-do turn the sacrament into a self-indulging feast and thereby humiliate the poor who come with nothing (1 Cor 11:21–22). Yet a third kind of shame is what Paul utilizes toward his readers to convict and invoke repentance (1 Cor 6:5; 15:34).[1]

Following Paul's lead, the church strives to avoid humiliating any member. Instead it "shames" in order to convict members to repent if they prove delinquent in Christian *furz*. Like Paul, the church instructs, exhorts, and reproves.

Filial piety is a fundamental Asian trait. The church can be Asian and Christian by redefining this trait along biblical lines. Respect for the older generation of disciples creates the opportunity for them to instruct and guide the younger generation and to model Christian *furz*.

At the same time, the church provides its members with a collective identity. Believers find their sense of self-worth in belonging to fellowship with the Father and the Son and with one another. The challenge comes, however, when the values, convictions, and priorities of the church clash with those

---

1. Paul uses two different words translated "shame." One word applies to the first two nuances that refer to humiliation with no thought to correct. Another word is used for the third nuance with the objective to correct.

of other groups to which members may belong, whether family, clan/tribe, or other.

Faced with "the intricate mosaic of its [Asia's] many cultures, languages, beliefs and traditions," the Asian church must develop an effective approach to engage society, characterized by filial piety and a strong sense of community.[2] A church member may be torn in allegiance and responsibility between the church and outside affiliations. It is at this critical juncture that the church must strike the balance between uncompromising faithfulness to its Lord as defined by 1 John and becoming a compelling presence in Asia. Can the church engage in meaningful dialogue with its Asian world characterized by urbanization; migration due to poverty, war, or ethnic conflict; industrialization; dehumanizing poverty and exploitation particularly of the young; and the marginalization of women?

The church faces two missions. First, it makes a difference in material and tangible ways both within its fellowship and outside in a hurting Asian world. To accomplish this objective its members must live a life of purity and compassion to help meet needs within the church and without in society. Secondly, it must tackle the hard questions of life. And those questions can be distilled into one theological focus, theodicy – the apologetics of upholding a holy, just, and good God in spite of the overwhelming presence of evil in the form of injustice and corruption, suffering and death, natural catastrophes, and conflicts.

The church points to Christ as the solution but the solution is eschatological, only when he returns. Its role is to humanize sufferers by treating them with dignity as people bearing the image of God. The church lifts up people by proclaiming that God loves them and wants to enter into an eternal relationship with them.

---

2. *The Church in Asia in the 3rd Millennium*, 10.

2 JOHN

Recently I came across an interesting and insightful online exposé of common mistakes people make when drafting a follow-up email.[1] One of the recommendations the writer offered to help improve follow-up emails is to determine the objective for such an email. He recognized four objectives: need for information; requesting a meeting; catching up with each other; and acknowledging something significant in the other person's or one's own life. When we examine 2 John, we get the impression that it reads like a follow up to 1 John. We discover that the elder's (the self-identified author) objectives align with two of the suggested objectives: request for a meeting (1:12) and acknowledging how well some of the readers are walking in the truth (1:4). However, the elder includes an additional objective – warning about false teachers who may come (1:10–11).

Both 1 and 2 John share the common themes of living in the truth, loving one another, and those who have gone into the world (the antichrists and false prophets in 1 John and the deceivers in 2 John). A crucial difference in the nature of each letter helps us better understand the possible relationship between them. Without a greeting or personal ending, 1 John appears more formal and impersonal, suggesting a more general readership. But 2 John addresses a specific group of readers from one church. Thus 2 John represents a specific application of the general tenets espoused by 1 John.

1:1–3 Family Greeting

The author begins with a self-designation, "the elder" (1:1a), without further description. This brief identification presumes familiarity. His readers know him well. The title invokes a sense of authority.[2] He seems to make a distinction between the lady and her children as two separate entities among the addressees of his letter.[3]

---

1. "The Ultimate Guide on How to Write a Follow Up Email." Online: http://www.hubspot.com/sales/follow-up-email.
2. Taking "lady" (1:1) as a metaphor for a church with ties to another church ("sister" in 1:13), "elder" signifies a spiritual authority responsible for the welfare of several churches, but nothing like a modern bishop. At most, "elder" designated a man whose spiritual stature was readily but informally acknowledged. See Judith Lieu, *The Second and Third Epistles of John: History and Background* (Edinburgh: T. & T. Clark, 1986), 52–64.
3. The construction "to the elect lady and to her children" appears to make two distinct references. For the two to allude to the same thing, the definite article associated with "children"

However, Paul identified his readers with the singular "church of God in Corinth" (1 Cor 1:2a) followed by the plural "those sanctified in Christ Jesus . . . the elect saints" (1 Cor 1:2b). The context supports taking the singular and plural forms as pointing to the same addressees. "Church" is a collective term for "those sanctified" and "elect saints." But in 2 John 1:1c, "and" separates "elect lady" and "her children" as two seemingly distinct references with the latter designating members of the church. However, if we understand "and" in an explanatory role, rendering the expression as "to the elect lady namely her children," then we have but one addressee.[4] Hence, "elect lady" alludes to the church collectively and "her children," in a distributed sense, of all the members seen as a whole.

The expression "her children" portrays a family. The regard the elder harbors toward them, "whom I love in truth" (1:1c), recalls close ties. The qualifier "in truth," as one commentator notes, refers to a love that evidences "integrity and sincerity."[5] The elder professes genuine affection and care for his readers that typify love within a family.

The family ties implied in 2 John reflect that of an Asian family. No matter how old the children may be, they are still children in the eyes of the parents, objects of care and concern. And regardless of age and marital status, they tend to be open to their parents' concerns and wishes, accommodating them when possible.

As the elder continues his greeting, he characterizes the love he has toward his readers, the family of the elect lady, as grounded in truth. Yet not only he, but "all who know the truth" (1:1f). The term "know" appears in a form that conveys a condition or characteristic.[6] All who subscribe to the truth and conform to it in their lives love those with similar traits. Exactly what this truth entails cannot be defined more precisely simply because the

---

ought to have gone with "lady" instead (BDF §276). Moreover, the presence of the possessive pronoun "her" makes the idea of a single referent difficult. If "her children" is the congregation, then "lady" seems to connote something else.

4. Generally commentators identity one addressee. Bultmann posits a "catholic" letter that circulated among churches such that while the letter remained in a given church it addressed that church (*Epistles*, 108).

5. Schnackenburg, *Epistles*, 279.

6. In the perfect tense, the substantive participle signifies a condition, state of being, or characteristic. All who know the truth, not only in a cognitive sense but also in an experiential sense as practitioners of the truth, love as the elder loves. And the object of their love is one another, everyone who is part of the family of God.

letter offers no substantial explanation.[7] However, "the truth that abides in us" (1:2a, ESV) recalls 1 John 1:8 and 2:4 where abiding truth correlates with acknowledging one's sin in the first incidence and keeping Jesus' commands in the second. Then this truth is not an inept system of doctrine encoded in a dry theological tome. But it represents a living and dynamic principle operative in a person.[8] It is a shared repository for both the elder and his readers that identify them as family such that those who do not possess this truth[9] are not members of the family. Lacking this truth implies lacking the ability to love as family because no truth abides within.

The elder promises that abiding truth will be with them forever (1:2) which implies that they have eternal life. The dynamic principle that fuels the eternal capacity of this family lies in abiding truth.

In 1:3, the elder draws his greeting to a close with a blessing of grace, mercy, and peace.[10] He identifies the source of blessing as God the Father and Jesus Christ his Son. The unusual "Jesus Christ, the Father's Son" (1:3c) highlights the family motif with the spotlight on the relationship between the Father and the Son. God is not only our heavenly Father; he is also Jesus' Father, thereby making the first two Persons of the Trinity family with us. As love and truth mark the horizontal relationship between the elder and his readers, and they among themselves, so too love and truth must describe the internal relationship between the Father and Son. What is true in heaven is also true on earth – family is central.

The greeting closes with "in truth and love."[11] The elder offers assurance that as truth and love characterize family relationships, each member will enjoy the blessings of grace, mercy, and peace. As abiding truth will be theirs forever, so too will be this triple blessing.

---

7. Judith M. Lieu suggests "principles of Johannine community" (*The Theology of the Johannine Epistles* [Cambridge: Cambridge University Press, 1991], 96). More helpful is Schnackenburg who finds "the truth that abides in us" (v. 2) reminiscent of 1 John 1:8; 2:4 (*Epistles*, 280).
8. Grayston highlights this truth as "less to do with orthodoxy than with orthopraxy" (*Epistles*, 151).
9. Yarbrough documents five nuances for truth: (1) what the Spirit imparts; (2) ethical standards to which believers should conform; (3) God's sanctifying presence that enables believers to manifest his traits; (4) what relates to God's omniscient wisdom; and (5) the gospel of Jesus Christ (*1–3 John*, 335–336).
10. Haas, de Jonge, and Swellengrebel define "mercy" as the compassion and pity of God's benevolence toward his people, "grace" as his initiative, and "peace" as the harmony between God and his people and among them (*Letters*, 161).
11. Brown surveys the different ways this expression has been interpreted (*Epistles*, 659–660). He prefers the simplest solution of taking truth and love as traits of the relationship between the elder and his readers.

This greeting prompts us to evaluate the adequacy with which we greet and communicate with one another in the church. Although meeting felt needs in tangible and practical ways manifests true love (1 John 3:16–18), sincere words of love spoken in a timely fashion can be equally effective. How often do we hear words of affirmation and affection in comparison to words that criticize, gossip, and disapprove? Encouragement can be powerful. If we give more forethought to our greetings, although brief, our relationships may grow more intimate and genuine, and the church warmer.

1:4–6 Walk the Talk[12]

The familiar metaphor of "walking" as a description of one's manner of life and conduct frequently appears in the NT. Hence, a journey or movement suggests something of the dynamic in one's life customs and habits, decisions and choices, and values and priorities. We move as we make choices, practice habits, and affirm values. As conscientious disciples, we want to live intentionally. So we want to "walk" purposefully in alignment with scriptural directives.

The elder expresses great joy over what he learns about some of his readers (1:4). They are walking in truth according to the Father's command. But we wonder whether the description implies a divided church, where only a portion of the members walk in the truth.[13] Ideally, all walk in the truth. But if this is not the case, we immediately suspect the possibility of some disunity. Yet, we also realize that no church, in reality, consists of all members living in an exemplary fashion. Even the "best" churches have some who drag their feet spiritually and make excuses about not becoming a purposeful disciple. There may even be a spectrum from the most fervent to the least with degrees of fervency in between.

However, in certain regions of Asia, simply attending church services may require courage and willingness to pay the ultimate price for being

---

12. Typically commentators view 1:4–11 as the body of the letter. However, to better highlight the theme of "walking," I treat 1:4–6 as a section while recognizing its link with 1:7–11. Schnackenburg, however, isolates 1:4–6 for discussion under the rubric "Test of Genuine Christian Life Is Fidelity to God's Commandments" (*Epistles*, 281–283). Westcott, on the other hand, groups 1:4–7 for his comments (*Epistles*, 226–229).

13. So Kysar, *I, II, III John*, 126. However, Brown hesitates to interpret "some of your children" to mean some but not all are walking in the truth (*Epistles*, 661). Theologically, he points out, those not walking in the truth would not have the truth abiding in them. Then, he asks, can they be considered "children"?

Christian.[14] The mandate for believers to be "walking in the truth" must be contextualized in order to instruct and challenge believers to appropriate expressions of faith.

Significantly, the writer of this letter rejoices greatly even if only some walk in the truth. Seemingly, he views the church like a partially filled glass, choosing to focus on it being half full than half empty. Those actively engaged in serving and bearing witness for the Lord can be regarded as the base on which to build and expand, hoping to encourage those inactive to become active by following the example of others. The writer's joy reveals hope that the church will continue to grow.

Three times in 1:4, 6, some form of the verb "to walk" appears.[15] The elder rejoices when he discovers that some members in the church family are walking in the truth (1:4b). Given the qualifying traits of truth and love that demarcates a member of God's family, anyone not possessing these cannot be part of the family.[16] Then we wonder whether the church addressed consists of a mixed group. In view of 1 John 2:19, the possibility must be acknowledged. However, another possibility may provide a scenario less problematic – the elder does not know everyone in the church but the ones he does know walk in the truth.[17] Nothing in the letter suggests that he was ever a member of the church. More likely, then, he is an outsider, although well known to his readers. He knows some of them well enough to commend their walk.

Then 1:4 concludes with the fact that they all received a command from the Father. Employing the first person plural "we," the elder includes himself along with his readers as the recipients of the divine command. Although he exercises authority over them, he submits himself under the authority of the Father to whom all must submit. All are accountable to him.

He then makes a request about a command they have had from the beginning, that they should love one another (1:5). The command not being new echoes 1 John 3:11 and 3:23. This repetition serves to tie the two

---

14. "Deadly Blasts Hit Pakistan Churches in Lahore" reports on two bomb blasts that killed at least 14 people and wounded many others near two churches in the Pakistani city of Lahore. Online: http://www.bbc.com/news/world-asia-31894708 (accessed July 15, 2015).
15. In 1:4, it occurs as an adjectival participle. Then it appears as a subjunctive verb twice in 1:6. Being in the present tense, all three verbal forms depict customary, ongoing conduct that defines the appropriate lifestyle. In the subjunctive, the two verbs convey projection and, in the context of a command (1:6), the verbs describe the divine expectation imposed on believers.
16. The prepositional phrase "in the truth" marks the sphere or realm within which believers should live out their faith. This expression recalls 1 John 1:6–2:6.
17. See Schnackenburg, *Epistles*, 281–282.

epistles together through a common theme. The elder urges his readers to love one another.

Strikingly, he softens the command to a request. As he notes in the previous verse, however, they have received the command from the Father.

In an Asian family, the authority figure, often the father, exercises unquestioned leadership to which all family members submit even if he should prove gentle. Within the family there exist the prominent elements of interdependence and, depending on the particular culture, filial piety.[18] What sociologists term interdependence our biblical author formulates as a command to love one another. Filial piety would be reinterpreted in 2 John as deference to the elder who urges the church to obey the command.

Whereas Asian fathers, at least among Chinese families, tend to take a more authoritarian role as disciplinarian characterized by emotional distance,[19] the elder freely expresses his affection for his "children" (1:1) and shows his unbridled joy at some who conform to the truth (1:4). Yet, he readily invokes the Father's authority to urge his readers to obey the Father's command rather than insisting on his own authority.

In explicating that the command is not new, the elder recalls the original giving of the command by Jesus (John 13:34) and its reiteration (1 John 3:11, 23; 4:7). Thus, he effectively ties the Gospel with 1 and 2 John by this theme. The continuity forms a bridge connecting the original generation of disciples who saw Jesus in the flesh and later generations including those to whom the epistles are addressed. If we should identify the elder as possibly the author of 1 John, then he represents an earlier generation who disciples the later generation in part through his writings.

A shift occurs between 1:4 and 1:5. Earlier (1:4), the elder expresses satisfaction with the elect lady's children in their walk. Yet, now (1:5) he makes

---

18. Ruth Chao and Vivian Tseng, "Parenting of Asians," in *Handbook of Parenting: Vol. 4 Social Conditions and Applied Parenting*, ed. M. H. Bornstein (Mahwah, NJ: Lawrence Erlbaum Associates, 2002), 59–93. In spite of the cultural diversity throughout Asia, the family has the prominent role of being "the prototype of all relationships" (64). D. Y. F. Ho, "Filial Piety and Its Psychological Consequences," in *The Handbook of Chinese Psychology*, ed. M. H. Bond (Hong Kong: Oxford University Press, 1996), 155–165; and U. Kim and S. Choi, "Individualism, Collectivism, and Child Development: A Korean Perspective," in *Cross-Cultural Roots of Minority Child Development*, eds. P. M. Greenfield and R. R. Cocking (Hillsdale, NJ: Lawrence Erlbaum Associates, 1994), 1–37. In the July 5, 2015 *Jubilee Day of Prayer* attended by 51,000 Christians to commemorate Singapore's 50th anniversary, organizers upheld filial piety as a virtue.
19. Chao and Tseng, "Parenting of Asians," 68.

a request, implying that something more needs attention.[20] He may be preparing them to face the potential threat of deceivers teaching false doctrine (1:7, 10–11).

Then in 1:6, the elder indicates what love entails – walking in accord with God's commands, particularly what the readers heard from the beginning. Love is an act of the will; it shows intention and submission. The critical phrase "from the beginning" in 1:6 recalls the very same phrase in 1:5 that speaks of the command to love one another. Then 1:6 likewise addresses the same love command.

But 1:6 speaks first of walking according to the commands (plural) and then of walking according to the command (singular). How do we explain and reconcile the difference in number?

Paul may provide the key to unlocking this puzzle. With regard to the Spirit-controlled life, he writes of fulfilling the whole law by loving our neighbor as ourselves. Obviously, many requirements make up the whole law. Instead of addressing each one individually, a person could fulfill the entire corpus by excelling in love.[21]

The parallelism in 1:6 facilitates repetition. Then "walk according to his commands" reappears as "walk in it." Thus, the singular form represents a collective reference to the many commands. Obedience to all of God's commands ought to be fulfilled in loving one another.

Summarizing 1:4–6, members of God's family delight the Father above and the elder below by living a life characterized by truth and love, not one or the other but both together. Two abiding principles operate in each member. First, walking in the truth (1:4) echoes 1 John 1:5–7 that portrays the believer walking in the light that is God himself, whereby God and believer enjoy intimate fellowship. This is possible because the believer's sins are cleansed by Christ's blood. Secondly, walking in love fulfills all of God's requirements by loving fellow family members. Hence, when truth and love abide in the family, they enjoy fellowship with God and with each other.

I see something of this relational dynamic in the family of one of my Filipino students. Before enrolling in seminary, she was employed making good money and was able to help her younger sister get through college. But as a student now she depends on her younger brother for occasional material

---

20. Brown marks the shift by translating the introductory conjunction as "but" in lieu of the usual "and" for 1:5 (*Epistles*, 663). He sees the shift as anticipation of false teachers. Then affirming the readers' walk in the truth serves to prepare for the threat.
21. Marshall makes a similar point (*Epistles*, 67–68).

support. The siblings enjoy close bonds with each other and with their parents. Such two-directional relationships mirror what 2 John 1:4–6 implores of God's family the church.

1:7–11 Remaining in the Truth about Christ

Recalling the warning of 1 John about the many false prophets who have gone out into the world prompted by the spirit of the antichrist (4:1–3), we find something quite similar in 2 John 1:7 about the many deceivers who have gone out into the world, denying Jesus' incarnation. Deception presumes a targeted potential victim. This verse warns of an external threat to the church family's well-being. Unless the family exercises truth and love they can be victimized. 1:7 provides the reason for the exhortation in 1:4–6.[22] Many deceivers have gone out into the world and presumably are looking for someone to subvert.[23] Hence, the character traits of truth and love not only define family, they serve as boundary markers to identify who is not family in lacking these traits and thereby potentially posing a threat.

The "many" deceivers depict a prevalent danger. Sooner or later some of them will invade and attack the church. It seems inevitable. The best strategy, then, is being preemptive by reinforcing the church's defenses before they come.

The particular deception is the denial that Jesus Christ came in the flesh, that is, a refusal to acknowledge his incarnation, a timeless or "abiding truth."[24] The reference is not limited to Jesus' time on earth, but points to the enduring union of God and humanity, not only in Jesus but, through Jesus, God and humanity can have fellowship of the most intimate kind. Apart from this christological truth, believers cannot walk in the truth nor love one another. And without this truth, they cannot discern truth from falsehood and so cannot resist the onslaught of false teachers.

---

22. The conjunction "because," that begins 1:7, links it with 1:6. Smalley notes that the threat discussed in 1:7–11 provides the rationale for the author urging his readers to manifest truth and love in 1:4–6 (*1, 2, 3 John*, 327).

23. "Into the world" may indicate that deceivers intentionally target believers. So Kysar, *I, II, III John*, 129. Anderson views them as false teachers who left the church (*1, 2, & 3 John*, 209). I find support for Anderson's contention in "they went out into the world" (1:7) and "they had went out into the world" (1 John 4:1) with a link to 1 John 2:19 through the common verb "went out." The verb in 1 John 2:19 and 2 John 1:7 appears in the perfect tense in 1 John 4:1 emphasizing the state of false prophets being in the world. Hence, the separatists (1 John 2:19), false prophets (1 John 4:1), and deceivers (2 John 1:7) all refer to the same group.

24. Glenn W. Barker, "2 John," in *The Expositor's Bible Commentary with the New International Version: Hebrews through Revelation*, 12 vols. (Grand Rapids, MI: Zondervan, 1981), 12:364. Also Bultmann, *Epistles*, 112, and Smalley, *1, 2, 3 John*, 329–330.

2 JOHN

In contrast to the many deceivers in the world, the singular "this is the deceiver and the antichrist" in referring back to the many suggests a collective sense rather than the prophetic and singular figure who embodies opposition to God and truth, the Antichrist with a capital "A."[25] In a collective sense, we can talk about the spirit of the deceiver and the antichrist that moves through the many who have gone out to ply falsehood. We see something similar in the episode involving false prophets energized by a deceiving spirit misleading Ahab into battle to meet his death (1 Kgs 22:19–23; 2 Chr 18:18–22).

Then the elder warns of the dire consequences of being deceived – losing[26] what he worked for. Instead, a full reward awaits those who resist. However, the elder does not explain what the reward entails.[27] But believers will receive it in the eschaton.

Rather than reading a works-righteousness idea into this verse, we remember how Jesus once responded to the query about what one must do to accomplish God's works by saying one must believe in the one whom God sent (John 6:28–29). The work of God centers on belief in the incarnation of Jesus as the union of God and humanity, a truth that believers must retain in order to claim their full reward someday. They must be ever vigilant in maintaining the twin traits of truth and love in order to finish well.

A pervasive heresy marked the analogy between the state church of Nazi Germany and present-day China. One scholar calls it the patriotic heresy where the state exerts influence on religion.[28] He writes:

> The problem with liberal theology is primarily its deconstruction of the authority of Scripture and of the reality of supernatural forces, as well as its exaggeration of the independence of human reason from God. Exploiting these weaknesses, worldly thinking entered the church and placed the idols of nation, race and human leaders on the altar of patriotism. Barth and Bonhoeffer

---

25. Brown, *Epistles*, 670. We find a parallel in 1 John 4:1–4 with the many false prophets and the spirit of the antichrist.
26. According to Johnson, this verb could be taken as "lose" or "destroy," the latter depicting a more active or aggressive role (*1, 2, and 3 John*, 157).
27. Bultmann takes it to be eternal life based on 1 John 2:25 (*Epistles*, 113). Either it is that or the reward for faithfulness (Anderson, *1, 2, & 3 John*, 211–212). The first option implies that believers may lose eternal life, something that Scripture does not support. Then the second alternative is preferable.
28. Mark C. Shan, "Beware of Patriotic Heresy in the Church in China," for the Chinese Christian Theological Association. Online: http://www.ccta.me/2014/06/mark-shan-beware-of-patriotic-heresy-in.html (accessed November 1, 2014).

both recognized the threat of liberalism and stood in opposition as its currents swept across Europe, preaching the return to and development of a theology centered on the Word of God.[29]

In the late 1990s, the Chinese government enforced the creed "love the country and love the church," in that order of priority through the Three-Self Patriotic Movement, a key aspect of Beijing Theology.[30] Because this was seemingly unrelated to clear biblical teaching, many Christians were not alarmed. Further, the civil authorities through their religious mouthpiece espoused a materialistic worldview denying, at the same time, the Bible's authority and belief in the supernatural. They advocated replacing "justification by faith" with "justification by love."[31] According to this tenet, a person is heaven-bound by acts of love regardless of having faith in Christ or not.

It requires discernment and courage to make a stand for the truth sometimes at great personal cost. Armed with the truth, a disciple can be alert to deviations often subtle yet dangerous. But taking an uncompromising stand may demand a willingness to face the consequences as occurred in Germany and China.

However, compromise results in spiritual loss. Those who do not retain the teaching of Christ[32] do not have God; but if they do, they have both the Father and the Son (1:9). The term "teaching" signifies orthodoxy. Hence, to go beyond orthodoxy enters the realm of heterodoxy. The teaching centers on Jesus' true identity. Confessing this identity results in having God, equivalent to having eternal life (1 John 5:12). Either people remain in the teaching of Christ or they do not. The form of the verbal idea "remain" depicts characterization.[33] Either people characteristically remain or conform to the teaching of Christ or they do not as a rule.

---

29. Ibid. However, not all Chinese Christians will agree with Shan's assessment that the "Three-Self Church and the House Church and their relationship are similar to that of Germany's Reich Church and Confessing Church," respectively. That conclusion is reductionistic. Evangelicals and heretics operate in both churches, so it is not an either-or situation.
30. Ibid.
31. Ibid.
32. The expression "teaching of Christ" can refer to teaching from Christ (subjective genitive) or teaching about Christ (objective genitive). Given the context of "confessing Jesus Christ coming in the flesh" earlier in v. 7, the second option seems preferable.
33. The verbal form is a substantive participle in the present tense. As such, it describes the normative character of people. The negation of the verbal form portrays them as not characteristically having that character, as a general rule. Positively, they remain faithful to the teaching.

2 John

The expression "teaching of Christ" may refer to Christ's teaching, he being the source, or to the teaching about Christ.[34] Certainly the point of contention with the false teachers concerns "Jesus Christ coming in the flesh" (1:7), teaching about Christ. Yet, at the same time, the spirit of "the deceiver and the antichrist" represents the source of false teaching which the author counters with the source of right teaching, Jesus himself. Thus, both the fact that Jesus is the source of truth and that that truth centers on him as the union of the divine and human determine who has God, and hence who belongs in the family of God. The fullest expression of that union is the family featuring God the Father, Jesus as the Christ, and all who walk in truth and obediently love those in the family.

The elder now turns from a general warning about deceivers in the world (1:7–9) to give a specific prohibition – do not receive them into your home or greet them because to do so makes you a partner in their evil works (1:10–11). The warning heightens if the visitation is imminent, any time.

Why would the elder bother to prohibit greeting them unless there is the possibility of it occurring? Normally people would be cautious toward strangers. But if the visitors are old acquaintances, being former members of the church, old ties may lull the readers to drop their guard.[35] Being forewarned, they must not let old friendships blind them to the threat.

These prohibitions may seem harsh and hardline. If these false teachers were once family members now gone astray, would not love compel one to reach out to them in order to win them back to the fold? However, a balance between love and truth must be maintained so that the purity of the family remains intact.[36] Defilement of the church family takes precedence, especially in view of the aggressiveness of these false teachers. Unrepentant, their boldness and shameless behavior and practice leave no other recourse but to resist them with uncompromising fervor.

---

34. Brown favors Jesus as the source based on John 16:14–15 (*Epistles*, 674–675). Haas, de Jonge, and Swellengrebel concur, but based on John 7:16–17 (*Letters*, 169). Contra, for example, Rensberger, *1 John, 2 John, 3 John*, 1997), 154; Kysar, *I, II, II John*, 130; and Bultmann, *Epistles*, 113.
35. Kysar regards these false teachers as separatists who were once part of the church but broke away (*I, II, III John*, 129–132). In the present tense, the two verbs "come" and "bring" convey complementary activities of coming and teaching. The second verb expresses the purpose of the first. They take a proactive role as teachers. See Anderson, *1, 2, & 3 John*, 213.
36. Thompson, *1–3 John*, 155–156.

1:12–13 Closing Remarks

Though brief, the letter still ends rather abruptly. Having received a serious warning about false teachers, the recipients may have follow-up questions for greater clarification and perhaps to discuss different scenarios. But the writer prefers not to elaborate. He hopes instead to make a personal visit at which point he can go into greater depth and entertain queries. In fact, he has many things to communicate but does not want to do so with papyrus and ink. He hopes[37] to come and have a direct conversation with them.

One commentator suggests the possibility of deferring unpleasant matters until a personal visit when the elder can work out relational issues with select members of the church.[38]

He expresses hope "that our joy may be fulfilled." This hope recalls his earlier declaration of great joy over some of the readers walking in the truth (1:4).[39] His and their joy, however, would become complete if they resist the false teachers.[40]

We have done something similar in our dealings with one another. We email highlights and arrangements for a personal meeting in order to flesh out the details. In such an encounter, interaction becomes more readily facilitated with questions and answers, points of contention or unclarity discussed, and the assessment of each other through our body language. These exchanges require a coming together to minimize misunderstanding and enhance the chances of our agenda being accomplished. Within the church, personal fellowship proves indispensable and effective.

The letter closes with a conveyed greeting from the sister church (1:13). Presumably, the elder writes from there. And since he represents them as well, the plural "our" joy of 1:12 would include members of the sister church, the elder, and the readers. The concept of family encompasses the individual congregation and even extends to multiple congregations.

---

37. Surprisingly, the author seems tentative in hoping to visit rather than to make definite plans to come. He does not explain unlike Paul in Romans 1:13.
38. Schnackenburg, *Epistles*, 288. Although Anderson concurs, he also allows for the possibility of more pleasant matters as well (*1, 2, & 3 John*, 216).
39. So Brown, *Epistles*, 695. Contra Bultmann referencing 1 John 1:4 (*Epistles*, 115).
40. In spite of the plural "our" joy, Schnackenburg thinks the elder refers only to himself (*Epistles*, 288–289). The singular may be viable provided 1:4 and 1:12 form an *inclusio*, "great joy" and "joy may be fulfilled," respectively. Haas, de Jonge, and Swellengrebel allow for the possibility of a singular reference but regard the plural as the more natural reading in view of the desired personal meeting with the readers (*Letters*, 172).

2 John

Historically, the elder embodied the bridge and bond between churches. Today perhaps the regional fellowship of pastors and church leaders from different churches serves a similar purpose. Nothing in 2 John suggests that any formal connection between the two churches existed. They knew of each other and extended greetings at least through the elder. Being an occasional document written in response to a given situation, this letter does not necessarily represent regular correspondence between the two churches.

Yet, a kindred spirit prevails between churches. Truth constitutes a linkage characterized by love. If two churches have members who know the truth, then they ought also to love each other in truth as like-minded disciples. Hence, what sort of relationship should exist between them is something their respective churches may explore for mutual edification. This letter, however, leaves the matter open and undefined.

How might the concerns of the elder align with the concerns of church leaders and members in Asia? The threat of itinerant false teachers entering through hospitality does not mirror the dangers Asian believers usually face. Typically, Asian Christians represent a minority living in a religiously pluralistic society. If religious tolerance is practiced, persecution may be minimal. In Singapore, for example, the religious harmony act holds liable,

> any priest, monk, pastor, imam, elder, office-bearer or any other person who is in a position of authority in any religious group or institution where the Minister is satisfied that the person has committed or is attempting to commit any of the following acts:
>
> (a) causing feelings of enmity, hatred, ill-will or hostility between different religious groups;
> (b) carrying out activities to promote a political cause, or a cause of any political party while, or under the guise of, propagating or practising any religious belief;
> (c) carrying out subversive activities under the guise of propagating or practising any religious belief; or
> (d) inciting disaffection against the President or the Government while, or under the guise of, propagating or practising any religious belief.[41]

---

41. Section 8 (1) of the Maintenance of Religious Harmony Act, enacted as law in 1990 and revised in 2001. Online: https://en.wikipedia.org/wiki/Maintenance_of_Religious_Harmony_Act (accessed July 17, 2015).

For the sake of community and religious peaceful coexistence of the various religious groups that largely reflect the country's ethnic demographics, the government can prohibit any activity it deems to be aggressive or "offensive" proselytizing.[42]

Although the government's enforcement of the Religious Harmony Act does not constitute religious persecution because the act applies to all religions equally, the constraints warrant caution on how Christians exercise their religious prerogatives, including evangelistic activities. Their challenge is to walk in the truth and to practice love toward one another in a manner that aligns with Scripture and yet conforms to the laws of the land.

But in other Asian regions where the majority religion proves assertive and even intolerant of minority religious practices, such as in Pakistan, Christians suffer and face the difficult decision to stay true to their beliefs or succumb to the pressure to convert to Islam. To confess Jesus coming in the flesh is tantamount to confessing him as sovereign Lord, greater than even the prophet Muhammed. That profession potentially puts one in harm's way.

Regardless of our particular situations, 2 John's call to abide in the teaching of Christ remains the same for us all. Will we be on guard against the deceivers in the world and remain true to the Father and the Son?

---

42. "Singapore Leader Says Religious Proselytizing Threatens Stability." Online: http://www.wtvy.com/community/headlines/53723047.html (accessed July 17, 2015).

3 JOHN

Xiao or filial piety has been a significant cultural feature in East Asia for centuries, although it tends to diminish in practice where western influence has made inroads. The familial-like relationship between the "elder" and his readers whom he addresses as "children" ten times[1] reflects the affection he harbors toward them and, at the same time, the expectation of compliance to his directives. Unlike *xiao*, however, the elder does not expect reciprocity from his spiritual children to care for his needs in old age. When we come to 3 John, the elder regards his principle addressee, Gaius, as his child (3 John 4) and by extension others in Gaius's church. The title "elder" pictures a man who possesses the recognition, respect, and affection of fellow believers. We find something similar as we read 3 John where the elder presumes on existing relationships with first his principle addressee, Gaius, and also with others in Gaius's church. The title "elder" pictures a man who possesses the recognition, respect, and affection of fellow believers.

If 1 John and 2 John document earlier correspondence between the elder and his readers, we can note an ongoing relationship in which he exercises spiritual authority in exhorting them to walk in the truth, to love one another, and to guard against the encroachment of the world's ideology into their thinking. He has already gained their trust and, being on familiar terms, he can point out specific issues to which they may respond.

As we begin examining this letter, we note a progression from a very general letter in 1 John, with no specific recipient identified, to a specific church in 2 John, and now to a specific individual (Gaius) in 3 John. The issues addressed in all three epistles remain the same in general. And so understanding 3 John requires us to first read 1 John and 2 John.

1:1 Greeting

The elder opens with words of affection to Gaius, affirming that he loves him in truth. He repeats "whom I love in truth" (2 John 1:1) here. We noted before that "in truth" connoted "integrity and sincerity." The elder testifies to the genuineness of his affection for Gaius. Yet, a christological nuance lies embedded in "truth." The phrase, or its equivalent form, occurs with regularity in 2 John 1:1–4 and earlier in 1 John 1:8; 2:4; 3:18. Being "in truth" refers to living in obedience to the commands of God, the primary one being

---

1. 1 John 2:1, 12, 14, 18, 28; 3:7, 18; 4:4; 5:21; 3 John 4.

to love one another, and to confessing Jesus' true identity that, on a practical level, alludes to his lordship. Hence, the elder loves Gaius in two significant ways – with sincerity and in obedience to Christ's commands.

Following the elder's example, we too ought to nurture relationships by loving one another with genuine care and affection in obedience to our Lord's admonition.

1:2–4 Walking in the Truth

The elder expresses his desire that Gaius prosper in all areas of life and remain healthy (1:2), a seemingly normal wish between two close associates, Christian or not. But the verse concludes with an acknowledgment that Gaius is already prospering. The elder wants this state of affairs to continue.[2]

The very next verse provides the context for the letter and sets its tone. The elder is elated by reports from other believers who testify to Gaius' manner of life, that he walks in the truth (1:3). This recalls 1 John 1:6, 8; 2:4; 3:19 and especially 2 John 1:4. Not only does the elder commend Gaius for his conduct and character, he adds his own observation ("just as you walk in the truth"). The testimonies were united and consistent.[3] The form of the verb "walk" underscores this consistency.[4] Evidently, Gaius has such an exemplary lifestyle that others have taken note and inform the elder. These witnesses include people in his church and other churches.[5]

Nowadays we receive reports about people through social media and blogs. Believers whom we would not otherwise know become known to us through the "cyber grapevine." In sharing their stories, Christians elsewhere receive encouragement.

In response, the elder rejoices greatly, no doubt offering praise to God for such a brother. His own observations are confirmed by others. This principle of multiple attestations serves the church well. Conduct and service are observable, even if done behind the scenes. Word gets out. This process should give us pause; "What kind of witness am I before others? Do I bring them joy?"

---

2. Haas, de Jonge, and Swellengrebel divide 1:2 in two, where the first part conveys a wish and the second depicts reality (*Letters*, 176). Then, "just as" recognizes Gaius as already conforming to the wish.
3. Anderson, *1, 2, & 3 John*, 222. The uniformity of witness strengthens the validity of any one witness.
4. In the present tense, the verb describes normative behavior in similar fashion to 1 John.
5. It is likely that believers from the two churches in 2 John knew Gaius. Marshall suggests that ordinary Christians traveling for business or itinerant missionaries may have come to the elder after having seen Gaius in action (*Epistles*, 83).

The construction "testify to your truth" appears abstract and, at first reading, puzzling.[6] But the following clause ("just as you walk in truth") clarifies the somewhat obscure "your truth." The conjunction "just as" links the two clauses together, with the second explaining the earlier rather enigmatic clause.

The elder adds that he has no greater joy than to hear of his children walking in the truth (1:4). As in 2 John, he highlights the familial relationship he and Gaius enjoy. The elder, being the spiritual leader, may have regarded Gaius as his disciple and mentee even though he may not have led him to Christ originally. And the elder also mentions other disciples, whom he refers to generically as "my children." Those others may have been in Gaius's church and members of the elder's own church. So those who come under an elder's spiritual oversight can become a source of joy if they walk in the truth. In fact, there is no greater cause for celebration and thanksgiving than one's disciples being obedient to the commands to abstain from loving the world, to discern the spirits of truth and deception, to overcome the evil one and the world by faith, and to pray with confidence.

This joy prompts us to consider what fills us with joy and thanksgiving. Although few of us ever attain to elder statesmanship in the faith, we who are further along in our faith journey and experience in life and ministry have a stewardship entrusted to our care – the nurture and development of the next generation of disciples (a major theme in 1 John). In recent years, efforts have been made to address the need for mentoring/coaching in the corporate world of Asia.[7] When it comes to developing an organization's next batch of leaders, some overlap occurs between the goals of a church and that of a corporation. The spiritual dimension as articulated in 1, 2, and 3 John should form the core of any mentoring implemented by the church.[8]

1:5–8 Showing Hospitality to Itinerant Ministers

Now the elder turns his attention to itinerant ministers and the need for Gaius to facilitate their ministry through hosting them in their travels. In

---

6. Lieu explains that "truth" alludes to the sphere in which believers walk or the standard by which they live (*I, II, & III John*, 270).
7. George Quek, *Coaching and Mentoring International*. Online: https://coachingandmentoringinternational.org/ members-worldwide-directory/asia-pacific/ (accessed July 18, 2015). He heads *Distinctions Asia* that targets the Asia Pacific region including Singapore, Hong Kong, and China.
8. From an Asian perspective, the pastoral team of Singapore's Covenant Evangelical Free Church (CEFC), for example, have spearheaded and facilitated mentoring and discipleship within the local church and globally.

doing so, Gaius partners with them in their work. Presumably, Gaius will recognize whom the elder is talking about. In view of the warning that many false prophets (1 John 4:1) and deceivers (2 John 1:7) have gone out into the world no doubt seeking to infiltrate unsuspecting churches, Gaius must have the anointing of the Spirit to discern truth from deception (1 John 2:20, 27; 4:4–6). He is to reject false ministers and to accept true ones. Thus, the church assumes a crucial role in repelling false teaching and promoting true teaching both within and without.

The elder commends Gaius for faithfully[9] hosting fellow believers, including strangers (1:5).[10] Using this incidence of hospitality, the elder exhorts Gaius to make it a general practice in facilitating the travels of other itinerant ministers in the future.[11] Gaius shows his faithfulness by his compliance. The instruction is, however, quite general, leaving room for Gaius to determine what seems proper and effective in hosting these travelers. The elder respects Gaius' wisdom. Even though the new arrivals may be strangers with no prior association with Gaius and his church, Gaius still has responsibility for their welfare and for meeting their basic need for lodging and food. No doubt fellowship will happen as they report on their work, progress, and challenges faced. The simple act of listening serves to encourage and affirm their work as legitimate and needful. Questions may be asked and answered. In response, Gaius and his fellow members probably talk about developments in their own work for the Lord. The fellowship will turn those who were once strangers into partners.

The elder then relays the testimony his own church has received from these ministers about Gaius' love (1:6a).[12] He encourages Gaius to send them on their journey in a manner worthy of God (1:6b). If Gaius proves hospitable and effectively ministers to these traveling ministers, he demonstrates love. He fulfills the command to love others, not only those within his church but those who belong to other churches and those who may be "at large."

---

9. The adjective "faithful" functions adverbially here. See Bultmann, *Epistles*, 98 n. 8.
10. The expression "and this" with the demonstrative pronoun in the neuter singular is extremely difficult to handle. According to Culy, the two words represent an ellipsis which, when expanded, would read "and you should do this for strangers" (*I, II, III John*, 160). The proposal seeks to parallel "you should do for brothers and sisters." Yarbrough, however, simply renders it as "and this strangers" where "this" refers to Gaius' good work (*1–3 John*, 371). Yet, Yarbrough agrees with Culy in the elder's meaning of the text.
11. Schnackenburg, *Epistles*, 294, Lieu, *I, II, & III John*, 269–270, and Yarbrough, *1–3 John*, 371.
12. Brooke, *Epistles*, 184.

3 John

The expression "you would do well" conveys the elder's hope.[13] Gaius' compliance with the elder's request will be an acknowledgment of the latter's authority. Since Gaius has demonstrated hospitality to the missionaries before, the elder implores him to continue doing so. Apparently, their itinerant ministry involves repeated forays through Gaius' region and so they will require repeated and perhaps frequent accommodation.

3 John 1:7 explains the concluding words ("worthy of God") in the previous verse (1:6). The elder reminds Gaius that these missionaries came out on behalf of "the Name," presumably the name of God. They received nothing from non-believers. Then support must come from believers, especially from churches. Hospitality honors God by honoring his servants.

In the above paragraph, I rendered the term normally translated as "Gentiles" or "pagans" as "non-believers." Given that Gaius' name is certainly not Jewish, implying that he was most likely ethnically Gentile,[14] the members of his church were likely also Gentiles. Given, too, that they are being asked to offer assistance, their ethnicity is clearly not a factor.[15] Rather, their status as disciples of Christ must be the sole factor prompting the elder to approach them to help the ministers who limited themselves to seeking support only from believers.

The churches I have attended over the years encourage members to participate in offering or tithing as a sacred duty. On several occasions, particularly when funds have to be raised above and beyond normal giving to support special events or ministries, the pastor has explicitly announced that visitors and those who have not made a decision for Christ were not expected to give. Of course, this was done tactfully, explaining that only God's people were being called upon to donate to God's work.

In Singapore, churches have to be very careful when soliciting money as they can become liable to litigation if someone complains that their actions violate the Religious Harmony Act. Soliciting money for a restricted purpose may be construed as an effort to proselytize. In terms of the Guidelines for

---

13. "Will do" in the future tense denotes projection which, in this verse, refers to the elder's hope projected onto Gaius that he will facilitate the missionaries' journey. This articulated hope becomes a request. The relationship of the elder with his children gives the request an imperatival impetus.
14. Lieu claims that the name "Gaius" was common among Roman families (*I, II, III John*, 266).
15. Plummer does not see the missionaries avoiding Gentile converts (*Epistles*, 147). Hence, believers, whether Jewish or Gentile, can help them. Ethnicity was not the issue; spiritual status was.

Public and Private Fund Raising, public fund raising must be directed toward charitable concerns that benefit the community at large.[16] Hence, any collection of funds from the general public to support church events is prohibited. Private fund raising, however, has fewer restrictions since it targets church members only.

The itinerant ministers of Gaius' day conscientiously pursued a course of conduct and action that kept them beyond reproach, maintained the purity of their motives, and safeguarded their mission by doing things God's way. The objectives of a ministry do not justify the use of any means to accomplish them. The journey is as important as the destination. The elder concludes that he and Gaius ought to receive missionaries such as these (1:8).[17] In doing so they become co-workers for the truth. Interestingly, the verse does not state that Gaius and the others become partners with the ministers; rather, they become partners with the truth.[18] In view of 1 John 2:21–23, "the truth" alludes to the proclamation that Jesus is the Christ.

By using "we," the elder encompasses all Christians.[19] We are all obligated to help itinerant ministers, even if only by offering hospitality to those who serve on the frontlines. This was brought home to me during a visit to a missionary couple in Kenya some years ago. We spent several evenings in deep conversation. Taking me into their confidence, they informed me that this level of sharing was not possible with their supporting churches. They simply did not understand. But because I was on the field to experience their lives and ministry firsthand, I could understand. One concern they shared related to the support staff who served as mechanics, secretaries, IT staff, and the like. All were important, though not all were on the frontlines.

Gaius and his church may have had a support role. They stayed home. But through their hospitality, they enabled those serving in the field to remain faithful and fruitful. Gaius and his fellow believers were an indispensable component of the ministry team.

---

16. Online: http://www.edb.gov.sg/content/dam/edb/en/industries/International%20Non%20Profit%20Organisation/downloads/5.%20Guidelines%20on%20Public%20and%20Private%20Fund-raising%20(Feb%202013).pdf (accessed November 7, 2014).
17. The demonstrative adjective "such as these" categorizes the ones Gaius helped as the standard by which to compare other itinerant ministers. If they measure up, then they too are qualified to receive help. See Yarbrough, *1–3 John*, 374.
18. Smalley suggests two ways to understand "the truth": (1) become co-workers in proclaiming the gospel; and (2) participate in the cause of the truth (*1, 2, 3 John*, 352–353). Brooke prefers the first option (*Epistles*, 187).
19. Marshall, *Epistles*, 87.

1:9–10 A Problem Person

In sharp contrast to Gaius, another member of the church, Diotrephes, poses a roadblock to the church's capacity to host and help itinerant ministers. He is an ambitious man who has attained a position of influence. Since Gaius is familiar with the situation, the elder omits the background information that would have proven enormously helpful for us.

He laments Diotrephes' disrespect for his authority, shown by his stopping an earlier letter to the church (1:9). Previous experience with Diotrephes arouses concerns about a potential disaster if the problem he poses is not dealt with swiftly and decisively. Perhaps the elder intends Gaius to relay his concerns to other church members.

Reviewing the qualifications for an overseer (1 Tim 3:1–7), we find that Diotrephes has disqualified himself. 1 Timothy 3:2 specifies that a spiritual leader ought to be hospitable, a quality described by a Greek word that is a compound of "to love" and "stranger." He must literally love strangers through welcoming them, something Diotrephes fails to do.[20] He also refuses to receive the itinerant ministers (1:5). Pride and arrogance prompt him to abuse his authority. He refuses to listen and rejects any cooperative venture. It must be his way or the highway.

The elder expresses his desire to come in person to deal with this problem in the church (1:10). But he seems a bit hesitant ("if I should come"[21]). Perhaps the reason for his uncertainty is related to the best timing to have maximum effectiveness or to the demands of his schedule. But when he comes, he intends to bring up the matter of Diotrephes and his disparaging words about the elder and his co-workers. Compounding his hurtful talk, Diotrephes does not receive the brothers and sisters, that is, the itinerant missionaries and perhaps other believers who are traveling. Moreover, he hinders those who desire to show them hospitality by throwing them out of the church. Diotrephes represents a problem so serious that it warrants a special visit by the elder. Apparently, anything short of his direct, personal intervention will be ineffective. Neither Gaius nor anyone else in the church can persuade Diotrephes to set aside his destructive agenda and activities. His

---

20. The statement "he does not receive us" refers to the elder and possibly those who accompanied him in attempting to visit the church. The present tense, "receive" indicates consistent refusal to host the elder and his companions.

21. The probable (third class) conditional statement depicts the elder as somewhat uncertain about his visit, perhaps because of Diotrephes' potent opposition. If the elder has apostolic authority, why would he be so hesitant?

position is too strong and entrenched for that. It is possible that Diotrephes owed his influence to the fact that the church may have met in his house. If he was wealthy enough to own a large home where believers could gather, they may have been in his debt.

The elder expresses his intentions clearly.[22] His visit will be no social call but a disciplinary one. Not specifying the venue in which he will present this case, he leaves us to speculate. Will he call a meeting with the church leadership? Will he gather the entire church in a congregational conference? Will he ask some of the leaders to accompany him when he confronts Diotrephes? Or will there be a one-on-one face-off with the man? We do not know. The only certainty is that the elder must come in order to break the gridlock; otherwise there will be no change in the corporate culture and useful ministry cannot be resumed.

All the verbs used to describe Diotrephes indicate that he has been abusing his authority for some time and will continue to do so unless something external forces change.[23] This strong-willed individual, totally in control, renders the church helpless.

Moreover, his words infect the congregation, conceivably poisoning the hearts of the members toward the elder and his associates. Diotrephes' malicious intent is evident in the use of the word "disparaging" to describe his customary speech pattern. The Greek word used here appears only one other time in the NT, in a context where it connotes gossip (1 Tim 5:13).[24] The intent behind the spoken words reveals the malicious heart of a person who fails to obey the command to love one another (1 John 3:11, 18, 23; 4:7, 11, 21; 5:2). Thus Diotrephes' spiritual status remains ambiguous in view of the following: the one who fails to love his brother cannot be associated with God (1 John 3:10) and abides in death (1 John 3:14); the one who does not love cannot know God (1 John 4:8) nor be able to love him (1 John 4:20).

Not content with malicious talk that harms the cause of Christ, Diotrephes seeks to inflict more damage. In a sense, his wicked passion parallels greed,

---

22. The future tense "will bring up" conveys the elder's intentions but not necessarily what will transpire given the uncertainty of his effectiveness. Plummer describes him as "half-hearted" (*Epistles*, 161). Perhaps we can characterize him as tentative. He is not in control of the situation; Diotrephes is.
23. The verbs and participles in the present tense depict normative and continuing activity. The tense suggests that his activities will continue until something forcefully terminates the action.
24. The adjective form of the verb appears once in the Greek version of the OT at 4 Maccabees 5:11, an apocryphal writing. There it alludes to something foolish or nonsensical.

which never finds satisfaction but is compelled to seek more and more, like the proverbial leech (Prov 30:15).

So in addition to refusing to show hospitality to the itinerant ministers ("the brothers and sisters"), he prevents members of his own church from showing them hospitality by expelling those members from the church. No one can challenge him as he operates with impunity.

This brings into question Gaius's position and role in the church. Has he been cast out along with the others? Or has he managed to stay although his place is precarious? Has he attempted to oppose Diotrephes albeit unsuccessfully? Or has he been cowed, so that this letter strives to encourage him? These questions cannot be answered as we do not have enough background information. All we know for certain is that the church faces a very uncertain future, possibly even a disastrous one. The elder must intervene; that is their only hope.

1:11–12 A Commendable Person

In this subsection, the elder begins by exhorting Gaius before commending Demetrius, who is virtually the opposite of Diotrephes. Whereas the latter is uniformly evil and harmful and poses a threat to the church, the former enjoys unanimous praise. Although his role and function remain unclear, he apparently has great potential. Undoubtedly, the elder has plans for him once Diotrephes is removed from leadership.

The elder exhorts Gaius not to imitate evil but to imitate good. He explains that those who do good come from God; but those who do evil have not seen God (1:11). The language of "good" and "evil" is foreign to 1 John and even 2 John, but the immediate context makes it clear that Diotrephes represents what is evil (1:9–10).[25] Evil is undergirded by pride that manifests itself in a desire to gain prominence and lord it over others. Evil is self-centered for it rejects God's sovereign authority. Evil harbors intolerance, as evidenced by unwillingness to dialogue and understand other points of view. An evil person is characterized by rigidity and stubbornness gravitating toward a hardened heart. Pride blinds them to others who have authority and even a position, as we can see in Diotrephes' rejection of the elder. Pride lacks sensitivity and love, does not care if others are hurt, and desires to reshape the church in one's own image.

---

25. Bultmann, *Epistles*, 102. The substantive "the evil" is neuter which, according to Schnackenburg, represents the elder's way of indirectly referring to Diotrephes's attitude and evil conduct (*Epistles*, 300).

Interpreting "the good" as the polar opposite of "the evil" yields a sober self-assessment: we are the recipients of divine grace, personified in Jesus Christ as our advocate (1 John 2:1), the propitiation for our sins (1 John 2:2), and our Savior (1 John 4:9, 14). We have entered into a new relationship with the Father and the Son and with other believers (1 John 1:3). This fellowship implies new marching orders, walking in the light as God is in the light (1 John 1:7; 2:6) and walking in truth (2 John 4) and according to God's commands (2 John 6). We inhabit a new realm where we abide in God (1 John 2:6; 3:6; 4:13), the Father and the Son (1 John 2:24d), in Christ who will return (1 John 2:28) and in the light (1 John 2:10). At the same time, there is a mutual abiding, we in God and God in us (1 John 3:24; 4:13, 16). We can do "the good" because of an indwelling of the word of God (1 John 2:14e, 24bc), his anointing (1 John 2:27b), his seed (1 John 3:9b), his love (1 John 3:17d), and his Spirit (1 John 3:24cd). And if we love others, then God's love is perfected in us (1 John 4:12bd).

In exhorting Gaius to imitate[26] good and not evil, the elder seems to imply that this may be challenging for Gaius. Here there is no commendation; only a command to lead an exemplary life. Gaius' present condition is not so set and hopeless that he cannot change for the better. He faces a decision about whether to comply or not. In calling him "beloved" or "dear friend" the elder softens the admonition so that if feels like a loving push in the right direction. Such love shows affection but also sees the situation clearly rather than through rose-colored lens. Love hopes for the best and holds the beloved accountable.

The choice between good and evil conforms to the typical dualism in the Gospel of John and the Epistles of John. No middle ground provides wiggle room when confronted with hard choices. The elder does, however, provide motivation by spelling out consequences of making the right choice. Those who do good align with God and his commands and enter into fellowship with him. Their faith overcomes the evil one and the world (1 John 2:13d, 14; 5:4–5).

---

26. The exhortation to imitate good and not evil alludes to both a general admonition to do good (what God approves) and a specific admonition concerning hospitality (Anderson, *1, 2, & 3 John*, 236). The elder may also be implicitly encouraging Gaius not to succumb to pressure from Diotrephes.

3 John

For those who do evil, their inability to see God brings a systemic problem to the surface.[27] Without transforming grace, people lack the capacity to perceive spiritual truth and to enter into a relationship with God. To "see" God connotes an experiential encounter with him, a communion, a mutual indwelling as discussed above. The inability to perceive reveals the lack of an inner reality to which only God can birth (1 John 2:29; 3:9; 4:7; 5:1, 4, 18). Again, the dualism stems from two possible conditions: either God has entered into people's lives and changed them permanently or he has not.

Eternal life is not mere existence without end (even the damned will continue to exist) but a relationship with the Father and the Son. To know Christ relationally is to have eternal life.

Lest we misinterpret 3 John in thinking that the elder writes of a salvation based on works, the whole tenor of 1, 2, and 3 John predicates our works on God's initiative, termed grace (1 John 2:5; 3:1, 16; 4:7–11, 16–17, 19; 5:1). All the commands, admonitions, and exhortations in these three epistles are directed to the children of God. They are not obeyed in order to become children. They are given because the recipients are already children of God.

Next the elder commends Demetrius, acknowledging the universal and uniform testimony by three categories of witnesses – all, the truth itself, and the elder and his associates (1:12). He emphasizes the truth of his own testimony and that of his associates. All who know Demetrius testify to his character and worthiness. This cloud of witnesses may include people from Gaius's church and that of the elder and perhaps from other churches. The extent of the witness is unknown since we have no clue as to how well known Demetrius was.

The other witness is the truth itself. Exactly what this entails remains ambiguous.[28] It may have doctrinal overtones, indicating that Demetrius concurs with the truth taught by the elder.[29] Or it may allude to Demetrius's life that conforms to the truth.[30] No doubt both ideas contribute to what the elder had in mind. The one substantial doctrine taught in these epistles is that

---

27. The perfect tense of the verb "to see" describes a condition or state of being that results from doing evil, namely the inability to see or perceive God. The substantive participle, "the one who does evil," uses the present tense to represent ongoing, customary behavior. Evil blinds. An evil person cannot perceive God which, on a practical level, means that they cannot pursue fellowship with God (Anderson, *1, 2, & 3 John*, 237).
28. Johnson suggests that the truth as witness consists of two complementary aspects: (1) acceptance of correct doctrine, especially as pertaining to Jesus' true identity; and (2) proper conduct, especially in loving one another (*1, 2, and 3 John*, 180).
29. Kysar, *I, II, III John*, 146.
30. Brown, *Epistles*, 723–724.

confession of Jesus' true identity demands obedience to his commands, primarily his command to love one another. The elder does not elaborate on this here. It is not an either-or proposition but a combination of right doctrine and right practice that conforms to the themes in these epistles.

If Demetrius is this exemplary, we wonder why there is a need for witnesses. Has some challenge arisen? Are these witnesses designed to oppose Diotrephes, who may have rejected Demetrius? The elder leaves us in the dark; we do not know. These questions spawn yet another question, who is Demetrius? Is he one of the itinerant ministers? If so, why is he singled out by name for commendation? Have his credentials been questioned? Or is he a member of Gaius' church who has come into conflict with Diotrephes? We have questions but no definite answers.

The juxtaposition of the exhortation to Gaius to imitate the good and the commendation of Demetrius suggests that the latter may be a model for the former to follow. Apparently, Demetrius is characterized as one who does the good and so sees God relationally. Gaius may be lagging behind in terms of doing good, which, in the context of 1 and 2 John, may mean loving others, particularly itinerant ministers according to the immediate context of 1:5–8. Demetrius, then, may have been held up as an example of one who practices hospitality and partners with others for the gospel's sake.

If we regard Gaius and Demetrius as a gauge to measure ourselves and others by, what might we glean? Gaius represents a disciple with potential who, with the right guidance, can advance in his spiritual development and service. He may already be serving and have attained a level of maturity. Further growth is not only possible but necessary. Demetrius, on the other hand, represents a disciple fully functional and actively engaged in the Lord's work. He has earned a favorable reputation among a fairly wide circle of acquaintances. Some may know him personally, having fellowshipped and served together with him. Others may know him by hearsay only. The witness of all, however, is uniformly positive. Another point of comparison is only implied – Gaius is localized in a particular church setting and fulfills his stewardship there, whereas Demetrius is more globalized, being involved in an itinerant ministry touching several churches and perhaps focusing his ministry on the unchurched in the world. Both men are or potentially can be commended and their respective ministries acknowledged. They represent a spectrum within which our responsibility is to discern our location and to serve faithfully there.

3 John

1:13–15 Desire to Dialogue in Person

The elder has more to share with Gaius, but not in writing. This brief note may represent only a cursory outline that he will elaborate in person. Details and even the tone cannot always be adequately conveyed in writing. Body language and facial expression cannot be encoded but must be acted out. Yet, the note serves an important purpose – it maintains contact when physical presence is not possible, and it anticipates future fellowship in preparing the recipient to receive what the sender has planned. The issues mentioned in the letter will not catch the recipient by surprise nor will he be unprepared when they meet.

The elder reveals that he has much more to discuss (1:13). He prefers to do so in person and not in writing. In alluding to the "many things" he desires to cover, he does not reveal his hand. Does the present letter contain the seeds of all he plans to discuss? Or are there other matters, perhaps equally important, that he is deferring until they meet? We do not know. If this letter is part of an ongoing dialogue between the two men, Gaius would probably have surmised what the "many things" entailed. But because we are not privy to their conversation and are confined to this note only, we have no clue and can only speculate. Did Gaius receive 1 and 2 John previously, and is 3 John a follow-up, personalized note just for him? Perhaps the "many things" not mentioned in 3 John are related to the contents of 1 and 2 John.

The basis for effective mentoring lies in cultivating functional relationships. This is particularly challenging today.[31] What we sense between the elder and Gaius is mutual respect. Obviously, "elder" is a title of authority and signifies wisdom and experience. For a man to assume that title without being presumptuous, he must have earned it through undergoing the trials of life and ministry, and must have proven his mettle through consistent living and performance in negotiating many challenges and even setbacks. Although he has earned the right to direct Gaius and to expect his compliance, the elder repeatedly pens words of endearment, four times addressing Gaius as "beloved." This may be something we would feel uncomfortable saying to each other. Asians tend not to express affection in words or actions.[32]

---

31. For a helpful discussion on person-to-person relationships as a basis for effective mentoring, see Martin Sanders, *The Power of Mentoring: Shaping People Who Will Shape the World* (Camp Hill, PA: Wing Spread, 2004), 25–40.
32. For an insightful article, read Jonathan Le, "Why Are Public Displays of Affection Taboo in Many Asian Families?" *Nha Magazine*. Online:http://news.newamericamedia.org/news/view_article.html?article_id=03759322f96951522c9345196098c80e (accessed November 8, 2014). Le is a Vietnamese American. Western men also find intimacy a bit foreign. See Sanders

The elder also voices a blessing (1:2) and indicates his joy if Gaius should prove to be walking in the truth (1:3). He alludes to his younger counterpart as one of his children (1:4). Such familial references close the gap and invite intimacy.

The elder expresses his hope that they will meet very soon (1:14). We do not know whether this meeting ever took place, although we may presume that it did. In expressing his desire to see Gaius soon, the elder implies the urgency of addressing his concerns. Things can quickly get out of hand unless immediate and decisive action is taken.

Concluding the letter, the elder sends greetings from friends who are with him to Gaius and his people, also referred to as "friends" (1:15). Although unnamed, these individuals were known by the elder and Gaius and did not need to be identified. They were part of the spiritual and social context in which both operated. If 2 John 1:13 offers a parallel, these "friends" may be members of the churches associated with the elder and with Gaius.

Common themes tie 1, 2, and 3 John together as a "family" of letters, possibly even a sequence. The command to love one another extends beyond the boundaries of a local church and its members to include believers from other churches and even those not affiliated with a single church who travel as ministers-at-large serving the cause of Christ in a global sense. Disciples such as Gaius exercise stewardship by showing love through hospitality in order to help these ministers by providing for their needs. Because these ministers deliberately resist seeking help from the world, they are absolutely dependent on the loving support of believers, even though they may be strangers to each other. In this manner, the church partners with those who work beyond its borders. In so doing, the church effectively extends its reach and influence.

Today, when technology enables travel and communication on a global scale, 3 John assumes special relevance to us. Yes, we devote the majority of our concern and resources to our local church. But we must also acknowledge our obligation to serve as stewards to the church universal that engages in God's work elsewhere. When we mobilize our resources, including our people, unity and collaboration will extend beyond individual churches to encompass the community of churches everywhere.

---

who identifies four levels of intimacy for men (*Mentoring*, 31–33). A sampling of personal experiences and opinions on Asians (including Chinese, Japanese, Thai) and displays of affection can be found at http://www.colorq.org/petsins/article.php?y=2006&m=5&x=5_4 (accessed November 8, 2014).

3 JOHN

The diversity of cultures and religions in our societies means that the Asian church often faces and struggles with the external realities of pluralism. The challenges of poverty, racial/ethnic and religious tensions, governments that may threaten the church's well-being, class conflicts, and the marginalization of women can prove so great that the church may neglect its internal challenges in channeling all its energies and resources outwardly. 3 John reminds us that sometimes the church's own leadership can be a roadblock to fulfilling its mandate.

TALE OF TWO REALMS – WITHIN THE CHURCH

In a previous article (Tale of Two Realms – Standing on the Truth, pp. 114–115), we explored the tale of two realms, the one characterized by light and truth and the other that denies the truth and dwells in darkness. Straddling the divide, the church must maintain the purity of its doctrine and practice because it belongs to the realm of light and truth as it ministers in the world. It carefully guards against any syncretism in its worldview, any compromise to Jesus as Christ and Lord. But what if darkness invades and seeps into the church?

To be light in the midst of darkness, the church must find the balance between being distinct and yet, at the same time, being relevant in its Asian world. Without proper contextualization the church remains foreign and non-Asian and hence will not be an inviting presence whereby Asians may be receptive to Jesus as the Savior. But if the church goes too far in striving to be accepted, it becomes syncretistic and darkness enters. It must establish several safeguards, then, to insure that it remains faithful to its profession of faith and allegiance to the Lord and still be culturally acceptable.[1] First, a reverent attitude toward the truth has top priority as mentioned earlier. Secondly, the anointment of the Spirit enables discernment (1 John 2:20, 27; 4:1–6; 5:6–9). Thirdly, armed with the truth and the Spirit's anointing, the church as a community must counter any syncretistic threat from a member, especially an influential leader who deviates from the truth (3 John 1:9–11). It may lead to church discipline and, if that does not work, the erring party must leave, either of their own volition or under compulsion, in order to preserve the purity of the church (1 John 2:19). Fourthly, someone in the role of the elder who authored 2 John and 3 John, and other key leaders like Gaius and Demetrius, respected in the church, must lead and guide its members and confront erring members.

---

1. The following discussion follows Paul G. Hiebert, *Anthropological Reflection on Missiological Issues* (Grand Rapids, MI: Baker, 1994), 88–92. Hiebert's third and fourth safeguards relate more to cultural diversity among believers enabling them to correlate in a *metacultural* and *metatheological framework*. I adapt my third and fourth factors to be more oriented to 1, 2, and 3 John.

BIBLIOGRAPHY

Akin, Daniel L., ed. *A Theology for the Church*. Nashville, TN: Broadman & Holman, 2007.

Anderson, John L. *An Exegetical Summary of 1, 2, and 3 John*. 2d ed. Dallas, TX: SIL International, 2008.

Anderson, Paul N. "The Community That Raymond Brown Left Behind: Reflections on the Johannine Dialectical Situation." September 2013. Online: http://www.bibleinterp.com/PDFs/Anderson.pdf.

Audi, Robert. "Theodicy." In *The Cambridge Dictionary of Philosophy*, 794–795. Cambridge; New York: Cambridge University Press, 1999.

Barker, Glenn W. *1 John* in *Hebrews through Revelation*. EBC. Grand Rapids, MI: Zondervan, 1981.

———. "2 John." In *The Expositor's Bible Commentary with the New International Version: Hebrews through Revelation*. 12 vols. Grand Rapids, MI: Zondervan, 1981.

Bauckham, Richard. *Jesus and the Eyewitnesses: The Gospels as Eyewitness Testimony*. Grand Rapids, MI: Eerdmans, 2006.

———, ed. *The Gospels for All Christians: Rethinking the Gospel Audiences*. Grand Rapids, MI: Eerdmans, 1998.

Berlin, Adele. *Poetics and Interpretation of Biblical Narrative*. Winona Lake, IN: Eisenbrauns, 1994.

Berling, Judith A. "Confucianism." In *Focus on Asian Studies,* Vol. 2, no 1: *Asian Religions*, 5–7, 1982. Online: http://www2.kenyon.edu/Depts/Religion/Fac/Adler/Reln270/Berling-Confucianism.htm.

Billings, J. Todd. "The Problem with 'Incarnational Ministry': What if our mission is not to 'be Jesus' to other cultures, but to join with the Holy Spirit?" *Christianity Today* 56 no. 7 (July/August 2012): 58–63. Online: http://www.christianitytoday.com/ct/2012/july-august/the-problem-with-incarnational-ministry.html?start=6.

Blomberg, Craig L. *From Pentecost to Patmos: An Introduction to Acts through Revelation*. Nashville, TN: Broadman & Holman, 2006.

Boo, Tan Eng. "Filial Piety and Burial Customs." *The Burning Bush* 9, 2003. Online: http://www.febc.edu.sg/bbvol9_2d.htm.

Borg, Marcus. *Meeting Jesus Again for the First Time: The Historical Jesus and the Heart of Contemporary Faith*. New York: HarperCollins, 1995.

Boyer, James L. "The Classification of Participles: A Statistical Study." *Grace Theological Journal* 5 (1984): 163–179.

Bräunlein, Peter J. "Spirits in and of Southeast Asia's Modernity: An Overview." *Dorisea Working Paper* Issue 1 (2013): 1–17. Online: http://www.academia.edu/4072136/Spirits_in_and_of_Southeast_Asias_Modernity.

Brey, Philip. "Evaluating the Social and Cultural Implications of the Internet." January 2000. Online: http://ethicsandtechnology.eu/wp-content/uploads/2012/10/a1-brey.pdf.

Brooke, A. E. *A Critical and Exegetical Commentary on the Johannine Epistles*. Repr. London, New York: T & T Clark, 2004.

Brown, Harold O. J. *Heresies: Heresy and Orthodoxy in the History of the Church*. Peabody, MA.: Hendrickson, 1984.

Brown, Raymond E. *An Introduction to the Gospel of John*. Edited by Francis J. Moloney. Garden City, NY: Doubleday, 2003.

———. *The Community of the Beloved Disciple: The Life, Loves and Hates of an Individual Church in New Testament Times*. Mahwah, NJ: Paulist, 1979.

———. *The Epistles of John: Translated with Introduction, Notes, and Commentary*. AB 30. Garden City, NY: Doubleday, 1982.

———. *The Gospel according to John (i–xii), Introduction, Translation, and Notes*. AB 29. Garden City, NY: Doubleday, 1966.

Brown, Rick. "Contextualization without Syncretism." *International Journal of Frontier Missions* 23 (2006): 127–133.

Brown, Tricia Gates. *Spirit in the Writings of John: Johannine Pneumatology in Social-scientific Perspective*. JSNTSup 253. New York: T & T Clark, 2003.

Bruce, F. F. *The Epistles of John: Introduction, Exposition and Notes*. London: Pickering & Inglis Ltd., 1970.

Bultmann, Rudolf. *The Johannine Epistles: A Commentary on the Johannine Epistles*. Translated by R. P. O'Hara, L. C. McGaughy, and R. W. Funk. Hermeneia. Philadelphia, PA: Fortress, 1973.

Burge, Gary M. *The Letters of John*. NIVAC. Grand Rapids, MI: Zondervan, 1996.

Busenitz, Irvin A. "The Sin Unto Death." *TMSJ* 1 (1990): 17–33.

Byron, John. "Slaughter, Fratricide and Sacrilege: Cain and Abel Traditions in 1 John 3." *Biblica* 88 (2007): 526–535.

Carr, David. "Torah on the Heart: Literary Jewish Textuality within Its Ancient Near Eastern Context." *Oral Tradition* 25 (2010): 17–40.

Carson, D. A. *Difficult Doctrine of the Love of God*. Wheaton, IL: Crossway, 2000.

"Caste Identity within the Church: Twice Alienation." Online: http://www.dalitchristians.com/html/castechurch.htm.

Chao, Ruth and Vivian Tseng. "Parenting of Asians." In *Handbook of Parenting: Vol. 4 Social Conditions and Applied Parenting*. Edited by M. H. Bornstein, 59–93. Mahwah, NJ: Lawrence Erlbaum Associates, 2002.

Bibliography

Chia, Edmund. "Asian Christianity: The Postcolonial Challenge of Identity and Theology." *Compass* 4 (2012): 9–13. Online: http://compassreview.org/autumn12/3.pdf.

Collins, Raymond F. "'A New Commandment I Give to You, That You Love One Another . . .' (Jn 13:34)." *Laval théologiqueetphilosophique* 35 (1979): 235–261.

Compton, R. Bruce. "Church Discipline: Separation from a Believer or Excommunication of an Unbeliever? Comparing Matthew 18:15–17, 1 Corinthians 5:1–13, and 2 Thessalonians 3:6–15." 2008. Online: https://www.dbts.edu/pdf/macp/2009/Compton%20Church%20Discipline%20and%20Excommunication.pdf.

Constable, Thomas L. "Notes on 1 John," 1–87. 2015. Online: http://www.soniclight.com/constable/notes/pdf/1john.pdf.

Covenant Evangelical Free Church in Singapore. 2013. Online: http://www.cefc.org.sg/index.php/training-resources/idt.

Cowan, Christopher. "The Father and Son in the Fourth Gospel: Johannine Subordination Revisited." *JETS* 49 (2006): 115–135.

Culy, Martin M. *I, II, III John: A Handbook on the Greek Text*. Waco, TX: Baylor University Press, 2004.

Davids, Peter H., Douglas J. Moo, and Robert W. Yarbrough. *1 & 2 Peter, 1, 2, & 3 John, Jude*. Grand Rapids, MI: Zondervan, 2002.

De Jong, Matthijs J. "The Fallacy of 'True and False,' in Prophecy Illustrated by Jer 28:8–9." *Journal of Hebrew Scriptures* 12 (2012): 1–29.

Derickson, Gary W. "What Is the Message of 1 John?" *BSac* 150 (1993): 89–105.

Dy, Aristotle. "Towards a Chinese Christology: Inculturation and Christology in the Chinese Context." *Landas* 15 (2001): 45–63.

Edwards, Ruth B. *The Johannine Epistles*. Sheffield: Sheffield Academic, 1996.

Ehrman, Bart D. *The Orthodox Corruption of Scripture: The Effect of Early Christological Controversies on the Text of the New Testament*. New York: Oxford University Press, 1993.

Elliott, William E. "Conditional Sentences in the Greek New Testament." ThD diss., Grace Theological Seminary, 1981.

En, Siau Ming. "External Threats Aplenty, but a United Nation Will Overcome Them: PM Lee." *Today*, September 9, 2015. Online: http://www.todayonline.com/ge2015/external-threats-aplenty-united-nation-will-overcome-them-pm-lee.

Engle, Richard. "Contextualization in Missions: A Biblical and Theological Appraisal." *Grace Theological Journal* 4 (1983): 85–107.

Erickson, Millard J. *Systematic Theology*. 3d ed. Grand Rapids, MI: Baker Academic, 2013.

Fanning, Buist M. *Verbal Aspect in New Testament Greek*. Oxford: Clarendon, 1990.

Fanning, Don. "Contextualization," *Trends and Issues in Missions* (2009): 1–28. Online: http://digitalcommons.liberty.edu/cgi/ viewcontent. cgi?article=1004&context=cgm_missions.

George, Sobin. "Dalit Christians in India: Discrimination, Development Deficit and the Question for Group-Specific Policies." *Working Papers of the Indian Institute of Dalit Studies* 6 (2012): 5–32. Online: http://www.academia.edu/6819127/Dalit_Christians_in_India_Discrimination_Development_Deficit_and_the_Question_for_Group-Specific_Policies.

Gold, Thomas, Doug Guthrie, and David Wank, eds. *Social Connections in China: Institutions, Culture, and the Changing Nature of Guanxi.* Cambridge: Cambridge University Press, 2002.

Grayston, Kenneth. *The Johannine Epistles.* NCBC. Grand Rapids, MI: Eerdmans, 1984.

Griffith, Terry. "'Little Children, Keep Yourselves from Idols' (1 John 5:21)." *TynBul* 48 (1997): 187–190.

Grudem, Wayne. *Systematic Theology: An Introduction to Biblical Doctrine.* Grand Rapids, MI: Zondervan, 1994.

Haas, C., M. de Jonge, and J. L. Swellengrebel. *A Handbook on the Letters of John.* New York: UBS, 1972.

Harris, R. Laird. "The Book of Job and Its Doctrine of God." *Grace Theological Journal* 13 (1972): 3–33.

Hays, Richard B. *The Faith of Jesus Christ: The Narrative Substructure of Galatians 3:1–4:11.* Biblical Resource Series. Grand Rapids, MI: Eerdmans, 2002.

Hendricks, Howard G. and William D. Hendricks. *As Iron Sharpens Iron: Building Character in a Mentoring Relationship.* Chicago, IL: Moody Press, 1995.

Hiebert, D. Edmond. "An Expositional Study of 1 John, Part 1 (of 10 parts): An Exposition of 1 John 1:1–4." *BSac* 145 (1988): 197–210.

———. "An Exposition of 1 John 2:7–17." *BSac* 145 (1988): 420–435.

———. "An Expositional Study of 1 John Part 2 (of 10 parts): An Exposition of 1 John 1:5–2:6." *BSac* 145 (1988): 329–342.

———. "An Exposition of 1 John 2:18–28." *BSac* 146 (1989): 76–93.

———. "An Exposition of 1 John 2:29–3:12." *BSac* 146 (1989): 198–216.

Hill, Charles E. *The Johannine Corpus in the Early Church.* Oxford: Oxford University Press, 2004.

Hills, Julian. "'Little Children, Keep Yourselves from Idols': 1 John 5:21 Reconsidered." *CBQ* 51 (1989): 285–310.

Ho, D. Y. F. "Filial Piety and Its Psychological Consequences." In *The Handbook of Chinese Psychology.* Edited by M. H. Bond, 155–165. Hong Kong: Oxford University Press, 1996. Online: http://blog.eteacherchinese.com/china-culture/taoism-a-philosophy-or-a-religion/.

Bibliography

Hodge, Caroline Johnson. *If Sons, Then Heirs: A Study of Kinship and Ethnicity in the Letters of Paul.* Oxford: Oxford University Press, 2007.

Hodges, Zane C. "Fellowship and Confession in 1 John 1:5–10." *BSac* 129 (1972): 48–60.

Houlden, J. L. *A Commentary on the Johannine Epistles.* London: Adam & Charles Black, 1973; Repr. London: Adam & Charles Black, 1976. Online: http://www.cprf.co.uk/articles/mutualindwelling.htm#.VA7GViwcTmI.

Huffman, Douglas S. *The Handy Guide to New Testament Greek: Grammar, Syntax, and Diagramming.* Grand Rapids, MI: Kregel, 2012.

Hummel, Charles E. *Tyranny of the Urgent.* Rev. ed. Downers Grove, IL: InterVarsity, 1994.

Jenkins, Michael H. "Religious Taoism vs. Philosophical Taoism." Online: http://people.opposingviews.com and http://religious-taoism-vs-philosophical-taoism-6900.html.

Jobes, Karen H. *Letters to the Church: A Survey of Hebrews and the General Epistles.* Grand Rapids, MI: Zondervan, 2011.

Johnson, Thomas F. *1, 2, and 3 John.* New International Biblical Commentary. Peabody, MA: Hendrickson, 1993.

Kausikan Bilahari Kim Hee P. S. "An East Asian Approach to Human Rights." *Buffalo Journal of International Law* 2 (1995–1996): 263-283. Online: http://tembusu.nus.edu.sg/docs/East_Asian_Approach.pdf.

Keiser, Thomas A. "The Divine Plural: A Literary-Contextual Argument for Plurality in the Godhead." *JSOT* 34 (2009): 131–146.

Kellemen, Robert. "Emotions: Why We Feel What We Feel?" March 26, 2014. Online: http://www.rpmministries.org/2014/03/emotions-why-do-we-feel-what-we-feel/.

Kempis, Thomas á. *The Imitation of Christ*, ch. 42 "On the Wonderful Effect of Divine Love." Online: http://www.worldinvisible.com/library/akempis/imitation/chapter%2042.htm.

Kennedy, George A. *New Testament Interpretation through Rhetorical Criticism.* Chapel Hill, NC: University of North Carolina Press, 1984.

Kim, U. and S. Choi. "Individualism, Collectivism, and Child Development: A Korean Perspective." In *Cross-Cultural Roots of Minority Child Development.* Edited by P. M. Greenfield and R. R. Cocking, 1–37. Hillsdale, NJ: Lawrence Erlbaum Associates, 1994.

Koh, Peter. "The Cell Group Church Structure: An Evaluation." *Church and Society in Asia Today* 6 (2003): 40–53. Online: http://www.disciplewalk.com/files/Peter_Koh_The_Cell_Group_Church_Structure_an_Evaluation.pdf

Kruger, Brent. "If God Is for Us: A Study of Pauline Theodicy in Rom 8:18–39." PhD diss., The Catholic University of America, 2013.

Kysar, Robert. *John, The Maverick Gospel.* 3d ed. Louisville, KY: Westminster John Knox, 2007.

Le, Jonathan. "Why Are Public Displays of Affection Taboo in Many Asian Families?" *Nha Magazine.* November 28, 2003. Online: http://news.newamericamedia.org/news/view_article.html?article_id=03759322f96951522c9345196098c80e.

Leffel, Jim. "Contextualization: Building Bridges to the Muslim Community." Online: http://www.xenos.org/essays/contextualization-building-bridges-muslim-community

Lewis, C. S. *A Grief Observed.* London, UK: Faber and Faber, 1961; Repr. Goshen, CT: Crosswicks, 1989.

Lewis, Jack P. "The Offering of Abel (Gen 4:4): A History of Interpretation." *JETS* 37 (1994): 481–496.

Lewis, Scott M. *The Gospel according to John and the Johannine Letters.* New Collegeville Bible Commentary 4. Collegeville, MN: Liturgical Press, 2005.

Lieu, Judith M. *I, II, and III John: A Commentary.* Louisville, KY: Westminster John Knox, 2008.

———. *The Second and Third Epistles of John: History and Background.* Edinburgh: T & T Clark, 1986.

———. *The Theology of the Johannine Epistles.* Cambridge: Cambridge University Press, 2001.

———. "Us or You? Persuasion and Identity in 1 John." *JBL* 127 (2008): 805–819.

McGhee, Michael, "Is Buddhism a Religion?" *The Guardian,* October 7, 2013. Online: http://www.theguardian.com/commentisfree/belief/2013/oct/07/is-buddhism-a-religion.

McKay, Kenneth L. "Aspect in Imperatival Constructions in New Testament Greek." *NovT* 27 (1985): 201–226.

McKinley, John E. "Four Patristic Models of Jesus Christ's Impeccability and Temptation." *Perichoresis* 9 (2011): 29–66.

Mayhue, Richard. "One God – Three Persons." *Master's Seminary Journal* 24 (2013): 161–165.

Merkle, Benjamin L. "What is the Meaning of 'Idols' in 1 John 5:21?" *BSac* 169 (2012): 328–340.

Metzger, Bruce M. *A Textual Commentary on the Greek New Testament.* 2d ed. Stuttgart: German Bible Society, 1994.

Moloney, Francis J. *The Gospel of John.* SP 4. Collegeville, MN: Liturgical Press, 1998.

———. *The Johannine Son of Man.* Biblioteca di Scienze Religiose 14. Rome: Libreria Ateneo Salesiano, 1978.

Bibliography

Morgan-Wynne, John Eifion. *The Cross in the Johannine Writings*. Eugene, OR: Pickwick, 2011.

Morris, Leon. *The Apostolic Preaching of the Cross*. 3d ed. Grand Rapids, MI: Eerdmans, 1965.

———. *The Gospel according to John*. Grand Rapids, MI: Eerdmans, 1995.

Moulton, James H., W. F. Howard, and Nigel Turner. *A Grammar of New Testament Greek: Volume II: Accidence and Word Formation*. London, New York: T & T Clark, 1963; Repr. Edinburgh: T & T Clark, 1976.

Ng, Kam Weng. "T. F. Torrance on Perichoresis (Mutual Indwelling of Persons within the Trinity)." May 24, 2006. Online: http://www.krisispraxis.com/archives/2006/05/t-f-torrance-on-perichoresis-mutual-indwelling-of-persons-within-the-trinity/.

Oldenburg, Ray. *Celebrating the Third Place*. New York: Marlowe & Co., 2001.

———. *The Great Good Place*. New York: Paragon, 1989.

Page, Sidney. "Satan: God's Servant." *JETS* 50 (2007): 449–465.

Petty, Richard E., John T. Cacioppo, and Martin Heesacker. "Effects of Rhetorical Questions on Persuasion: A Cognitive Response Analysis." *Journal of Personality and Social Psychology* 40 (1981): 432–440.

"Pew Research: Global Attitudes Project." Online: http://www.pewglobal.org/2012/06/13/chapter-2-attitudes-toward-american-culture-and-ideas/.

Pickering, Ernest, with Myron Houghton, *Biblical Separation: The Struggle for a Pure Church*. 2d ed. Schaumburg, IL: Regular Baptist, 2008.

Pink, A. W. *An Exposition of the First Epistle of John*. eBook edition. Online: http://www.chapellibrary.org/files/2213/7547/5526/1joh.pdf.

Plummer, Alfred. *The Epistles of St. John*. Cambridge: Cambridge University Press, 1886; Repr. Grand Rapids, MI: Baker, 1980.

Porter, Stanley E. *Idioms of the Greek New Testament*. 2d ed. Repr. London: Continuum, 2007.

Porter, Steven L. "The Gradual Nature of Sanctification: Σάρξ as Habituated, Relational Resistance to the Spirit." *Them* 39 (2014): 470–483.

Quek, George. *Coaching and Mentoring International*. Online: https://coachingandmentoringinternational.org/ members-worldwide-directory/asia-pacific/.

Rainbow, Paul A. *Johannine Theology: The Gospel, the Epistles and the Apocalypse*. Downers Grove, IL: InterVarsity Academic, 2014.

Reese, Robert J. "Filial Piety in Chinese Religion." 2003. Online: http://www.casawomo.com/essays/filial-piety-in-chinese-religion.

Rensberger, David. *1 John, 2 John, 3 John*. Abingdon New Testament Commentaries. Nashville, TN: Abingdon, 1997.

———. *The Epistles of John*. Louisville, KY: Westminster John Knox, 2001.

———. "The Messiah Who Has Come into the World," 15–23. In *Jesus in Johannine Tradition*. Edited by Robert T. Fortna and Tom Thatcher. Louisville, KY: Westminster John Knox, 2001.

Richards, E. Randolph. "Reading, Writing, and Manuscripts." In *The World of the New Testament: Cultural, Social, and Historical Contexts*. Edited by Joel B. Green and Lee Martin McDonald. Grand Rapids, MI: Baker Academic, 2013.

Rittgers, Ronald K. "Luther on Private Confession." *LQ* 19 (2005): 312–331.

Robertson, A. T. *A Grammar of the Greek New Testament in the Light of Historical Research*. 5th ed. New York: Richard R. Smith, n.d.

Sanders, Martin. *The Power of Mentoring: Shaping People Who Will Shape the World*. Camp Hill, PA: Wing Spread, 2004.

Schilbrack, Kevin. "Religious Pluralism: A Check-up." *RelSRev* 40 (2014): 1–7.

Schmutzer, Andrew. "Jesus' Temptation: A Reflection on Matthew's Use of Old Testament Theology and Imagery." *Ashland Theological Journal* 40 (2008): 15–42.

Schnackenburg, Rudolf. *The Johannine Epistles: Introduction and Commentary*. Translated by Reginald and Ilse Fuller. New York: Crossroad, 1992.

Schreiner, Thomas R., and Ardel B. Caneday. *The Race Set Before Us: A Biblical Theology of Perseverance and Assurance*. Downers Grove, IL: InterVarsity, 2001.

Schuchard, Bruce G. *1–3 John*. Concordia Commentary. Saint Louis, MO: Concordia Publishing House, 2012.

Section 8 (1) of the Maintenance of Religious Harmony Act, enacted as law in 1990 and revised in 2001. Online: http://en.wikipedia.org/wiki/Maintenance_of_Religious_Harmony_Act.

Segovia, Fernando F. *The Farewell of the Word: The Johannine Call to Abide*. Minneapolis, MN: Fortress, 1991.

Senior, Donald. *Invitation to Matthew in Invitation to the Gospels*. New York: Paulist, 2002.

Shan, Mark C. "Beware of Patriotic Heresy in the Church in China." *Chinese Christian Theological Association*, June 4, 2014. Online: http://www.ccta.me/2014/06/mark-shan-beware-of-patriotic-heresy-in.html.

Simpson, A. Rae. "Young Adult Development Project." Online: http://hrweb.mit.edu/worklife/youngadult/changes.html.

"Singapore Leader Says Religious Proselytizing Threatens Stability." August 19, 2009. Online: http://www.wtvy.com/community/headlines/53723047.html.

Smalley, Stephen S. *1, 2, 3 John*. WBC 51. Waco, TX: Word, 1984.

Smith, David. "The Epistles of John." In *The Expositor's Greek Testament*, vol. 5. Peabody, MA: Hendrickson, 2002.

Smith, Terry L. "A Crisis in Faith: An Exegesis of Psalm 73." *ResQ* 17 (1974): 162–184.

Bibliography

Sternberg, Meir. *The Poetics of Biblical Narrative: Ideological Literature and the Drama of Reading*. Bloomington, IN: Indiana University Press, 1985.

Stott, John R. W. *The Letters of John: An Introduction and Commentary*. TNTC 19. Repr. Downers Grove, IL: InterVarsity Academic, 2009.

Sun, Catherine Tien-Lun. *Themes in Chinese Psychology*. Singapore: Cengage Learning, 2008.

Sunquist, Scott W. "Asian Perspectives on Theological Pluralism." *Theology Matters* 5 (1999): 1–7. Online: http://www.theologymatters.com/SepOct991.PDF.

Talbert, Charles H. *A Literary and Theological Commentary on the Fourth Gospel and Johannine Epistles*. Rev. ed. Macon, GA: Smyth & Helwys, 2005.

———. *Reading John: A Literary and Theological Commentary on the Fourth Gospel and the Johannine Epistles*. New York: Crossroad, 1994.

Tan, Jonathan Yun-Ka. "A New Way of Being Church in Asia: The Federation of Asian Bishops' Conferences [FABC] at the Service of Life In Pluralistic Asia." *Missiology: An International Review* 33 (2005): 72–94.

Thatcher, Tom. "'Water and Blood' in AntiChrist Christianity (1 John 5:6)." *Stone Campbell Journal* 4 (2001): 235–248.

The Church in Asia in the 3rd Millennium: A Guidebook to the Apostolic Exhortation, The Church in Asia, Ecclesia in Asia (FABC Papers 98). 2001. Online: http://www.fabc.org/fabc%20papers/fabc_paper_98.pdf

Thompson, Richard P. *Keeping the Church in Its Place: The Church as Narrative Character in Acts*. New York: T & T Clark, 2006.

Trick, Bradley R. "Sons, Seed, and Children of Promise in Galatians: Discerning the Coherence in Paul's Model of Abrahamic Descent." PhD diss., Duke University, 2010.

van der Merwe, Dirk. "The Identification and Examination of the Elements that Caused a Schism in the Johannine Community at the End of the First Century CE." *HTS* 63 (2007): 1149–1169.

Vermeulen, Karolien. "Mind the Gap: Ambiguity in the Story of Cain and Abel." *JBL* 133 (2014): 29–42.

Vine, W. E. *The Epistles of John: Light, Love, Life*. Grand Rapids, MI: Zondervan, 1970.

Vitrano, Steven P. "The Doctrine of Sin in 1 John." *Andrews University Seminary Studies* 25 (1987): 123–131.

Ward, Tim. "Sin 'Not Unto Death' and Sin 'Unto Death' in 1 John 5:16." *Churchman* 109 (1995): 226–237.

Westcott, Brooke Foss. *The Epistles of St John: The Greek Text with Notes*. Repr. Grand Rapids, MI: Eerdmans, 1976.

Whiteman, Darrell L. "Contextualization: The Theory, the Gap, the Challenge." *International Bulletin of Missionary Research* 21.1 (January 1997): 2–7.

Wilkes, Nicola J. "Life and Health: Bonhoeffer's Normative and Divergent Accounts of Private Confession of Sin." *Theology Today* 71 (2014): 58–68.
Yarbrough, Robert W. *1–3 John*. Grand Rapids, MI: Baker Academic, 2008.
You, Young Gweon. "Shame and Guilt Mechanisms in East Asian Culture." *The Journal of Pastoral Care* 51 (1997): 57–64.
Zerwick, Maximilian. *Biblical Greek*. Rome: Editrice Pontificio Istituto Biblico, 1994.

Asia Theological Association
54 Scout Madriñan St. Quezon City 1103, Philippines
Email: ataasia@gmail.com Telefax: (632) 410 0312

OUR MISSION

The Asia Theological Association (ATA) is a body of theological institutions, committed to evangelical faith and scholarship, networking together to serve the Church in equipping the people of God for the mission of the Lord Jesus Christ.

OUR COMMITMENT

The ATA is committed to serving its members in the development of evangelical, biblical theology by strengthening interaction, enhancing scholarship, promoting academic excellence, fostering spiritual and ministerial formation and mobilizing resources to fulfill God's global mission within diverse Asian cultures.

OUR TASK

Affirming our mission and commitment, ATA seeks to:

- **Strengthen** interaction through inter-institutional fellowship and programs, regional and continental activities, faculty and student exchange programs.
- **Enhance** scholarship through consultations, workshops, seminars, publications, and research fellowships.
- **Promote** academic excellence through accreditation standards, faculty and curriculum development.
- **Foster** spiritual and ministerial formation by providing mentor models, encouraging the development of ministerial skills and a Christian ethos.
- **Mobilize** resources through library development, information technology and infra-structural development.

To learn more about ATA, visit www.ataasia.com or Facebook /AsiaTheologicalAssociation

Langham Literature and its imprints are a ministry of Langham Partnership.

Langham Partnership is a global fellowship working in pursuit of the vision God entrusted to its founder John Stott –

> *to facilitate the growth of the church in maturity and Christ-likeness through raising the standards of biblical preaching and teaching.*

Our vision is to see churches in the majority world equipped for mission and growing to maturity in Christ through the ministry of pastors and leaders who believe, teach and live by the Word of God.

Our mission is to strengthen the ministry of the Word of God through:
- nurturing national movements for biblical preaching
- fostering the creation and distribution of evangelical literature
- enhancing evangelical theological education

especially in countries where churches are under-resourced.

Our ministry

Langham Preaching partners with national leaders to nurture indigenous biblical preaching movements for pastors and lay preachers all around the world. With the support of a team of trainers from many countries, a multi-level programme of seminars provides practical training, and is followed by a programme for training local facilitators. Local preachers' groups and national and regional networks ensure continuity and ongoing development, seeking to build vigorous movements committed to Bible exposition.

Langham Literature provides majority world preachers, scholars and seminary libraries with evangelical books and electronic resources through publishing and distribution, grants and discounts. The programme also fosters the creation of indigenous evangelical books in many languages, through writer's grants, strengthening local evangelical publishing houses, and investment in major regional literature projects, such as one volume Bible commentaries like *The Africa Bible Commentary* and *The South Asia Bible Commentary*.

Langham Scholars provides financial support for evangelical doctoral students from the majority world so that, when they return home, they may train pastors and other Christian leaders with sound, biblical and theological teaching. This programme equips those who equip others. Langham Scholars also works in partnership with majority world seminaries in strengthening evangelical theological education. A growing number of Langham Scholars study in high quality doctoral programmes in the majority world itself. As well as teaching the next generation of pastors, graduated Langham Scholars exercise significant influence through their writing and leadership.

To learn more about Langham Partnership and the work we do visit **langham.org**

www.ingramcontent.com/pod-product-compliance
Lightning Source LLC
Chambersburg PA
CBHW051927160426
43198CB00012B/2064